IT and European Bank Performance

IT and European Bank Performance

Elena Beccalli

London School of Economics, UK

and

Università Degli Studi Di Macerata, Italy

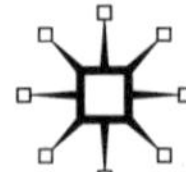

First published 2007 by
PALGRAVE MACMILLAN
Houndmills, Basingstoke, Hampshire RG21 6XS and
175 Fifth Avenue, New York, N.Y. 10010
Companies and representatives throughout the world

PALGRAVE MACMILLAN is the global academic imprint of the Palgrave Macmillan division of St. Martin's Press, LLC and of Palgrave Macmillan Ltd. Macmillan® is a registered trademark in the United States, United Kingdom and other countries. Palgrave is a registered trademark in the European Union and other countries.

ISBN-13: 978–0–230–00694–2 hardback
ISBN-10: 0–230–00694–9 hardback

This book is printed on paper suitable for recycling and made from fully managed and sustained forest sources. Logging, pulping and manufacturing processes are expected to conform to the environmental regulations of the country of origin.

A catalogue record for this book is available from the British Library.

A catalog record for this book is available from the Library of Congress.

10   9   8   7   6   5   4   3   2   1
16   15   14   13   12   11   10   09   08   07

Printed and bound in Great Britain by
Antony Rowe Ltd, Chippenham and Eastbourne

To my husband Francesco.
To my parents Luigi and Maria.

Contents

List of Tables and Figure

Tables

Figure

Foreword

It is almost 25 years (1983) since we first stated the need to redefine the cost function of a financial intermediary in order to capture the pervasive effect of information technology (IT) on the structural business, and specially to define the cost function of technology and its components. The original idea was to view the technological function "as a complex variable whose configuration is such as to necessarily involve the very nature of the production function" and "as the element of constitutive interconnection between the flux in environmental variables, strategy, structure and operational mechanisms" (Fusconi, 1996, pp. 480–481). A collateral effect of this phenomenon was the need to focus the attention on the relevance of organisational themes and operating performance as strategic variables, in a context of market globalisation where the role of interest rates diminished in favour of operating efficiency. Notwithstanding the pervasiveness of technology was – and remains – a certainty, the impact of technology on performance remained uncertain: it was not clear whether technology was able to generate improvements in bank performance (either as cost minimisation or revenue maximisation) or was only motivated by organisational reasons. Now, this distinguished book does so and represents a concrete approach to verify not only on a theortical but also on an empirical basis the majority of the questions overlooked.

Nowadays, there still remains some doubt as to whether the massive spending on IT by banks has positively influenced performance or productivity in the sector. In fact, there is some evidence that the so-called "productivity paradox" still exists in US banking – where IT appears to have had a negative impact on bank productivity. Also, a recent debate has emerged emphasising the strategic role to attribute to IT investments (IT as a strategic necessity vs a strategic opportunity) that also appears to have inconclusive views as to whether significant IT spending really boosts bank performance.

In spite of its importance, no great body of literature is devoted to the study of IT spending in banking, especially with reference to European banks. This comprehensive book will be the first to provide a systematic appraisal of this area and will be the first to analyse whether the billions of dollars spent on IT by European banks have impacted on their performance.

In this unique publication, the author provides an insight into the role of IT in European banking and investigates whether IT investments in hardware, software and other IT services have influenced on bank performance. In particular, the author proposes a scientifically rigorous methodological approach capable of isolating the effects of investment in technology on the performance of banks. The approach aims to bring together two broad areas: the IT literature (that focuses on the theories of competitive strategy) and the banking literature (in order to evaluate how IT spending has influenced bank performance and the production process).

The thesis is that a new paradox, the so-called "profitability paradox", exists in European banks: operational profit efficiencies did not improve when investment in IT increased. The introduction of IT into European banking in the latter part of the 1990s seems to be geared towards the production of products and services when, how and where the market requires. There is a shift from the use of technology in keeping with a paradigm involving the rationalisation of production processes to the use of technology in accordance with a paradigm privileging operational adequacy and the market. It seems that generally technology represents a strategic necessity as opposed to a variable capable of generating a competitive advantage. The adoption by the banks of information systems that are more and more expensive seems to be a structural component of the form of competition that exists in the industry – they are essential in order to enter and remain in the industry.

The text will be of interest to practitioners in the banking and IT areas as well as researchers and students interested in the role of technological developments in the financial area. It will enable bankers, IT consultants, policymakers, researchers and other interested parties to get a detailed insight into the effects of IT investments on European bank performance, and to contribute to the strategic debate on IT spending.

The banking community is enriched by this book, and I am delighted to have the opportunity to present it after having had many occasions to discuss its contents with the author, Elena Beccalli, who took her PhD under my guidance here at the Università Cattolica del Sacro Cuore of Milan, and now joins the school of distinguished researchers of our university.

Agostino Fusconi
Full Professor of Economics of financial markets and intermediaries
Università Cattolica del Sacro Cuore, Milan

Preface

The aim of this book is to provide an insight into the role of IT in European banking and to investigate whether IT investments in hardware, software and other IT services has influenced on bank performance. The study of IT investment in banking is an important issue because banks are the main spenders on new technology and it is widely accepted that technological developments have had a major impact on re-shaping banks' front- and back-office operations. However, there still remains some doubt as to whether the massive spending on IT by banks has positively influenced performance or productivity in the sector. In fact there is some evidence that the so-called "productivity paradox" exists in US banking – where IT appears to have had a negative impact on bank productivity. Also a recent debate has emerged emphasising the strategic role to attribute to IT investments (IT as a strategic necessity vs. a strategic opportunity) that also appears to have inconclusive views as to whether significant IT spending really boosts bank performance.

This book seeks to address these issues in relation to the IT investments in European banking. The aim is to provide a text that enables bankers, IT consultants, policymakers, researchers and other interested parties to get a detailed insight into the effects of IT investments on European bank performance, and to contribute to the strategic debate on IT spending. The approach aims to bring together two broad areas – the IT literature (that focuses on the theories of competitive strategy) and the banking literature (in order to evaluate how IT spending has influenced bank performance and the production process).

Given that so little is written about IT spending in banking this book will be the first to provide a systematic appraisal of this area and will be the first to analyse whether the billion of dollars spent on IT by European banks has impacted on their performance. In particular, it proposes a scientifically rigorous methodological approach capable of isolating the effects of investment in technology on the performance of banks. The text is of interest to practitioners in the banking and IT areas as well as researchers and students interested in the role of technological developments in the financial area.

Acknowledgements

I would like to express special thanks to Professor Phil Molyneux, who contributed enormously to every aspect of this book. Special thanks must also go to Professor Agostino Fusconi for his teaching and his tireless, thought-provoking criticism, which have been of incalculable help. In addition, I would like to thank Professor Francesco Cesarini and Professor Peter Miller for the constant support and the many precious suggestions they have offered me. Thanks must go also to Professor Mauro Marcóni, for his support. A further special thanks must go to Francesco Virili for the endless passionate discussions that have enabled me to confront the literature on information systems with so much more depth. I am also grateful for the constructive comments offered by Andrea Sironi, Mario Anolli, Pascal Frantz, and the participants at the Wolpertinger Meeting 2005, the European Accounting Association Conference 2005, the Financial Management Association Conference 2006, and the research colloquia at Università Cattolica del Sacro Cuore (Milan) and Università di Macerata. I would also like to take this opportunity to thank Financial Insights, an IDC Company, Convenzione Interbancaria per i Problemi dell' Automazione and the European Commission (Enterprise Directorate General, e-Business) for making available their data on investments in technology – data that would otherwise have been extremely difficult to obtain. Thanks must also go to the DIEF Department of Macerata University and to the Accounting and Finance Department of the London School of Economics for all the support they offered me in the course of my research. A final heartfelt thanks goes to Banca delle Marche for the financial support offered to publish the book, edited by Nicholas Crotty.

1
Introduction: Banks and Investment in IT

1.1 Introduction

By its very nature, activity in the banking industry consists to a considerable extent in the handling of information. It is hardly surprising, then, that investments by banks in technologies related to the handling of information (hereafter referred to as information technology or IT) are substantial – higher, indeed, than those of any other sector in the economy. The measurement of the performance of such investments, however, is extremely problematic. What is more, the measurements that have been taken so far in respect of the banking industry have proven negative. In fact, the relating small number of US empirical studies conducted to date have identified a negative relationship between bank's investment in IT and productivity. This phenomenon is known as the productivity paradox. The finding appears surprising for two reasons. In the first place, investments in IT show a positive performance in a large number of the other industries of the economy. Secondly, no other industry invests as much in IT as do the banks. The counterintuitive evidence of the productivity paradox in the US banking industry – high levels of IT investment resulting in a negative performance – constitutes the underlying reason for pursuing the central objective of this book: an investigation into the complex relationship between performance and IT investment in European banking.

1.2 The definition of the concept of information technology

The concept of information technology[1] cannot be reduced to a single definition. As Orlikowski (1992) effectively argued, two important considerations come together to determine this interpretative complexity: the breadth of the object defined (what are the elements that make up technology) and the role of technology (the relationship between technology and organisation).

Regarding the first of the two factors identified (the so-called *"scope"* of technology), the most commonly proposed definitions are situated at the two ends of a *continuum* in terms of which the debate is conducted: on the one hand, technology as "hardware", and on the other, "social technologies". In respect of the former interpretation, technology is taken to be "the equipment, the machines and the tools that people use in their productive activity, whether these instruments be of an industrial or computing nature" (Orlikowski, 1992, p. 339). So far as the latter is concerned, technology is understood as inhering to the whole productive process, and includes "the generic tasks, techniques and knowledge utilised when humans engage in any productive activity" (ibid., p. 399).[2]

In this book the definition of the scope of technology lies in an intermediate position between the two interpretations cited above, unfolding in terms of three key constitutive components: hardware (computers, large-scale units of memory, printers and other peripheral equipment), software (commercial applications whether of a standard nature or internally developed) and IT services (consultancy services, implementation services, operational services, training and staff development and technical assistance services).

Our intention is to maintain a distinction – at least from a theoretical point of view – between the "technological input" employed in the productive process and the human activity of the people that make use of that input. The ultimate subject of the study, in fact, is the performance of investments in IT, which is measured in relation to the productive process of the bank. One part of the input in that process – apart from the physical capital, the financial capital and the human resources – takes the form of the technological factor in all its various manifestations. More specifically, this particular form of input is constituted by its three modular components (hardware, software and IT services),[3] given that today these components make up the "IT resources" that are employed conjointly by the banks in their productive process.

So far as the interaction between technology and organisation is concerned, it is possible to distinguish between an "objective" view and a "subjective" view of technology (Orlikowski, 1992). In the case of the former,[4] the role of technology is objectively given (the so-called "technological determinism"), that is technology constitutes an external force with deterministic impacts on the structure of organisations. By contrast, in the subjective view,[5] technology is considered a product of a human nature, in which a significant role is played by the interpretation and action of the people involved.[6]

The contrast between the objective and the subjective views can be overcome by way of employing the concept of "interpretative flexibility", or, in other words, by taking into consideration the degree to which users can exercise some form of control in their interaction with technology.[7] Taken in this sense, the notion of interpretative flexibility refers to the extent to which the users of a technology are engaged in the constitution of it (technical and/or social) in the course of the developmental and operational phases. Thus, there exists a certain degree of flexibility in the design, use and interpretation of technology, which is not limitless and which can vary for each type of technology in accordance with a series of factors.[8] This varying degree of flexibility is determined, on the one hand, by the particular material characteristics of the technology itself, and, on the other, both by the institutional context in which the technology is deployed and by the different levels of knowledge and power exercised by the actors that play a role in the development and use of the technology (Orlikowski, 1992, p. 409).

In this book, then, technology will be viewed as an external force that exerts an impact on organisations. At the same time, however, that impact will be assumed to be shaped by human actors and organisational contexts in accordance with varying degrees of interpretative flexibility. Even accepting that technology is understood here as an input employed in the productive process, and that, as such, it rates as an external force; nonetheless, it should not be overlooked that technology plays a vital role in all the areas of management in a bank, so much so that any measuring of its performance must necessarily relate to the firm as a whole. In what follows, then, the measurement of performance will relate to the whole productive process, in which, it will be argued, that the part played by the effects of external forces (amongst which technological input) are no more important than those played by the interpretation of those forces by the subjects involved in the productive process itself and by the organisational units of the entity in question.

1.3   Investment in IT and the performance of banks

The existence of different degrees of interpretative flexibility makes it extremely difficult to measure the economic effects of investment in technology. Indeed, each technological artefact has a technical component with particular features and outcomes that are largely predictable and a human component whose effects depend upon the free interpretation of the user. The degree of interpretative flexibility associated with the use of technology can vary considerably and with it the predictability of returns on investment in IT. Technologies with a low level of interpretative flexibility generally have impacts and economic returns that can be forecast more easily; technologies with a high level of interpretative flexibility, on the other hand, have effects that are less easy to track.

The unpredictability of the effects of technology essentially takes the form of a difficulty in estimating the consequences provoked by the technology's so-called "human component". It is sufficient to think of the consequences of the introduction of a new operating procedure. In fact, investment in technology cannot be reduced to the mere acquisition of hardware and software applications. Very often it has the effect of profoundly affecting knowledge, job roles, the partition of responsibilities, operational behaviour and the distribution of power – and all of this with effects that are as substantial as they are difficult to foresee in advance (as well as difficult to quantify after the event). In more recent theories the point has even been reached of hypothesising a tendency towards the occurrence of the so-called "organisational drift" (Ciborra, 2000) or, in other words, towards the impossibility of controlling the impact of technological infrastructures on the organisation of firms.

It goes without saying that the approach adopted in this book implicitly assumes that the degree of interpretative flexibility of the technology subject to investment is not so great as to produce significant collateral effects or a significant amount of "organisational drift". This assumption would seem to be a reasonable one for the banking industry, where the degree of operational control is generally maintained at a high level, with a very limited amount of discretionary power being granted to the people involved in the use of the technology.

What we have said so far makes it necessary to spell out certain interpretative steps involved in the definition of technology so as to demonstrate explicitly how it is possible to measure its economic impact empirically. In this way the analysis of the concept of technology allows us to bring out its distinctive characteristics, in particular that of pervasiveness.[9] Within this perspective, the complex definition of the object of the research in this book makes it necessary to relate the very broad set of phenomena identified as technological change back to the concept of the pervasiveness of technology.

A development of this theme in a way that can be usefully extended to this book is offered in Fusconi (1996, p. 480),[10] where the technological function is understood "as the element of constitutive interconnection between the flux in environmental variables, strategy, structure and operational mechanisms". Viewed in this way, the pervasiveness of technology emerges clearly. Once it is recognised that technology plays a role in underpinning all the areas of managerial activity in a bank, it becomes difficult to identify any particular cost–benefit relationship that, together with the relevant IT investments, should be associated with a given area. In essence, the decision to estimate the economic impact of technology on the firm in its entirety makes it possible to obtain a measurement – albeit, an imperfect one – both of the objective component and (of part) of the effects of the subjective interpretation of technology. The complex specification of the concept of technology is achieved, then, by way of acknowledging the dimension of the pervasiveness of technology. This latter assumption opens the way to measuring at the microeconomic level – or, in other words, at the level of individual banks – the impact associated with investment in IT.

1.4   Overview of the research themes

1.4.1   Banking: An industry with an intensive use of information and a high level of investment in IT

In embarking upon an investigation of the particular subject of this book, the European banking industry, it is necessary to start out by taking into consideration the degree to which IT is employed and the weight of the influence it has. In point of fact, the industry is generally considered to be one that involves an intensive use of information[11] and that, as such, is characterised by a strategic use of technology (Porter and Millar, 1985). Although the very nature of banking activity points clearly to the presence of information intensity, the notion that it also involves a strategic employment of technology does not appear to be entirely self-evident and, thus, warrants some discussion.

The management of information has always constituted both the core and the foundation of banking activity just as it always has of banking products. It is in this sense that the industry is classified as one involving an intensive use of information in its productive processes and a high level of informational content in its products (Porter and Millar, 1985). In the view of the two aforementioned authors, which has long been accepted and adopted in the literature (Goddard *et al.*, 2001), information intensity expresses itself through the strategic use of technology. The industries with a high level of information intensity, amongst which, in fact, stands banking, appear to be more inclined than those with a low level to engage in a strategic application of technology. Within this logic, IT transforms not only products and processes[12] but even the nature of competition itself. It does so in three fundamental ways: creating a lever with which to achieve competitive advantage (be this expressed in terms of a reduction of costs or an increase in revenues as a result of policies of differentiation), generating completely new business and changing the structure of the industry.[13]

The adoption of this position in relation to the strategic use of technology on the part of the banking industry[14] raises a fundamental question. In fact, at this point it is clear that it is necessary to specify the qualitative nature of this strategic use: is technology to be understood as a strategic necessity for the banking industry (or, in other words, a resource that it is absolutely necessary to acquire so as to be able to respond to structural changes in the industry) or does it represent a strategic opportunity (capable, that is, of generating a strategic advantage)? The methodological framework developed in this book (and the consequent empirical examination, the results of which are presented in Section 4.6) will provide an opportunity to offer a response to this question.

Even at this early stage, however, given the empirical evidence in support of it, the high level of information intensity in the banking industry emerges clearly. The intensive use of information manifests itself indubitably in the sheer magnitude of the phenomenon under consideration: in fact, as far as the US economy is concerned, the banks constitute the industry with the highest level of investment in technology (Council of Economic Advisors, 2001); and a comparable level of investment is also apparent in respect of the European banking industry especially starting from the second half of the 1990s (European Information Technology Observatory, EITO, 1996–2002). In particular, the total amount of investment in European Union banks doubled between 1995 and 2005: from US$21,871 millions to US$54,290 millions (Financial Insights – IDC, 2006). Nonetheless, differences in the magnitude of the phenomenon are apparent in respect of the five major European banking industries taken into consideration in the present study (France, Germany, Italy, Spain and the United Kingdom): the highest level of investment in IT took place in the UK banking industry (25.92 per cent of the total amount invested in IT by European banks in 2005), while the lowest took place in the Spanish industry (5.36 per cent in 2005). The French and German banking industries each accounted for 14.82

and 16.43 per cent of the total amount of investment in IT by European banks, whereas the proportion of Italian banks was 11.65 per cent in 2005. In the period between 1995 and 2005 the most substantial increase in investment in IT was registered in the German banks ($+147.64$ per cent) while the most limited increase took place in the Italian industry ($+100.73$ per cent).

1.4.2   The performance of investments in IT in banks: from the difficulty of measurement to the productivity paradox

The high level of investment in IT in the banking industry is accompanied by a marked difficulty in evaluating its performance. This has been described clearly by Fitzgerald (1993). Organisations have great difficulty in effecting an evaluation of their investments in technology and, as a result, use unverified or imaginary values to determine the advantages they bring (which generally result in a substantial underestimation of costs).[15] The reasons for this situation are to be found in the lack of information on the performance of technology as well as in the difficulty involved in classifying and identifying the information itself. A further contributing factor lies in the fact that investment in IT is often founded more on faith in the benefits that it might bring as opposed to concerted efforts to measure what those benefits are. This latter observation seems to be true for all industries of the economy and the banking industry is no exception. In particular, the position of Child and Loveridge (1990) appears more than credible: the huge investments that the banking industry makes in technology can be traced back not just to the assumption that they will generate a reduction in other costs (in particular, labour costs) but also to the expectation that they will lead to an improvement in the quality of the products and services offered to clients. Nonetheless, the majority of banks have not made any systematic attempt to verify whether such benefits have been realised in actual fact, much less identify the impact of them or their effects. Among the factors put forward to explain the reasons for such a lack of information about the performance of technology, particular attention should be given, on the one hand, to the perception that it is clearly feasible to realise benefits and, on the other, to the difficulty of distinguishing between the various projects towards which investment in IT is directed.

Notwithstanding what we have so far said about the undoubted difficulty of engaging in an evaluation of investments in IT and about the scarcity of attempts to undertake such an enterprise on the part of banks, this book will focus on the problem of measuring the impact of IT investment on performance in the banking industry. Can investment in technology contribute to improving the performance of this industry?

Debate about the evaluation of the performance of investments in IT was dominated for a long time – and in certain respects still is today – by the so-called "productivity paradox", which was put forward by Robert Solow: "We see computers everywhere except in the productivity statistics" (Solow, 1987). In essence, it seems that there has been no proof – up to the first half of the 1990s – that the productivity of the economic system has been increased by the substantial investments in IT put in place in almost all industries of the economy. It is difficult to identify empirically where positive payoffs have occurred and even whether such positive payoffs have in actual fact materialised. The impact of investments in technology on productivity was not obvious for a long period of time and that was particularly so in the services sector.

The uncertain impact on productivity of investments in technology has become a paradox for economic theory, a worry for the management of firms and a concern for the people responsible for economic policy. The issue has also attracted the attention of numerous scholars who, by developing new and more sophisticated models, have gradually managed from the second half of the 1990s onwards to provide even more satisfactory explanations as well as demonstrate empirically that for a large number of industries in the US economy the productivity paradox does not constitute a real problem (for an extensive review of the literature, see Dedrick *et al.*, 2003). In particular, the industries characterised by an intensive use of IT have experienced increases in productivity levels that have been greater than those of industries not so characterised (Stiroh, 2001b). Has the productivity paradox, then, been resolved definitively?

Although recent empirical work suggests that for a large number of industries investments in technology are productive (above all, if the industry is characterised by an intensive use of IT), it has emerged quite clearly that the productivity paradox remains unscathed so far as the US banking industry is concerned (Council of Economic Advisors, 2001; McKinsey Global Institute, 2001): there is clear evidence that for banks there has been no positive relationship between investments in technology and productivity in the post-1995 period. The existence of the productivity paradox in the US banking industry is surprising for a number of reasons. In the first place, investment in IT leads to a positive performance in a large number of other industries in the economy; indeed, it is precisely the industries characterised by an intensive use of IT that experience the highest rates of growth in productivity. Secondly, the information intensity in banking products and services is particularly high and no other industry invests as much in IT as do the banks.

It should be recognised, however, that all the relevant empirical evidence relates exclusively to the US economy. In fact, it would appear that there is not a single comparative empirical analysis dealing with the European banking industry.[16] The surprising confirmation of the productivity paradox in relation to the US banking industry – in contrast to what has been observed in the rest of the US economy – constitutes in itself the fundamental reason for undertaking this book, which aims to provide an insight into the role of IT in European banking and to investigate whether IT investment has had an impact on bank performance. This particular approach lends to the book, which will investigate the experience of the five major banking industries in Europe in the period between 1995 and 2000,[17] a character of novelty.

1.5   The methodology

The main contribution of this book is that it presents a new methodological approach, bringing together the literature on information systems and banking, in order to arrive at scientifically rigorous quantifications of the effects of investment in IT on bank performance.[18] To this end a methodology is developed which integrates models derived from strategic competition as originally employed in the literature on information systems on the basis of accounting measures of profitability. This is then related to an appropriate measurement of performance that reflects the characteristics of the productive process of banks and captures the various dimensions of the impact of technology.

In fact, while the literature on information systems has developed models for examining the achievement of positions of competitive advantage (or of reductions in costs) as a result of investment in IT, the banking literature, in an almost totally uniform manner, has viewed the measurement of technological change by way of the inclusion in the analysis of a temporal (time-trend) variable that seeks to identify shifts in cost functions over time. (We shall argue later that this, however, seems to have little significance for the measurement of the phenomenon, as will be seen in Chapter 5.) On the other hand, the specification of a performance measure capable of taking into consideration the peculiarities of the productive process of banks and of capturing the various dimensions of the impact of technology (such as X-inefficiencies)[19] has been the object of immense interest (and empirical investigation) in the banking literature, but has not (as far as we are aware) been investigated in the context of information systems.

Given the economic considerations at the basis of the interest in the performance of IT investments, the problem of the definition of a methodology unfolds in terms of the selection of a pertinent economic theory. In recent studies on the US banking industry the economic theory at the basis of the analysis has been the theory of productivity, which has been employed to investigate whether technology has provided for the production of a greater quantity of outputs for a given quantity of inputs (including technological input). However, considering the magnitude and the variety of the dimensions in terms of how the impact of technology on banks unfolds (to list just a few: the quality of products and services, multiple distribution channels, customisation and rationalisation of the organisational processes), it would seem more appropriate in this book to refer to the theory of strategic competition, which is geared towards investigating whether investment in technology reduces the costs of banks or improves their revenues. In other words, are banks able to use technology so as to gain competitive advantage and realise profits that are higher than what they would otherwise achieve?

Within this framework, our methodology is designed to investigate the relationship between bank performance and their investment in IT in various European countries with a view to examining whether technology generates a significantly positive (or negative) impact on the performance of banks both in respect of the short term and in respect of the medium-to-long term. In other words, our intention is to respond to the following questions:

1. How much does an investment in IT impact upon accounting profitability in the period in which it was effected or over the course of a subsequent period of time?
2. How much does it impact upon revenues over the short-to-medium term?
3. How much does it impact on costs over the short-to-medium term?
4. How much does it impact on costs in the medium-to-long term?

In order to respond to these questions, it is necessary to introduce some appropriate methodological guidelines and, at the same time, proceed towards a definition of the performance variables that are necessary to examine the relationship under investigation:

1. With regard to the first question, the degree of interaction between technology and global profitability (for the bank as a whole) takes the form of the result of a regression analysis, where the independent variables are the traditional accounting measures of financial profitability or, in other words, return on equity (ROE) and return on assets (ROA).

2. With regard to the second question, the impact of IT investments on revenues requires the specification of a stochastic measure of operational efficiency called profit X-efficiencies. Such an approach makes it necessary to ask whether it is possible for investments in IT to contribute to rendering a bank profit-maximising. In other words, do investments in IT result in the production of more outputs (or outputs of a higher quality) though still using the same amount of inputs, and/or do they allow banks to apply a price premium in recognition of their higher quality?

3. With regard to the third question, the specification of the impact on costs makes it necessary to introduce the measure of cost X-efficiencies. Do investments in IT contribute to rendering a bank cost-minimising or, in other words, to placing it in a position of being able to produce the same amount of outputs while employing less inputs and consequently experiencing cost savings?

4. Finally, the identification – in the form of a first approximation – of a measure of the impact of technology on costs in the medium-to-long term is obtained by way of another methodology based on the estimate of a stochastic cost frontier where the time variable takes the form of a measure of technical change. However, this technique, which has traditionally been proposed for the measurement of the effects of IT on cost efficiency, requires that caution be adopted in that the time variable captures not only the effects of technological progress but also the effects produced by other factors such as environmental changes.

Up to the present the relevant literature has provided an investigation of the theory of strategic competition only in relation to the first question or, more precisely, only in relation to the relationship between traditional accounting measures of profitability and investments in IT in the short term.[20] These analyses, moreover, have focused on the US economy as a whole and not in particular on the banking industry. The fourth question, too, or, more precisely, the relationship between costs and investment in IT over the medium-to-long term, has been the subject of extensive discussion, and in this case, by contrast, with specific reference to the banking industry.[21]

By contrast, the second and third questions, which relate to the relationship between investments in IT and a global measure of operational efficiency, have been formulated for the first time in this book. This extension of what the literature has offered to date in the form of methods for examining the theory of strategic competition and, therefore, for specifying performance measures goes hand in hand with a belief that the traditional accounting profitability measures used up to the present involve substantial interpretative limits in two major directions. Above all, these measures involve a measure of global profitability that does not allow for the identification of the factors that determine competitive advantage: reductions in costs and increases in revenues. Secondly, the traditional accounting profitability measures are not capable of quantifying and taking account of the large number of IT impacts[22] – originally identified as "soft benefits" by Brynjolfsson (1993) – that determine the competitive position of a bank and, therefore, its performance. In fact, investments in technology impact not only on the outputs of the productive process but also on many other elements of operational performance such as services to users, quality, the speed and flexibility of delivery, customisation and the informational content of products and services. They also impact on costs of an operational nature such as depreciation and current operating costs (mainly labour costs).

In order to overcome these limitations, alongside the traditional accounting measures of financial profitability, we add a global measure of operational efficiency, the so-called "X-efficiencies" (in other words, the distance of the position of equilibrium of each bank from the optimal operative frontier). Quite apart from the fact that they are superior in general terms to the traditional accounting measures of profitability,[23] X-efficiencies also make it possible to capture delays, errors and uncertainties in the decision-making process, that is to measure the capacity of management to control costs (cost X-efficiencies) or to maximise revenues (profit X-efficiencies). In other words, X-efficiencies are measures of the impact of IT or, more precisely, of the improvements/deterioration in organisational capacities, in the quality and variety of the services and products offered, in the rapidity and flexibility of delivery, in the simplification of administrative processes, in the productivity of labour and in operational productivity and, what is more, they are capable of distinguishing between impacts on costs and impacts on revenues. Never used before in analogous studies, they constitute an absolute novelty in the measurement of the performance of investments in IT. Their use in this context, moreover, brings some clear advantages compared with the accounting measures that have been employed traditionally. These are manifest, on the one hand, in terms of the quantification of the various dimensions of the impact of technology and, on the other, in terms of the possibility of breaking down the possible sources of competitive advantage of the bank (reduction in costs versus increase in revenues).

1.6   Outline of the book

Below we provide a description of how the book is organised.

Chapter 2 analyses the role and the various forms of investments in technology put in place by European banks in the second half of the 1990s. This is done in the light of the nature and objectives of the banks' strategic plans (merger and acquisition operations, the multi-channel approach and e-banking) as well as in the light of the institutional factors that impacted upon them (for instance, the reorganisation of payment systems).

Chapter 3 offers a critical overview of the literature on the evaluation of the performance of investment in technology. The debate was dominated for a long time – and, so far as the banking industry is concerned, still is – by the so-called "productivity paradox". In this chapter we endeavour to respond to the absence of an interpretative, analytical framework to explain the persistence of the productivity paradox in relation to investment in technology in an industry, like the banking industry, that makes intensive use of information. The review of the literature, the object of which is to provide an analytical framework to use as a theoretical reference point in the empirical enquiry, seeks above all to identify the economic theories and key variables taken into examination in the relevant studies as well as the depth with which they have been investigated. The particularly significant aspect of the review consists in the fact that it identifies clearly the various economic theories that underlie the analysis of research questions that are of a very different nature. In this way a range of economic theories are explicated: the theory of production (conceived to examine whether investments in technology contribute to increasing productivity), the theory of strategic competition (aimed at investigating whether banks are capable of using technology with a view to gaining competitive advantage and realising profits that are higher than what they would be otherwise) and the theory of the consumer (directed towards investigating the creation of value for consumers by technology). The clarification of the differences involved in these positions, which up until now have produced a considerable amount of confusion in the relevant literature, also impacts upon the definition of the measures of performance that are adopted in our later empirical work.

Although the recent empirical research suggests that investments in technology have been productive for a large number of industries in the United States, the only two studies dealing with the banking industry clearly point to the absence of a positive relationship between investments in technology and productivity in the period after 1995. This counterintuitive confirmation of the productivity paradox in the US banking industry – in contrast to what has been observed in the rest of the economy – reveals by itself the fundamental reasons for undertaking this study, which takes the form – in Chapter 4 – of an examination of the relationship between performance and investments in technology in the European banking industry. In order to contextualise in an appropriate manner the problem under examination, a first methodological choice is made in the form of selecting a theoretical reference point from among the economic theories laid out in the review of the literature presented in Chapter 3. As our preference is for the theory of strategic competition, we aim to investigate whether IT investments improve business performance (and not simply productivity, as traditionally is done in respect of banks) for, if this is the case, it can be inferred that such spending impacts positively on organisational capabilities, thereby resulting in improved competitive advantage. Given that economic theory of competitive advantage proves preferable, a further methodological choice is made in relation to the following factors:

- the measure of the performance of banks (traditional accounting measures of profitability versus those based on optimising techniques that control for business mix and other features, namely efficiency measures that relate to both the revenues and the costs side);
- the measure of different types of investments in IT (the total amount and the value broken down into its various components);
- the scope of the analysis of the phenomenon: in particular, an attempt is made to compare the situations in various European banking industries.

The results of the analysis are then presented and discussed.

After confirming the existence of the profitability paradox in the European banking industry in relation to the short-to-medium term, we move on to Chapter 5 to examine the impact of investments in technology on performance over the medium-to-long term. In other words, we endeavour to measure the so-called "technical change" in the period between 1993 and 2000. Although this methodology must be used with caution in that the time variable involved generally captures the effects produced by environmental and circumstantial factors (and not just technological ones), it is particularly valuable to the extent that it involves an empirical examination of the impact of technical change on the characteristics of production as well as on the cost structure of the banking industry over the medium-to-long term. There are two major reasons for this. On the one hand, technical change is widely recognised as one of the principal sources of change in the industry. On the other, very few studies have either estimated the effects of technical change on factors like the costs for European banks of supplying services or attempted to determine the optimal bank size in respect of IT investments.

In short, the empirical evidence suggests that the strengthening of IT resources is accompanied by savings in costs over the medium-to-long term and, to a certain extent – just in so far as investments in hardware and software are concerned – also over the short term. Nevertheless, it seems that a series of factors impede the transformation of technological innovations into profitability and, above all, into improvements in revenues. In an attempt to identify the reasons for this paradox, in Chapter 6 we offer an analysis of the objectives and obstacles related to IT initiatives so as to arrive at an identification of the factors that determine the negative direction of the relationship that has been established empirically. Thus, we identify the objectives that lie behind IT investments in banks as well as the reasons – and the circumstances – on account of which investments in IT have not produced improvements in performance in the banking industry. In addition, an analysis is offered of the factors that influence decisions relating to the role that IT investments should play in the pursuit of increases in profitability. Finally, we examine the impact of IT investments on individual activities in the value chain of banks, and highlight factors that transform costs and revenues in various business areas.

2
New Strategic and Structural Tendencies in the European Banking Industry and Investment in IT

2.1 Introduction

Historically, investments in technology in the banking industry were effected initially as mere instruments for reorienting organisations towards the objective of achieving greater efficiency in traditional areas of activity (Fusconi, 1996). In the initial phase of automation the corresponding organisational initiatives were conceived for the most part in terms of maximising the outputs that could be obtained from the production function and did not involve a great deal of attention to the effects on costs (in particular, costs of a financial nature). In this way the expansion and the control of the volumes of deposits and loans constituted the fundamentals of the bank financial management. In fact, banks used information technology, on the one hand, to deal more efficiently with the information relating to deposits and loans, on the other, to transmit that information and process payments more quickly, all the while employing less resources. The effect of these initiatives at the organisational level was a rationalisation of the production process and a simplification of the work with a view to reducing the unit costs of production. A further effect related to the dimensions of the activity itself, in particular, in regard to the volumes of deposits and the payment instruments handled.

In a later period, as a consequence of the pressure exerted by the innovation taking place in the financial industry, there emerged a requirement that technological change offers support to banks in implementing strategies to diversify products and markets. Such strategies had been rendered necessary both by disintermediation and by the changing requirements of customers in the form of a greater and more widespread sensibility towards the price and the quality of the services offered as well as to the degree of their sophistication and of the speed with which they were executed (Fusconi, 1996). Among other things, technology had facilitated the development of new and more sophisticated financial products (Tufano, 2002), as had the introduction of new distribution channels that complemented traditional networks of bank branches (White, 1998). Thus, it became important not just to rationalise production by lowering costs, but also to produce appropriate products and services at the same time, in the manner and in the location that the market demanded. Moreover, new technology was widely employed to effect a more efficient evaluation of risk aimed at disaggregating and reconstituting risks in new ways (Allen and Gale, 1994). Finally, the development of low-cost technology, together with the process of deregulation, intensified competition in the banking industry. In this way technological change provided banks with a new strategic lever to achieve the objectives of rationalisation and cost management (De Bandt and Davis, 2000).

Overall, as clearly shown in Berger (2003), the advances in back-office technologies determined improvements in cost and lending capacity, as well as the improved front-office technologies produced consumer benefits. Also, IT generated significant overall productivity increases in terms of improved quality and variety in banking services. In addition, technological progress likely may have effects on the structure of the industry, facilitating consolidation by making it more or less efficient at the margin for banks to be larger and/or more geographically dispersed.

2.2   The nature and objectives of the strategic plans of European banks and investments in IT

The role and the modularity of the investments put in place by European banks in the second half of the 1990s can be appreciated by considering the set of institutional factors that impact upon the strategic plans of banks as well as the nature and objectives of those strategies. In this respect we can identify the following forms of intervention:

1. Merger and acquisition operations (M&A);
2. The multi-channel approach;
3. E-banking;
4. The reorganisation of payment systems.

2.2.1   Merger and acquisition operations

The consolidation of the banking industry has been very marked in the EU during the 1980s and 1990s. So far as investment in IT is concerned, this tendency has obliged the banks to make an enormous effort to integrate the complex and often heterogeneous IT system that has resulted.

In fact, the number of mergers and acquisitions increased rapidly and substantially following the liberalisation of the financial services market that – starting from the beginning of the nineties – was introduced legislatively at the European level within the context of the Single Market Programme. The wave of merger operations that took place in the European banking industry in the course of the 1990s – above all, at the national level – has resulted in a smaller number of institutions of a bigger size: in the period between 1997 and 2002 the number of banks in the EU decreased by 1300, that is by about 14 per cent (Table 2.1).[1]

An analysis of the decline in bank numbers across countries, however, shows that there has been considerable variation in this trend. The most marked reduction in the number of banks has taken place in Germany. Substantial reductions have also occurred in France and, to a lesser extent, in Italy and Spain.

Since 2000, however, the trend towards a reduction in the number of banks has basically flattened out: in 2001, the number (and the value) of merger and acquisition operations underwent a marked decline compared with 2000 (in 2001 the value of domestic M&A operations was about 26 billion Euro, i.e. 40 per cent less than the figure for the previous year). The same downward trend continued in 2002. Nonetheless,

Table 2.1   The number of banks in European countries

Number of banks	Year						Change (%) 1997–2002
	1997	1998	1999	2000	2001	2002	
EU15	9077	9260	8809	8368	8023	7756	−14.55
France	1273	1226	1159	1099	1050	1011	−20.58
Germany	3577	3238	2992	2792	2526	2363	−33.94
Italy	935	934	890	861	843	822	−12.09
Spain	411	402	387	368	367	359	−12.65
UK	480	521	496	491	452	440	−8.33

The table shows the number of banks in the banking industry in the EU15 as well as in each of the countries examined in this study. Figures are provided for each year over the period 1997–2002.
Source: European Central Bank (2003a, p. 23).

merger operations continue to take place regularly between medium-sized banks as well as between certain types of banking intermediaries (such as savings banks and co-operative banks and building societies), where the phenomenon is essentially driven by considerations relating to market competitiveness and to economies of scale.

The reduction in the number of banks in Europe has led inevitably to an increase in the degree of concentration. As can be seen in Table 2.2, this phenomenon was widespread in the European banking industry in the period 1997–2002. In keeping with the downturn in the trend towards a reduction in the number of banks, the intensity of the phenomenon of concentration has also diminished. An analysis of the two indexes of concentration employed for each national banking industry (the value of the assets of the five biggest banks in each country as a percentage of the combined value of the assets of all the banks in that country and the Herfindahl index) shows that in spite of the proliferation of merger and acquisition operations, the German banking industry still has the lowest level of concentration among the five countries taken into consideration in this study. It is enough to note that the five largest banks control only 20 per cent of the national banking market. By contrast, Spain reveals the highest level of concentration: the five biggest banks have a market share of 53 per cent. If we extend our analysis to the entire EU banking industry, however, it might well be observed that the degree of increase in the level of concentration that has taken place in the last few years in some countries (Belgium, the Netherlands, Finland and Sweden) gives cause for some concern – if not worry – in relation to the overall competitiveness of the industry.[2]

The role that investment in technology has played in merger and acquisition operations has shown itself to be not so much a driving force in strategic terms as a factor that can produce a retarding effect on such operations or, at any rate, some form of difficulty (European Central Bank, 1999). Indeed, there have even been cases where it has constituted an impediment, given the difficulties – and the short-term costs – associated with the integration of incompatible systems and the consequent reduction in the resources that can be channelled into IT for other purposes.

Nonetheless, it seems clear that following upon merger and acquisition operations it is possible to achieve cost savings in the medium-to-long term by means of the use of more efficient technology (European Central Bank, 1999). This suggests that the very perception on the part of banks of a need to dedicate ever more resources to technology may

Table 2.2 The degree of concentration in the European banking industry (according to country)

	Level of concentration (in percentage terms) – CR5						Herfindahl index				
	1997	1998	1999	2000	2001	2002	1997	1998	1999	2000	2001
France	40	41	43	47	47	45	0.0449	0.0485	0.0509	0.0589	–
Germany	17	19	19	20	20	20	0.0114	0.0133	0.0140	0.0151	0.0158
Italy	31	26	26	23	29	31	0.0306	0.0210	0.0220	0.0190	0.0260
Spain	45	45	52	54	53	53	0.0496	0.0488	0.0716	0.0874	0.0844
UK	24	25	28	28	29	30	0.0207	0.0216	0.0263	–	0.0292

The table shows the degree of concentration in the banking industry of the relevant European countries for each year over the period 1997–2002. The indexes employed are in order: the total value of the assets of the five biggest banks of each country as a percentage of the combined value of the assets of all the banks in that country (CR5) and the Herfindahl index relating to total assets.
Source: European Central Bank (2002b, p. 55; 2003a, p. 24).

itself constitute an economic reason to justify merger and acquisition operations. This last observation may be explained in terms of the need to effect a critical mass of investments in technology so as to pay off the investments themselves as well as adopt technological innovations as they become available with a view to maintaining competitiveness in the industry.

2.2.2 The multi-channel approach

In relation to the second structural characteristic of the industry, the organisational nature of the set of distribution channels, investment in technology again plays a significant role. It is necessary to recognise at the outset that, even though there has clearly been a move towards a multi-channel approach, the automation of branches still claims more than 50 per cent of the IT investment allocated by banks to distribution policies (International Data Corporation, 2000). The relative importance of such investments, however, seems destined to diminish: this rate of growth of IT spending in bank branches for the period 2000–2005 has been estimated at 3.6 per cent, compared with an IT investment growth rate for non-branch distribution channels as a whole of 11.3 per cent. In essence, this means that the policy of strengthening or building up new distribution channels – such as automated teller machines (ATM), point of sales (POS), phone-banking and e-banking – is now pursued in an increasingly radical manner.

It is clear, then, that the European banks now prioritise a multi-channel approach to distribution, in which there is a widespread co-existence of new and traditional distribution channels. This situation gives us good reason to expect that an analogous strategy will continue to prevail in the European banking industry in the future (European Central Bank, 1999). Banking activities are conducted ever more frequently outside traditional branches, or, in other words, beyond the points at which there is personal contact with customers. This does not mean that branches have lost their role in the strategic policies of banks but, rather, that new distribution channels are enjoying an increase in popularity. The fundamental justification for the presence of multiple distribution channels is to be explained by reference to the players involved in banking activity. On the one hand, customers place increased emphasis on simplicity and speed of services (in respect of the timing, the location as well as the velocity of the actual provision of services) as well as on the immediate availability of information and services.[3] On the other hand, banks themselves can extract advantages from the use of new distribution channels, especially remote ones, in the form of potential cost savings and the achievement of greater revenues consequent upon the policies of differentiation associated with the provision of such services.

Notwithstanding such developments, it is apparent that European banks' networks of branches remain extensive. Nor has there been any clear evidence to suggest that the development of alternative distribution channels has led to any excess capacity (European Central Bank, 2002b). In fact, European banks are readjusting the dimensions of their networks of branches more slowly than might have been expected. Indeed, in some countries (for example, Italy and France) – in contrast to expectations – there has been a further expansion in recent years, both in terms of the overall number of branches and in terms of the ratio of bank branches to inhabitants (Table 2.3).[4] It is expected that in the short term the network of branches, which, as has been said, constitutes the point of contact between bank and customer, will maintain a role of foremost importance for European banks. A physical presence is still considered necessary in many countries for two major reasons: on the one hand, remote channels are not yet considered to be a full substitute for branches, given the uncertainty that characterises the demand for such new channels;[5] and on the other hand, in some European countries constraints of a legislative and regulatory nature require the continued presence of branches.[6] A further thing to note is that a considerable number of banks offer access to remote channels essentially with a view to self-defence, in particular, because their major competitors adopt the same approach to distribution.

It seems clear, however, that in the medium term the problem of optimising the use of resources requires that the banks decide whether they intend to consider remote channels as substitutes for the physical network of branches and how they intend to direct customers towards more efficient channels. If the number – and the dimensions – of branches were not reduced, then, in the case that those branches were maintained alongside remote channels, the banks would actually run the risk of losing market share in favour of competitors who were more cost-efficient on account of a distribution policy based exclusively on remote channels. In other words, there is a risk of a duplication of the distribution channels and consequent cost inefficiency.

Presumably, in the long term, banks will consolidate their multi-channel distribution policies with a view to providing services in accordance with principles of cost saving/price reduction and customer satisfaction. In this context, it is quite likely that banks will put in place

Table 2.3 The number of branches maintained by European banks (according to country)

	1998		1999		2000		2001		2002	Variation in number of branches (%) (1994–2000)
	No. of branches	No. of branches per 1000 inhabitants	No. of branches	No. of branches per 1000 inhabitants	No. of branches	No. of branches per 1000 inhabitants	No. of branches	No. of branches per 1000 inhabitants	No. of branches per 1000 inhabitants	
EU15	199,796	0.53	199,027	0.53	–	0.52	–	0.51	–	2.6
France	25,428	0.43	25,501	0.43	25,657	0.43	26,049	0.44	0.43	−1.52
Germany	59,929	0.73	58,546	0.71	56,936	0.69	53,931	0.66	0.62	13.9
Italy	26,283	0.46	27,154	0.47	28,189	0.49	29,266	0.51	0.52	21.9
Spain	39,039	0.99	39,376	0.99	39,311	0.98	39,024	0.97	0.96	8.7
UK	15,873	0.27	15,470	0.26	14,225	0.24	–	0.25	–	−20.9

The table shows the number of branches and the number of branches per 1000 inhabitants for the banking industry of each of the relevant European countries and for the banking industry of the EU15 as a whole in the years 1998–2002. It also indicates the variation that occurred in the number of branches in each of the national banking industries over the period 1994–2000.
Source: European Central Bank (2002b, pp. 52–53; 2003a, p. 23).

a policy to reduce the number of branches. They will do so essentially for two reasons. First, as a response to the spread of e-banking and the competition and pricing pressures exerted by the more efficient banks present in the industry, which we can presumably identify in the form of those banks that will make extensive – if not exclusive – use of remote channels. Secondly, in response to the need for banks to create new demand for their products and services as well as to differentiate between components of the existing demand on the basis of the distribution channels that customers use (traditional versus remote). In this regard, it would seem that the areas of banking activity most likely to provide for substantial increases in the numbers of customers are payment services, services connected with the management and provision of information and services relating to financial securities (in particular, asset management services).

Keeping in mind what has been said so far about the current and probable future importance of multi-channel distribution policies in the European banking industry, it is necessary now to specify how widely spread is each of the alternative channels (listed in ascending order of innovativeness): ATMs, phone banking and e-banking (for this last case, see Section 2.2.3).[7]

So far as ATMs are concerned, it is likely that there will be a progressive, moderate reduction in the investment directed towards this technology following upon the increasing use of e-banking. Nonetheless, ATMs will presumably continue to play a role as a supplementary channel both for the traditional physical channels and for the remote ones. Basically they will come to form an important component of a multi-channel distribution policy, above all in view of the role they will be able to play in providing innovative services in support of banking strategies oriented towards customers. (One need to only think of the simple transmission of marketing messages or of Customer Relationship Management (CRM), which we will discuss later.) The principal factor leading to the maintenance of ATMs is to be ascribed to the fact that they facilitate significant cost savings.[8]

The ratio of ATMs to inhabitants and the number of ATM transactions *per capita* have increased constantly over the period 1998–2001 (Table 2.4). The customers of European banks have been making increasingly intensive use of electronic infrastructures to perform highly standardised operations. The particular manner of using these infrastructures, however, varies significantly from country to country, above all, because

Table 2.4 Number and unit value of operations performed with ATMs

	No. of ATMs per 1,000,000 inhabitants				No. of operations per capita				Average value per operation (in Euro)			
	1998	1999	2000	2001	1998	1999	2000	2001	1998	1999	2000	2001
UE	533	578	623	654	18.8	20.2	21	22	110	111	111	114
France	487	535	582	606	15.0	16.9	18	19	58	61	61	61
Germany	556	563	580	603	17.1	18.4	20	19	152	146	146	157
Italy	487	524	549	593	8.5	8.7	9	10	160	161	163	162
Spain	962	1062	1123	1167	16.2	16.8	18	17	83	87	85	84
UK	415	476	575	612	31.2	33.1	34	37	78	83	91	94

	Increase in the number of ATMs (in percentage terms)				Increase in the number of operations per capita (in percentage terms)				Increase in the average value of operations (in percentage terms)			
	1998	1999	2000	2001	1998	1999	2000	2001	1998	1999	2000	2001
UE	8.7	8.3	9.1	6.7	10.6	6.9	7.9	3.5	12.4	9.7	7.4	6.9
France	9	10	8	5.0	9	13	5	7.6	7	18	5	8.3
Germany	10	1	3	4.1	–	8	11	−4.7	–	3	10	2.4
Italy	10	8	5	8.3	18	2	6	6.6	17	3	7	5.9
Spain	12	10	7	4.8	5	4	10	−5.5	7	9	7	−6.0
UK	6	15	25	11.1	6	6	3	8.2	9	10	5	13.3

The table shows in relation to the relevant national banking industries three indexes relating to the use of ATMs over the period 1998–2001: the number of ATMs, the number of transactions performed per capita at ATMs and the average value (in Euro) of ATM operations. It also shows the average increase (in percentage terms) for each index over the course of the period 1998–2001.
Source: European Central Bank (2002a, p. 355; 2003b, p. 13).

banking intermediaries themselves have implemented a distinct variety of policies. So far as the ratio of ATMs to inhabitants is concerned, the Spanish banking industry is characterised by the most intensive deployment (1167 ATMs per million inhabitants in 2001). By contrast, the figure for the Italian banks is about half of that (593 ATMs per million). In regard to the number of ATM operations *per capita*, however, it is the UK system that is characterised by the most intensive use of the channel (37 transaction per head in 2001). The country with the least intensive use of ATMs, on the other hand, is Italy (10 transactions per head), where, however – as might be expected – the average value per operation is highest: in other words, while the ATMs are used less frequently than elsewhere, the transactions involved are of considerable value (see Table 2.4).

Another alternative channel used by banks is phone banking. This form of banking is offered both by financial institutions without physical branches and direct contact with customers and by mainstream banks. Typically services are provided via telephone, through call centres or through telephone systems with an automatic response facility (keyboard or vocal). For a significant number of banks, phone banking constitutes the only alternative channel that up till now has enjoyed a moderate degree of success in respect of both the banking institutions themselves and their customers. This situation is strictly linked to the fact that phone banking services involve a high degree of standardisation and presumably for this reason facilitate cost savings. Such considerations explain the rapid growth in Europe of the phone banking, which seems to have already been operating for some years at a state of full maturity (European Central Bank, 1999). Particularly interesting is the situation in the banking industries in the United Kingdom and France, the two systems which, compared to the average, appear to be quite advanced as regard to phone banking. In fact, the degree of penetration in these countries (10 per cent) is the highest in absolute terms in the European scene (Table 2.5).[9] In Italy the number of users of phone banking services stood at more than 2.7 million in 2002 and there was a moderately upward trend up until the 3rd quarter of 2003 (Osservatorio Phone Banking, 2003; 2004a,b). Another feature to

Table 2.5 The spread of phone banking in European banks

France [a,b]	10%
Germany [c]	6%
Italy [c]	3%
Spain [a]	6%
United Kingdom [a]	10%

The table shows various indexes relating to the spread of phone banking in Europe between 1997–1998. In particular, it represents phone banking in terms of the following:
[a] the percentage of retail customers;
[b] the percentage of retail bank deposits; and
[c] Minitel users.
Source: European Central Bank (1999, p. 13).

note is the high level of concentration in the use of the channel: about 55 per cent of users are customers at one of the country's five biggest banks.

2.2.3   e-Banking

The third and most innovative distribution channel – commonly referred to as e-banking, be it in the form of on-line PC banking or Internet banking[10] – appears to be the focus of attention of much of the efforts of the European banks to introduce technological innovation. The degree to which the channel has spread – something which depends mostly on the extent to which customers accept it – is closely tied to a number of specific factors, including the socio-economic condition of customers (which manifests itself essentially in terms of the degree of familiarity with the Internet), the type of technological infrastructures that are available (it is enough to think of the recent developments in the technology relating to mobile phones and digital television which have contributed to improving the access of customers to Internet banking) and the creation of an adequate legislative and regulatory framework (just one example is Directive 1999/93/EC on the regulation of the electronic signature in the European Community). It is necessary to recognise, however, that the relative importance of these factors is presumably decreasing in the face of the simplicity, speed and ease of access to banking services provided by the Internet channel.

Given the above considerations, it is likely that the different national systems in Europe will adopt increasingly similar ways of deploying e-banking. The range of services offered includes not only on-line consultation and correspondence with customers, the payment of household bills and money transfers between domestic accounts, but also wholesale international payment services and services relating to financial securities. Further on-line banking services include such things as on-line financing services and payment services for the retail banking clientele.

With a view to providing an authoritative view as to how widespread e-banking is at present, it is worth furnishing some results provided by E-Business W@tch (2003a), the only empirical study – as far as we are aware – that deals with e-banking in Europe. In regard to the spread and use of e-business infrastructures in the relevant countries (for a summary of the technical characteristics, see Inset 1 and Table 2.6), it is apparent that in the majority of cases there is a widespread use of personal computers, Internet, e-mail, Intranet and Local Area Networks (LANs); less widespread, it appears, are Extranet, Wide Area Networks (WANs) and Electronic Data Interchange (EDI).

Inset 1   The most widely used e-business infrastructures

Internet is a world-wide system of computer networks – a kind of network of networks – in which users who use a given computer can, with the appropriate authorisation, obtain information from any other computer on the network (as well as communicate directly with the users of other computers). Developed by a US government agency (Advance Research Project Agency) in 1969 and initially known by the name of ARPANET, it was designed with the intention of creating a network that allowed the users of a computer in one university to communicate with the computers in another university. One additional advantage of ARPANET consisted in the fact that because communications could be directed or diverted in more than one direction, the network could continue to function even if parts of it were destroyed in the course of a military attack or some other type of external disaster. Today, the Internet is a public, co-operative and self-financing instrument accessible to billions of people all over the world.

E-mail (electronic mail) consists in the exchange of messages stored in computers by way of telecommunications. Electronic mail constitutes one of the major forms of use of Internet and to this day is the most widespread; a large percentage of the total amount of traffic on Internet is made up of e-mail.

Intranet is a private network that is developed and deployed within a firm. Generally, it is made up of a number of inter-connected local networks based on TCP/IP (Transmission Control Protocol/Internet Protocol, which are the basic communication and addressing protocols of the Internet). The fundamental reason for adopting the Intranet is that it allows people to share information within a firm. Intranet can also be used to facilitate the work of groups of people and videoconferencing. Normally, large-scale firms allow their Intranet users to have access to the Internet (the public network) by way of a system of firewalls or, in other words, servers that provide protection for communications in both directions in such a way that the security and confidentiality of the firm are guaranteed.

Local Area Networks (LANs) A local area network (LAN) is made up of a group of computers and supporting equipment which rely on a single line of communication (or on a wireless connection) with a view to sharing the resources of a given micro-processor (or server) within a geographic area of limited dimensions (for example, an office building). Generally, this microprocessor or server contains applications and data that can in this way be shared by users on different computers, be they just a few or some thousands.

Extranet has the characteristics of a private network that uses the Internet protocol and public telecommunications systems with a view to sharing in a secure manner certain information about company activities and operations with suppliers, customers, partners and other firms. Thus, the Extranet is a kind of extension of the Intranet directed towards users who stand outside the firm itself. It has also been described as an approach wherein the Internet is perceived as a model for conducting business relations with other firms and for selling products to customers. Firms can use the Extranet with a view to (a) exchanging large quantities of data through Electronic Data Interchange (EDI); (b) providing or having access to services provided by a firm to a group of other firms, as in the case of on-line banking applications managed by one firm on behalf of a group of affiliated banks; (c) collaborating with other firms on joint development projects; (d) developing and using together with other firms programmes for staff development and training; and (e) sharing information of common interest with associated or controlled firms.

Wide Area Network (WAN) A Wide Area Network is a telecommunications network that is spread out geographically. The term serves to distinguish this form of telecommunications network – that is one that extends over a large geographical area – from a Local Area Network (LAN). A wide area network may be privately owned or rented but, generally, the term presupposes the inclusion of a public network that is shared by multiple users.

> **Electronic Data Exchange (EDI)** is a standard format for the exchange of company data. EDI is one form of electronic commerce (e-business). An EDI message contains a sequence of data elements, each one representing a specific item of data (for example, the price and code of a financial instrument). The entire sequence is known as a data segment. One (or more) data segment – preceded by a heading – makes up a transaction set, which constitutes an EDI transmission unit (the equivalent of a message). A set of transmission units is essentially equivalent to what is generally contained in a typical document or commercial form. The subjects that exchange EDI messages are known as commercial partners.
>
> *Source:* various page www.whatis.com

Table 2.6 The availability and use of e-business infrastructures in the European banking industry

	Computers	Internet access	E-mail	Internet use	Intranet	Extranet	LANs	WANs	EDI
France	98.4	93.6	91.9	88.8	47.9	16.5	67.8	26.9	26.2
Germany	99.0	95.9	92.8	93.9	61.2	36.8	66.3	37.2	8.9
Italy	100.0	98.4	95.1	72.1	42.9	15.3	57.5	19.8	5.8
Spain	100.0	96.8	93.6	79.3	49.7	21.1	71.9	28.0	22.8
UK	98.4	93.4	90.2	86.9	38.6	5.2	49.5	9.6	9.1
EU7	98.9	94.9	92.2	84.6	44.9	14.2	58.6	19.9	13.9

The table shows a series of indexes relating to the availability and use of e-business infrastructures in the relevant countries and in the EU7 with reference to the year 2002. The figures reported show in percentage terms the number of banks – of those that participated in the E-Business W@tch survey – that made use of each of the various infrastructures.
Source: E-Business W@tch (2003a).

With regard to the banking industry and, in particular, to e-business infrastructures that are used by European banks, the empirical evidence shows that the use of e-business mainly depends on the size of the banks themselves (measured in terms of the number of employees (Table 2.7)). In particular, medium-sized banks tend to adopt new technology more quickly than larger and smaller banks. This variation can be explained by the fact that medium-sized banks have greater flexibility and propensity to innovate. In this regard it is interesting to note that in many European countries medium-sized players include the popular banks and the savings banks, which have often played a pioneering role

Table 2.7 The availability and use of e-business infrastructures in European banks (according to size)

	Computers	Internet access	E-mail	Internet use	Intranet	Extranet	LANs	WANs	EDI
All industries									
	94.4	84.3	80.6	73.4	30.0	9.1	42.7	9.3	9.4
Banks									
0–49 employees	98.7	94.5	91.6	84.0	41.6	11.8	55.6	16.2	12.6
50–249 employees	100.0	100.0	99.6	98.1	80.8	41.8	87.2	54.7	17.3
250+ employees	100.0	94.1	94.1	94.1	79.9	31.9	100.0	76.6	36.1

The table shows a series of indexes relating to the availability and use of e-business infrastructures with reference to the EU7 banking industry for the year 2002 (The banks are divided according to size, measured in terms of the number of employees). The table also shows the same indexes in reference to all industries in the economy. The figures reported show in percentage terms the number of banks – of those that participated in the E-Business W@tch survey – that made use of each of the various infrastructures.
Source: E-Business W@tch (2003a).

in the adoption of sophisticated technological platforms for the provision of retail and SME (Small and Medium Enterprise) financial services (E-Business W@tch, 2003b). By contrast, the smaller banks – generally in the institutional form of rural banks or co-operative banks – do not have sufficient financial resources to invest in new technology and, therefore, tend to prioritise direct contact with customers.

In order to analyse the role of alternative e-banking channels it is necessary to establish more clearly the degree to which e-commerce has spread within the European banks or, more precisely, the number of purchase and sales operations that are realised on-line. Referring once again to the study conducted by E-Business W@tch (2003a), it is immediately apparent that only 11.6 per cent of banks effected sales operations on-line[11] (Table 2.8). Moreover, the number of banks that made on-line purchases is much higher than the number of banks that effected on-line sales (36 versus 11.6 per cent). This indicates that the banking industry is more advanced as a user of e-commerce than as a provider. The higher number of on-line procurements as opposed to on-line sales can be explained in terms of the fact that the peculiar nature of the activity makes it difficult for the banks to convince their customers to make purchases on-line. Breaking down the data in terms of country, it is apparent that the German banking industry stood well above the European average in terms of the number of banks offering on-line

Table 2.8 On-line sales and procurement by European banks

	On-line sales/ procurement	Projects for on-line sales/ procurement	On-line services for more than 2 years	On-line services from 1 to 2 years	On-line services for less than 1 year
On-line sales					
France	11.1	6.7	79.1	4.7	16.2
Germany	25.9	18.0	53.7	34.7	7.7
Italy	11.5	11.9	49.9	33.5	16.6
Spain	11.6	14.8	27.1	63.8	9.2
UK	8.5	6.8	21.0	58.6	20.4
EU7	11.6	9.1	49.2	34.2	15.3
On-line procurement					
France	31.8	4.9	35.7	36.4	26.9
Germany	58.1	2.9	56.7	38.1	3.4
Italy	21.1	3.7	66.4	32.2	1.4
Spain	26.5	12.2	43.9	52.1	0.0
UK	45.2	8.3	54.8	15.8	29.3
EU7	36.6	6.0	51.1	27.2	20.9

The table shows the number of banks in the EU7 and in each of the countries surveyed (as a percentage of the total number of banks in the sample) that had on-line sales and procurement operations in place in the year 2002. It also shows the number of years that the banks had conducted on-line sales and procurement operations as well as the number of banks that planned to begin such operations.
Source: E-Business W@tch (2003a).

sales (25.9 per cent), while The United Kingdom was the country with the least number of banks offering on-line sales (8.5 per cent). So far as purchases are concerned, on the other hand, it was the Italian banking industry that made the least use of e-business (21.1 per cent), while the German industry was the one most inclined to use it.

Taking into consideration the number of years that the banks have practised on-line sales and procurements (see Table 2.8), it is important to highlight that one-third of banks had practised on-line sales for more than a year and that almost a half had done so for more than 2 years. This points to the great speed with which these new technologies have been introduced into sales policies in the European banking industry. Similarly, the banks were among the first to use e-business on the procurement front, as is testified by the fact that many had been making on-line purchases for more than 2 years.

A distinction between different types of on-line sales in terms of the segment of the market to which the service is provided (retail customers,

Table 2.9 On-line sales of European banks according to the segments of the clientele

	Retail customers	Corporate clients	Public administration
France	95.2	83.3	5.2
Germany	76.7	73.6	31.6
Italy	41.2	37.2	19.1
Spain	72.7	45.7	40.8
UK	79.0	20.5	21.7
EU7	74.7	52.8	20.0

The table shows the number of banks in the EU7 and in each of the countries surveyed (as a percentage of the total number of banks in the sample) that had on-line sales operations in place in respect of the various segments of their clientele (retail, corporate and public administration) in the year 2002.
Source: E-Business W@tch (2003a).

corporate clients and the public administration) shows, as expected, a greater volume of sales to retail customers as opposed to corporate clients or the public administration (Table 2.9). In fact, it would seem reasonable to argue that the on-line banking services offered to retail customers are less sophisticated than those offered to corporate clients and that, therefore, they can be distributed more easily through the Internet channel (it is enough, for example, to think of on-line trading). Note, however, that – compared with the European average – the German and French banking industries were notably more orientated towards the provision of on-line services to the corporate segment.

In order to represent more precisely the magnitude of on-line sales and procurements in the banking industry, it is necessary to classify the banks themselves in terms of the quantity of on-line operations as a percentage of total operations (Table 2.10). In terms of the aggregate for the European banking industry, the level of on-line purchases as a proportion of overall purchases again confirms how on-line activity has had a greater impact on the procurement side than it has on the sales side: only 17.8 per cent of banks had a figure for on-line sales that was greater than 10 per cent of total sales. In respect of on-line procurements that figure rises to 27.8 per cent. These figures provide further evidence of the greater propensity of banks to engage in on-line procurements than in on-line sales. Examining the magnitude of the phenomenon according to country, so far as Italy is concerned, it is apparent that, when the banks choose to position themselves in the on-line sales segment, the strategic choice becomes a determining one. Indeed, for more than a third of such banks, on-line sales represented more than

Table 2.10 On-line sales as a percentage of total sales and on-line procurements as a percentage of total procurements in European banks

	Percentage of sales/procurements on-line				
	50%	**26–50%**	**11–25%**	**5–10%**	**<5%**
	On-line sales				
France	0.0	0.0	3.6	2.2	94.2
Germany	4.5	0.0	17.7	26.5	51.3
Italy	35.5	17.7	3.3	3.2	40.3
Spain	0.0	10.9	0.0	22.5	66.6
UK	0.0	0.0	0.9	25.2	73.9
EU7	7.9	3.9	6.0	15.2	67.0
	On-line procurements				
France	0.0	10.6	5.3	32.4	51.7
Germany	9.2	11.2	16.4	27.3	35.9
Italy	0.0	8.4	23.7	32.9	35.0
Spain	0.0	2.2	17.4	17.4	63.0
UK	7.4	0.5	22.7	30.6	38.8
EU7	4.7	5.6	17.5	30.4	41.9

The table shows the number of banks in the EU7 and in each of the countries surveyed (as a percentage of the total number of banks in the sample) classified in terms of the magnitude of their on-line sales (expressed as a percentage of total sales) and their on-line procurements (expressed as a percentage of total procurements) for the year 2002.
Source: E-Business W@tch (2003a).

50 per cent of total sales. By contrast, in Germany, where the largest number of banks engage in on-line sales activity, the corresponding figure was less than 5 per cent for about half of the relevant banks.

2.2.4   The reorganisation of payment systems

A final factor of an institutional nature, which impacts deeply on the operational activity of banks, takes the form of the reorganisation of the payments system in the European financial sector. Given the presence of a substantial technological component in almost all bank investments effected in this area, it follows that for our purposes it is very important to effect an examination of the cost savings and increases in efficiency achieved as a result of such technological innovation.

In order to analyse the effects of reorganisation of the payment systems resulting from technological developments, it is necessary first of all to examine briefly – in an essentially empirical manner – the operations that are normally involved in payment services. Observing the aggregate figures for all EU countries in 2001, it is evident that credit transfers continued to represent the most widely used form of payment at the European level (31.36 per cent), immediately followed by debit and credit cards (27.73 per cent) and direct debits (24.51 per cent)[12] (Table 2.11). The figures for 1999 show a different picture: credit transfers made up half of non-cash payments and direct debits constituted a third of these. It is particularly interesting to note – in view of the implications it has for the use of technology in banking – that the importance of automated payment systems (above all debit and credit cards) has increased considerably (so much so that it has resulted in a change in the relative importance of the different forms of payment), while the number of cash payments and bank cheques, while still underspread, has diminished.

Survey information from multiple sources indicate that an electronic payment only costs one-third to one-half as much as its substitute paper-based alternative (Humphrey *et al.*, 2001). Since a country payment system can account for 3 per cent of the GDP, the shift to electronic payment from paper-based payment determines marked reductions in bank operating costs, and similar benefits for consumers if all the cost reduction is passed on in the form of price adjustment (Humphrey *et al.*, 2006).[13] Similarly Berger (2003) documents that IT advances appear to have increased productivity and scale economies in processing electronic payments that have reduced costs dramatically over time (in some cases by more than 50 per cent during the 1990s); this may explain some of the recent shift of customers from paper to electronic payments.

The use of credit and, in particular, debit cards has expanded considerably in the Euro zone above all as a result of the growth in the acceptance on the part of shopkeepers of payment instruments different to cash. In fact, in the EU more than one-fifth of all non-cash payment operations in 2001 were effected by way of card-based payment instruments (see Table 2.11). Breaking down the overall figures, it is clearly apparent that the situation varies considerably from one country to another. While card-based payments represented the most widely used payment instrument in Great Britain (39.04 per cent of all payment operations), they constituted a much less important instrument in Germany, where only 11.33 per cent of payment operations were effected by way of card-based instruments. The figures for other European countries were more or less in line with the European average: France: 29.96 per cent; Spain: 26.32 per cent and Italy: 24.63 per cent. In order to appreciate this data fully, however, it is necessary to correlate the figures for the use of the various payment instruments with the number of inhabitants, thereby obtaining a better proxy of the use of the respective payment

Table 2.11 The use of traditional and electronic payment instruments

	Bank cheques				Payments with credit/debit cards				Credit transfers				Direct debits				Cards based on e-money				Total	
	1999		2001		1999		2001		1999		2001		1999		2001		1999		2001		1999	2001
	N	%	*N*	%	*N*	%	*N*	%	*N*	%	*N*	%	*N*	%	*N*	%	*N*	%	*N*	%	*N*	*N*
EU	9,268	19.33	8,486	16.19	11,163	23.29	14,538	27.73	15,933	33.24	16,436	31.36	11,450	23.89	12,847	24.51	88	0.18	113	0.22	47,936	52,419
France	4,480	40.10	4,339	35.42	2,912	26.07	3,671	29.96	2,051	18.36	2,175	17.75	1,731	15.49	2,064	16.85	–	–	3	0.02	11,172	12,251
Germany	424	3.15	319	2.28	1,199	8.90	1,583	11.33	7,025	52.13	6,958	49.81	4,806	35.67	5,080	36.36	21	0.16	29	0.21	13,475	13,970
Italy	665	25.17	606	20.25	477	18.05	737	24.63	1,003	37.96	1,038	34.69	497	18.81	611	20.42	0,4	–	–	–	2,642	2,992
Spain	209	10.65	167	7.34	476	24.26	599	26.32	284	14.48	354	15.55	991	50.51	1,154	50.70	2	0.10	1	0.04	1,962	2,276
UK	2,859	28.81	2,565	23.52	3,406	34.32	4,257	39.04	1,797	18.11	1,931	17.71	1,863	18.77	2,152	19.73	–	–	–	–	9,925	10,905

The table shows the number (in millions) of transactions in the payment services area effected by way of bank cheques, credit/debit cards, credit transfers, direct debits and cards based on e-money as well as the numerical relationship (in percentage terms) between the number of operations effected by each instrument and the total number of payment instruments in the years 2001 and 1999.
Source: European Central Bank (2003b, pp. 19–20).

Table 2.12 The use of electronic payment instruments per inhabitant

	Bank cheques		Payments with credit/debit cards		Direct debits		Credit transfers		Cards based on e-money		Total	
	1999	2001	1999	2001	1999	2001	1999	2001	1999	2001	1999	2001
EU	25	22	30	38	32	35	42	42	0.59	0.58	131	138
France	74	71	48	60	29	34	34	36	–	0.05	185	201
Germany	5	4	15	19	59	62	86	85	0.3	0.4	165	170
Italy	12	10	8	13	9	11	17	18	–	–	46	52
Spain	5	4	12	15	25	29	7	9	0.1	0.03	50	57
UK	48	43	57	71	31	36	30	32	–	–	167	182

The table shows the number of transaction – per inhabitant – performed by way of the various forms of payment services (bank cheques, credit/debit cards, credit transfers, direct debits and cards based e-money) with reference to the years 2001 and 1999.
Source: European Central Bank (2003b, pp. 21–22).

instruments (Table 2.12). Taking into consideration the number of inhabitants, then it is interesting to note that while the evidence relating to France and the United Kingdom shows a relative widespread use of credit and debit cards (coherently with the evidence shown as regard to the number of transactions not taking into account the number of inhabitants), the figures for Italy and Spain show that the use of these payment instruments was very limited (differently from the evidence shown not taking into account the number of inhabitants).

Comparing the different forms of card-based payment, it emerges that debit cards were more widespread than credit cards both in terms of the number of transactions performed and in terms of the number of cards in circulation (Table 2.13). On the other hand, it is important to recognise that the average amount per transaction was much higher for credit cards than that for debit cards (Euro 57.70 versus Euro 101.80 in 2001). If we also take into consideration the number of inhabitants, it emerges that the relative importance of debit and credit cards remains unaltered both in terms of how widespread the use of the instruments was and in terms of the extent to which they were used (Table 2.14). In 2001, at the level of the EU as a whole, there were 928 debit cards for every 1000 inhabitants as against a figure of 434 for credit cards (however, compared with an increase (in respect of 1999) of 48.63 per cent in the number of credit cards, there was an increase of only 17.47 per cent in the number of debit cards). Moreover, debit cards were

Table 2.13 Debit cards and credit cards

	Debit cards				Credit cards			
	No. of transactions	Value per transaction	Increase in no. of transactions	Increase in value of transactions	No. of transactions	Value per transaction	Increase in no. of transactions	Increase in value of transactions
EU	30.4	57.8	22.5	23.7	10.5	90.3	10.4	11.3
France [Francia]	60.3	46.4	11.5	11.2	–	–	–	–
Germany [Germania]	14.7	73.4	16.7	16.6	4.5	100.6	5.4	11.4
Italy [Italia]	7.3	68.6	33.0	26.1	5.4	92.4	15.4	16.0
Spain [Spagna]	8.4	41.0	18.7	23.7	6.4	60.0	16.8	14.6
UK [Regno Unito]	46.0	57.7	15.6	25.0	29.1	101.8	7.8	10.5

The table shows with reference to debit cards and credit cards the number of transactions performed per inhabitant and the average unit sum per transactions in 2001. It also shows the variation (expressed in percentage terms) in the number of transactions per inhabitant and the average value per operation over the period 2000–2001.
Source: European Central Bank (2003b, pp. 14–15).

Table 2.14 Number of debit cards and credit cards per inhabitant

	Cards with a cash function			Cards with a debit function			Cards with a credit function			Cards with an e-money function		
	Number		Variation	Number		Variation	Number		Variation	Number		Variation
	1999	2001		1999	2001		1999	2001		1999	2001	
EU	1039	1194	0.1492	790	928	0.1747	292	434	0.4863	351	484	0.3789
France [Francia]	619	711	0.1486	552	652	0.1812	20	–	–	–	5	–
Germany [Germania]	1201	1480	0.2323	1099	1405	0.2784	200	228	0.1400	739	818	0.1069
Italy [Italia]	369	394	0.0678	351	370	0.0541	214	345	0.6121	1	–	–
Spain [Spagna]	1103	1281	0.1614	1085	1256	0.1576	400	441	0.1025	205	244	0.1902
UK [Regno Unito]	1882	2124	0.1286	775	906	0.1690	755	936	0.2397	3	–	–

The table shows the number of debit cards and the number of credit cards per 1000 inhabitants in 1999 and in 2001 as well as the variations in percentage terms over the period 1999–2001. In particular, the numbers and variations are provided in relation to four types of cards: prepaid cards with a cash function, cards with a debit function, cards with a credit function and cards based on e-money.
Source: European Central Bank (2001, p. 359; 2003b, p. 17).

used for 30.4 transactions per person per year, compared with a figure of 10.5 transactions for credit cards.

The degree to which clients accept these new channels as a way of effecting payment operations depends primarily on the ease with which they can be employed and the cost structure of the underlying technologies. The technologies themselves vary considerably from one country to another. In particular, there are two different technologies that are employed prevalently at the European level: the magnetic card,[14] which is used in the majority of continental countries, and the "chip and PIN" card,[15] which has been introduced recently in the United Kingdom. It is expected that European countries will be the first in the world to pass on to payment technologies based on chips. In fact, by 2006 a substantial number of European credit and debit cards already incorporate chip technology.[16]

This has meant that the reorganisation of payment systems has been closely connected with another development that has impacted significantly on the use of technology by banks, namely the recent, but very marked, tendency of clients to issue and transmit electronic payment instructions to banks (European Central Bank, 2001). Actively exploiting recent advances in the technological infrastructures available, the banks themselves have offered ever more widely payment services based on forms of Internet banking, thereby extending the services they provide through more traditional remote distribution channels (such as self-service banking and phone banking, as discussed earlier). A clear manifestation of this are the initiatives in the banking industry to standardise and simplify the use of these channels in payment operations as well as improve the security features of Internet banking, the electronic payment of household bills and e-money schemes.[17]

This last point in relation to e-money merits further consideration. Although considerable interest has arisen in relation to the use of e-money and its importance,[18] it has not yet been widely used. In 2001, only 0.58 payment operations per inhabitant were conducted in EU countries by way of e-money, even though that figure constituted an increase of 37.89 per cent in respect of the figure for 1999. Underlying this expansion was the development and monitoring of a substantial number of payment schemes tied to e-money. The objective consists in perfecting the features of electronic cards so as to produce a strengthening in the demand on the part of the clients as well as an increase in familiarity with such payment instruments that would presumably encourage more people to use them (especially for low-value transactions).[19]

It follows that, in order to reach the critical mass required with respect to IT investments in remote channels, the banks have to be able to amortise the increase in IT investment necessary to take advantage of the rapid, substantial and innovative developments in payment systems in order to remain competitive. In this context the banks have put in place strategic alliances and co-operative agreements on both the production and the distribution sides. In fact, the problem of economic viability implicit in such operations makes it necessary to consider the nature of the incentives at the basis of such co-operative agreements. In respect of this the following considerations are of particular note: the need to distribute IT development costs among banks participating in the agreement, the need to achieve economies of scale and the importance of design compatible systems. Some concrete examples of such alliances take the form of the following: common platforms for the deployment of ATMs, compatible payment instruments (such as debit cards that are accepted on a world-wide basis) and the definition of compatible technical standards (such as agreements on digital security).

On the other hand, such alliances cause banks to become concerned that they may suffer competitive disadvantages in the case that they are not able to offer payment instruments in advance of competitors who are involved with them in the same co-operation agreements. One further related concern is that in this way the banks become increasingly dependent on external suppliers and partners.

Nowadays all large commercial banks own and run payment systems based on alliances and co-operative agreements. Big banks tend to join-up with other big banks and to run the bulk of the countries payment system. Although this can be quite costly, these banks have the largest number of customers so they need to supply these services anyway. Such co-operation agreements are widely spread also among co-operative and savings banks, where they are set in place by the central institute on which the banks of the particular category are dependent. The bigger central institute can cover the fixed costs required for the development of such new technology better than the individual banks. Moreover, the individual banks benefit from the know-how acquired by the institute and together with the other participating banks they are able to develop commercial synergies to help spread the service. This allows each bank to achieve economies of scale (and to benefit from associated cost reductions) as a result of the centralised collection and processing of information, the rationalisation of production and distribution structures (in particular, the extension of the distribution network) and the centralised management of application software.

3
Evaluating the Performance of Investments in IT: Reflections on the Productivity and Profitability Paradox

3.1 Introduction

Discussion about the evaluation of the performance of investment in technology was dominated for a long time – and in certain respects still is today – by what Solow (1987) referred to as the "productivity paradox". Solow sought to examine the relationship between technology and performance by evaluating the various inputs involved in the production function: labour, capital and, in particular, technology. His analysis revealed that the residue of the function – this amount being understood as the measure of the impact of technology – decreased from the mid-1970s onwards, or, in other words, roughly over the same period from the beginning of which investment in technology became increasingly widespread.

This unexpected and controversial result in respect of the business value of investment in IT meant that it became essential to identify and evaluate the nature and the relative importance of the variables that either make up technology or that impact upon it as well as the nature of the relationship that ties them to performance. In fact, since its emergence, the productivity paradox and its various implications have given rise to a vigorous debate among a large number of economists including – to cite just a few names – Baily and Chakrabarti (1988), Roach (1989), Loveman (1994) and Gordon (1987).[1]

The idea of the productivity paradox has attracted increasing interest as a result of the confirmation on the part of the above-mentioned scholars that the impact of investment in technology on productivity was not obvious. Indeed, it was found that rising levels of investment in IT were actually associated with decreasing levels of productivity, a phenomenon that was particularly evident in the services sector.[2]

In their effort to deal with the productivity paradox, the initial reaction of scholars consisted simply in an attempt to explain its existence (Brynjolfsson, 1993). Departing from the assumption that "a shortfall of evidence is not necessarily evidence of a shortfall", Brynjolfsson (1993) identified a series of possible explanations for the absence of empirical evidence testifying to the possible positive effects of investment in technology on productivity (see discussion in Section 3.4.1).

A later reaction, which unfolded at the beginning of the 1990s in response to the explanations of the productivity paradox offered in the initial work, took the form of an effort to develop more sophisticated models at a microeconomic (at the level of individual firms) and macroeconomic level (at the country or industry level) so as to be able to better examine the relationship between technology and productivity. A reawakening of interest in performance evaluation is also evident in the literature on information systems. The wide array of studies in this direction (Brynjolfsson and Hitt, 1993, 1995, 1996, 1998; Landauer, 1995; Lichtenberg, 1995; Bresnahan, 1999; Jorgenson and Stiroh, 2000; Council of Economic Advisors, 2001; Kraemer and Dedrick, 2001a) provided a range of very clear empirical evidence confuting the productivity paradox (see discussion in Section 3.5).

On the basis of what has been observed so far, it is possible to draw some useful guidance as to how to best focus on the problem of measuring the performance of investments in technology. Although recent research has substantially confirmed the existence of a positive relationship between IT investment and productivity in a large number of industries in the US economy (see the extensive review offered in Dedrick *et al.*, 2003), a number of important questions remain without an answer. In particular, so far as the objectives of our own research are concerned, it must be underlined that it is not at all clear why industries that make intensive use of IT – banks, insurance companies and building societies – have not registered gains in labour productivity in spite of a huge amount of investment in technology. Although the difficulties involved in measuring outputs in such industries may constitute a possible explanation for such results, the more recent literature on the performance of technology (Dedrick *et al.*, 2003) suggests that future research activity should dedicate far greater attention to actually explicating and interpreting them.

In this chapter we seek to address the absence of an interpretative analytical framework for dealing with the reasons for the apparent persistence of the productivity paradox in relation to investments in technology in an industry – like the banking industry – that makes intensive use of IT. Our interest lies in seeking to understand the fundamental issues relating to the mechanisms through which technology realises its effects on performance in the banking industry. The review of the literature presented in this chapter is aimed at providing an analytical framework to use as a theoretical reference point in the course of conducting the empirical study – carried out in Chapter 4 – of the effects on company performance of the investments in technology put in place in the European banking industry over the period 1995–2000.

3.2   An analytical framework for the evaluation of the value of investments in IT

In order to offer a critical overview of the literature on the evaluation of the value of technology, we adopt an analytical framework that outlines the main economic theories and performance measures used in various studies to investigate IT/performance issues and also quote the context in which the studies are undertaken.

3.2.1   Economic theories and methodological reflections on the value of technology

So as to be able to interpret the results put forward in the literature on the productivity paradox, it is necessary first to spell out the particular characteristics of the problem. From the theoretical point of view this involves assigning the existing studies to three, logically distinct, theoretical and methodological, frameworks that together facilitate the identification of the various issues involved in examining the value of technology (in this regard, see Hitt and Brynjolfsson, 1996):

a. The economic theory of production, aimed at identifying whether investments in technology contribute to increasing productivity. In other words, does technology allow for the production of a greater quantity of outputs for a given quantity of inputs?
b. The theory of strategic competition, aimed at enquiring into whether investments in technology improve business profitability. Are firms able to use technology to obtain competitive advantage and realise profits that are higher than those they would achieve otherwise?
c. The theory of the consumer, geared towards investigating the creation of value for consumers by technology. In other words, to what extent does technology generate benefits that are either delivered to the consumer or demanded by him or her?

The framework outlined in (1) above has been traditionally used to evaluate the productivity of various inputs including capital, labour and expenditure on research and development (Berndt, 1991). In more recent years proponents of the theory have introduced the concept of the production function, which explicates in mathematical terms the method that firms use to transform inputs into outputs. On the assumption that there is a correspondence between the production function and certain mathematical assumptions, it can be demonstrated that the employment of various combinations of inputs will result in the production of a given level of outputs. Employing a particular form of the production function (generally, quasi-concavity and monotonicity), it is possible to estimate econometrically the contribution of each input to total outputs in terms of gross marginal productivity.[3] The theory implies, therefore, that rationally managed firms should continue to invest in a given input up until the time that the last unit of this input generates a value superior to its cost. Moreover, given that every input involves a cost, according to the theory, gross marginal productivity should be positive. In a state of equilibrium, then, the theory of production assumes that investments in technology have a positive gross marginal productivity (i.e. they contribute positively to the total amount of outputs – to the margin).[4] In other words, the theory predicts that lower prices for technology should be capable of generating benefits in the form of a reduction in the costs of production for a given output. Well known in this regard is Moore's Law.[5]

The framework deriving from the theory of strategic competition, outlined in (2) above, is proposed with the aim of overcoming a limitation in the theory of production, in particular the inability to identify whether firms can extract a competitive advantage out of technology and, thereby, realise higher profits (in other words, increases in the value of the firm itself). The possibilities that might arise are twofold. On the one hand, if a firm has exclusive access to a given technology, it may be in a position to generate higher profits precisely by virtue of that access. On the other hand, technology does not enable a firm to make an abnormal profit, if all the other players in the industry have ready access to it.[6] In this latter case, there is no reason to expect *a priori* that a firm that spends more (or less) on technology compared with its competitors will achieve a higher (or lower) level of profit. On the contrary, all the firms will use the amount of technology that they judge to be optimal in a state of equilibrium. In any case, no single player will be in a position to obtain competitive advantage from investments in technology. This line of argument is consistent with what is maintained by Clemons (1991) and, more recently, by Carr (2003): that technology has become a "strategic necessity" and not a source of competitive advantage. The only situation in which technology (or any other input) enables firms to achieve abnormal profits is where there exist barriers to entry into the industry.[7] There are basically two circumstances in which technology can act as a barrier to entry. In the first place, in industries with pre-existing barriers to entry it may be possible for firms to increase profits by way of an innovative use of technology, provided that the barriers to entry remain intact. Secondly, the very use of technology itself may reinforce or weaken already existing barriers to entry, or, indeed, it may create new ones, bringing about in this way a change in the profitability of the individual firms or the industry as a whole. The impact of technology on barriers to entry is not clear. On the basis of what has been observed so far, it would seem that the theory of strategic competition does not allow us to predict in an unambiguous manner how technology impacts upon barriers to entry in a given industry and, therefore, is not capable of identifying a unidirectional relationship – whether positive or negative – between technology and profits. The hypothesis, then, is that technology is not correlated with abnormal profits. Out of this arises the issue of whether it is possible to identify an empirical test for the relationship in question.

The framework based on the theory of the consumer, outlined in (3) above, and it, too, like the previous framework, derived from microeconomics, can be used to estimate the overall benefits that the purchase of a given product bestows on consumers. The consumer demand curve represents how much consumers are willing to pay for every additional unit of product. Actually, in reality, consumers simply have to pay the market price. Thus, if they attribute to a given product values that are higher than that of the market price, then, in this way, they obtain a surplus. Adding together all the benefits of each additional unit of product, the total benefit can be represented in terms of the area that intervenes between the demand curve and the offer curve. Moreover, in a competitive sector of the economy even the surplus deriving from the inputs into production is transferred to consumers. In this way, in respect of an input – like technology – the area under the demand curve represents an appropriate estimate of consumer surplus (Schmalensee, 1976). The principal problem tied to the adoption of such an approach is the identification of the *locus* of the demand curve (Berndt, 1991). Nevertheless, in the case of technology the natural occurrence of a dramatic reduction in the cost of microprocessors makes it possible to trace the evolution in the actual amount of technology purchased. This makes it possible to trace the demand curve and, thereby, calculate consumer surplus (Brynjolfsson, 1996). In a state of competitive equilibrium a reduction in the price of a given input generates an increase in expenditure for that input and an increase in consumer surplus. Thus, if firms effect optimal investments, the marginal consumer surplus should be higher than (or, at least, equal to) the related costs. Assuming that the theory is valid, consumer surplus originating from technology should emerge as positive and increasing over time.

3.2.2   The definition of the economic concept of performance

The second dimension of the analytical framework outlined above relates to the concept of performance. This concept can be summed up in terms of the output of the production process. The distinction between the various analytical perspectives outlined above implicitly creates grounds for deriving from each of them a particular measure of performance or, seen from another angle, allows us to assemble a variety of ways in which to specify – in economic terms – the notion of performance. Looked at in this way, the theory usually distinguishes the following classes:

a. at the level of the country and of the particular industry, which have been the focus up to date of much of the discussion as well as the empirical results available in the literature, the notion of performance has been perceived in terms of economic growth, the wealth of consumers and growth in the productivity of labour. While economic growth is expressed in terms of variations in gross domestic product (GDP) and is measured at the level of the country, growth in labour productivity acts as a measure of the efficiency with which resources are used to create value and is used principally in relation to particular industries;
b. at the microeconomic level of individual firms, economic performance can be expressed in terms of the following indicators: labour productivity, profitability, intermediate measures of economic results, the composition of the production mix, multi-factor productivity (MFP), market share and the wealth of consumers.

To better demonstrate the legitimacy of the above-mentioned indexes, it is worth making some additional observations. A firm has a higher level of productivity when, for a given number of outputs produced, it employs a smaller number of inputs (and in this way enjoys a cost advantage); or when, with the same amount of inputs, it produces outputs of a higher quality (and, therefore, charges a higher price, the so-called "premium price"). In this way labour productivity, profitability, intermediate measures of economic results, the composition of the production mix and multi-factor productivity all constitute appropriate measures of performance. If one accepts that a firm interacts in a variety of ways with the institutional environment in which it operates, it becomes necessary to characterise the concept of performance in a broader fashion and, as a corollary, to identify for it other indicators. On the assumption that competition induces competing firms to bridge any differences in terms of productivity, the achievement of higher profits by a particular firm – thanks to productivity gains – would imply that firm had the capacity to maintain levels of profitability higher than those of its competitors. In essence, this means that in terms of this line of reasoning market share constitutes a good indicator of performance. Finally, it should be noted that we can assume that over the long term, profits are eroded to the benefit of consumers. This benefit relates to the aggregate value realised by consumers from their purchase of goods after the price paid for the goods has been deducted. Viewed in this way, the performance of firms can be measured in terms of the wealth of consumers (consumer surplus).

By way of summary, in the literature the concept of performance – both at the level of the firm and at the level of the industry or country – has generally been quantified by way of the use of two measures of productivity: first, labour productivity, which, it is assumed, increases in the moment that the workforce is provided with more capital; and secondly, multi-factor productivity, which consists in the realisation of a higher output for given levels (and qualities) of inputs.

Such reflections on the concept of performance raise a number of questions in relation to the validity of the various particular positions that have been traditionally adopted in the literature. In fact, parting from the assumption that a distinctive feature of technology is its ubiquity, it is necessary to ask which definition of productivity is best able to capture the particular characteristics of technology. The nature of technology implicitly creates the grounds for introducing as a measure of performance production efficiency (otherwise known as operating efficiency or, in the terminology originally introduced by Leibenstein in 1966, X-inefficiencies). This measure makes provision for taking into consideration the productivity of an organisation and its resources (not just its financial resources), for distinguishing between results that can be attributed to institutional factors as opposed to structural factors and for attributing importance to organisational matters (in particular, those relating to the professional skills of a firm's staff). For these reasons, in this book we have worked on the assumption that measuring performance is only possible by way of a complex procedure which does not neglect to take into consideration how an investment in technology can have indirect effects on all the inputs and outputs in the production process – and which, therefore, as will be elaborated in Sections 3.4.3 and 4.4.2, makes use of X-efficiencies.

3.2.3   The level of analysis

In order to better illustrate the analytical framework developed so far, it is necessary to examine the third dimension referred to above, focusing attention on the implications of the "level of analysis". In fact, this third dimension takes the form of the level – in terms of the relevant economic aggregate – to which performance relates, in that it is assumed, as has already been shown, that the nature of payoffs should be broken down in accordance with the economic context in relation to which a given enquiry is conducted. In particular, it is possible to distinguish the following levels:

a. the aggregate of the industry;
b. the aggregate of the entire economic system (national or international);
c. the separate entities constituted by production units (the single firm).

The analysis of the impact of technology at the macroeconomic level of the entire economy, as in (a) and (b) above, enables researchers to deal with a wide range of critical questions, even though investments in technology distribute their immediate effects in the microeconomic context of the firm. Reference to the entire economic system makes it possible to understand the role that technology and the IT industry, too, play in strengthening economic growth and, in the final analysis, increasing the wealth of a country. In addition, it makes provision for discussing the existence of stable, high growth rates in economies characterised by an intensive use of IT, a typical and central component of which is represented by the banking industry. Finally, it allows for the identification and understanding of the differences between the various industries and an examination of the role that the structural, institutional and regulatory characteristics of each industry play in influencing the returns that are achieved as a result of investments in technology. One critical matter in this regard consists in examining whether productivity gains do actually take place in industries that make intensive use of IT and, in the event that they do, investigating whether these gains can be attributed to the investments in technology. The research question can be put broadly in the following terms: has the intensive use of technology allowed such industries to adopt production methods that are superior to those that would otherwise have been adopted?

In our analysis of the European banking industry, the macroeconomic approach at the level of the country or at the industry level involves us pursuing, among others, the following distinctive objectives (in this regard, see Dewan and Kraemer, 1998 for a general overview, the relevant parts of which have been drawn on here):

1. investigating the productivity paradox at the level of analysis in respect of which its existence has been identified, in particular, at that of the industry as a whole;
2. verifying whether technology leads to a better economic performance for the entire banking industry or whether it simply effects a redistribution of the economic performance among the various banks;
3. bringing together data relating to various countries with similar characteristics with a view to obtaining evidence in relation to the performance of investment in technology in each of the countries;
4. broadening the scope of the empirical analysis undertaken to date in the studies at the microeconomic level, which have concentrated exclusively on large-scale listed firms in the United States and which, for this reason, do not necessarily reflect the experience of the European banking industry, the object of this study.

On the other hand, the analysis of the impact of technology at the microeconomic level, as in (c) above, is justified because investments in technology are in actual fact put in place by individual organisations, in particular firms, whose interest lies in the performance of their own investments and not in that of the national economic system as a whole. Although the productivity paradox was originally put forward and formulated with reference to statistics on levels of aggregate productivity, it is individual general managers and financial managers who make decisions about investing in technology and who, in performing this role, use investment evaluation criteria that relate to performance at the level of the firm. The confirmation that the productivity of technology improves overall productivity at a macroeconomic level does not imply that individual firms necessarily draw analogous benefits. In fact, it may well be that investments in technology generate significant social benefits which find expression in a higher level of consumer wealth or higher overall economic growth but which are not enjoyed by the firms that actually make the investments. Therefore, for managing directors as well as financial managers – not to mention people working in the IT area – it is a matter of great concern whether their investments in technology produce positive payoffs for the firm.

3.3   The productivity paradox: its origins and underlying causes

At the end of the 1980s (and the beginning of the 1990s), when investment in technology had been experiencing – and would continue to experience – a long period of apparently inexorable growth, there began to be expressed in the academic literature and, in particular, in the economics literature considerable doubts and concerns in relation to the impact of technology on the productivity of organisations. This was reinforced by many high-profile macroeconomic studies – conducted at both the level of the national economy and that of individual industries – that suggested that if there had been any positive payoff from investment in technology, it had been minimal (and, in any case, not substantial enough to justify the enormous expenditure that had been sustained).

One of the first influential scholars to investigate the theme from a macroeconomic perspective – at the level of the entire system or at the inter-sectorial level – was Roach (1986, 1989).[8] Interest in the matter first arose when scholars began to reflect on how at the beginning of the 1970s there had been a sharp downturn in productivity in the entire US economy. This downturn, in fact, had more or less coincided with the rapid increase in the use of technology. The negative correlation between overall productivity at the level of the national economic system and the advent of computers was what stood at the basis of many lines of reasoning that held that technology would not help to generate increases in productivity in the United States or even that investments in technology *per se* were counter-productive. This argument was put forward in Roach (1989), where attention was focused specifically on "the workforce involved in information" (information workers) independently of the industry to which they belonged. The statistics analysed by Roach showed that the productivity of workers engaged in the manufacturing sector grew by 16.9 per cent between the mid-1970s and 1986, whereas the productivity of information workers diminished over the same period by 6.6 per cent. He concluded that the reason for the fall in productivity in the United States was essentially clear, specifying that it had been concentrated in that portion of the economy which constitutes the major supplier of white-collar work and which is most densely endowed with high technology capital (Roach, 1989, p. 104).

Focusing attention on the literature dealing with the services sector, it is immediately apparent that there is ample documentation to show that much of the downturn in productivity took place precisely in that sector (Roach, 1991).[9] Before the 1970s, productivity growth in the services sector remained at levels more or less the same as those in the manufacturing sector but, starting from those years, the trend showed what appeared to be a significant inversion. Against this, at the same time there began to take place in the services sector a substantial increase in the share that the sector provided of total employment and, albeit in a less marked fashion, the share that it generated of total production. Given that the services sector used about 80 per cent of technological resources, this situation was taken to be indirect evidence of the limited contribution IT made to productivity.

An important reservation, which may discredit the very validity of the argument, must be expressed immediately. It is very clear that a failure to identify benefits and productivity increases in the use of technology may derive equally either from an inept management of the development and use of the technology or from deficiencies in the methods used for measuring and the rigor with which they are employed. In particular, the principal limitations of the measurements in the studies on the services sector stem from the fact that many of the transactions that take place in it are effected by idiosyncrasy (Brynjolfsson and Hitt, 1993) and, as a consequence, are subject to problems of statistical aggregation and arbitrariness in classification.

Moreover, it is also evident, as suggested by Brynjolfsson (1993), that the alarming correlation between increases in investment in IT and reductions in the productivity of the entire US economic system should not be taken as absolute and definitive in that a whole series of other factors can impact upon productivity. What is more, on the assumption that growth in investment in technology had taken place at substantial levels – and this was true of the period in question – Brynjolfsson predicted plausibly that, in view of the growth rates at the time and on the further assumption that computers do actually help to increase productivity, there would be increases in the aggregate level of GDP in the immediate future.[10]

3.3.1 The productivity paradox in the original studies on the banking industry

A body of research that has even more relevance for this book relates to the many studies on the impact of technology on the performance of the various types of intermediaries operating in the financial services industry. Parsons *et al.* (1993) estimated a production function for banking services in Canada and showed that the impact of IT on multi-factor productivity was quite low in the years from 1974 to 1987. The hypothesis advanced in this study was that investments in technology placed the industry in a position to be able to obtain higher levels of growth in the future. Similarly, from a productivity analysis on US retail banks for the years 1993–1995, Prasad and Harker (1997) conclude that additional investment in IT capital may have no real benefits and may be more of a strategic necessity to stay even with the competition. However, their results indicate that there are substantially high returns to increase in investment in IT labour and that retail banks need to shift their emphasis in IT investment from capital to labour. Similar conclusions were proposed in a study by Franke (1987), where it emerged that investments in technology are tied to a clear decrease in the productivity of capital and to stagnation in the productivity of labour. Nonetheless, the author remained optimistic about the future potential of technology, pointing to the time lags associated with previous "technological transformations". Similarly, Willcocks (1992) calculated that 30–40 per cent of IT-related projects fail to produce a net benefit for the activity. One particularly relevant aspect of this study was that in the evidence presented there were many examples that related to the banking industry. Willcocks (1992) maintained, moreover, that at least 20 per cent of expenditure in IT was useless. This finding strongly suggests that it would be a good idea to introduce a strict method of financial evaluation to determine which IT proposals should be supported. In other words, approval should be given only to those IT investments for which clear financial advantages have been demonstrated. Alpar and Kim (1990a,b) also provided an estimate – with reference to a sample of 759 American banks over the period 1979–1986 – of the variation in costs provoked by investments in technology. They compared two approaches based respectively on microeconomic theory (i.e. a translog cost function including IT attributes) and on accounting ratios (i.e. return on common equity). The empirical evidence based on the translog cost function shows that IT has been cost reducing (a 10 per cent increase in IT capital is associated with a 1.9 per cent decrease in total costs) whereas the accounting ratio does not show any significant correlation with IT investments. Therefore, as they noted, the methodology used to make the estimate heavily conditioned the results. Specifically, the approach based on standard accounting ratios emerges as particularly misleading, if compared with that based on the microeconomic theory of productivity.[11]

So far as the European banking industry is concerned, there is again a notable lack of information on the performance impact of investments in technology. According to a study conducted by Child and Loveridge (1990), European banks have invested in technology in the expectation that other costs, in particular, those relating to personnel, would be contained and that, as a consequence, the quality of the service to clients would be improved. However, not only have the majority of the banks not made any systematic attempt to verify whether such benefits have actually been realised but (as far as we are aware) they have not even tried to identify their impact or effects. The reasons put forward to explain the lack of information on the performance impact of technology investment probably relate to the view that the benefits derived from IT are obvious and are also related to the difficulties involved in distinguishing between the various projects into which investment in technology is channelled.

3.4   Four possible explanations of the productivity paradox

3.4.1   The original contributions in the literature on information systems

Although similar conclusions about the productivity paradox have been reached in a large number of empirical studies in the field of information systems (that typically refined the analysis to the point of redefining the paradox as a "productivity mystery"), Brynjolfsson (1993) argued that "A shortfall of evidence is not necessarily evidence of a shortfall".[12] In the context of this debate, Brynjolfsson (1993) suggested four possible explanations for the apparent productivity paradox, relating to:

1. the measurement of outputs and inputs;
2. delays in learning and adjusting to technology;
3. the redistribution and dissipation of profits;
4. bad management of information and technology.

The first two explanations propose as determinants of the productivity paradox deficiencies in the methodology of the related research and not phenomena of an objective nature. In the first place, it is possible that the benefits of investment in technology are substantial but that a valid indicator for measuring its actual impact has not yet been identified. The traditional measures of the relationship between inputs and outputs have not succeeded in taking account of the non-traditional sources of value. In the second place, if there exist significant time lags between the moment in which the investment in technology is effected and the subsequent moment in which the benefits associated with it become apparent, results over the short term may very well seem modest. Nonetheless, in the ultimate analysis the payoffs may well be proportionately greater over the long term. In fact, these time lags may be due, for example, to widespread problems of an organisational nature brought on by the adoption of the technology such as difficulties in learning how to use the hardware and the software on the part of the workforce and changes in organisational procedures.

The other two explanations suggest that in reality investments in technology may not produce positive payoffs (either in the present or potentially). This implies that it is necessary to investigate why in spite of contraindications managers continue to invest systematically in technology. The argument about the redistribution of profits suggests that, although the organisations that invest in technology do benefit from it on an individual basis, this could come about at the expense of others. In this way no net benefit would be generated at the aggregate level. The last explanation is that there has been a systematic mismanagement of technology: there must be something in the very nature of technology that leads firms – or, indeed, entire industries – to make investments even when they ought not to or, alternatively, to allocate technology investment in an erroneous way even to the point that the technology itself, rather than promote productivity, acts as a factor that causes delays and shortfalls.

The first reason, given as (1) above, relates to errors in measuring inputs and outputs. In practice such problems of measurement seem to be particularly serious in the services sector, where, moreover, the majority of IT capital is directed. One extremely important category of benefits that is typically associated with investment in technology takes the form of the so-called "soft benefits" including, for example, improvements in quality, additional services provided to the user, the speed and the rapidity of operations and customisation in the form of tailoring products and services to the specific needs of clients. After all, it is precisely the soft benefits that constitute the component of output that is taken into consideration only partially in the statistics on productivity and in traditional accounting data.

The second explanation ((2) above) relates to time lags due to the learning process and to organisational adjustments associated with (and provoked by) technology. The benefits deriving from IT may require many years before they manifest themselves in a substantial way in financial terms. Because of the complexities and innovations produced by technological change, users need to have a certain amount of experience before they can become proficient.[13] In addition, it should be recognised that many IT projects require months, if not years, before they can be brought to completion. Because of this, if the costs and benefits are measured only on a short-term basis,[14] the investments in technology will appear inefficient. The literature on information systems has stressed that, in order for investments in technology to show a positive payoff, it is necessary that from the time of the investment there elapses a period of at least 5 years. This thesis finds confirmation in a range of studies (Brynjolfsson *et al.*, 1994; Brynjolfsson and Hitt, 2000). In particular, Brynjolfsson and Hitt (2000) suggested that the positive impact of technology on the growth of multi-factor productivity was at its peak only after a lapse of time that goes from a period of 4 to 7 years from the time of the investment.[15]

A third possible explanation of the productivity paradox, as outlined in (3) above, relates to the redistribution of profits. In this context, it is necessary to point out that, although technology can produce benefits at the microeconomic level of the single firm, at the macroeconomic level, it may turn out to be unproductive from the point of view of either the entire industry or the national economic system as a whole.[16] Moreover, Brynjolfsson (1993) stressed that such a redistribution hypothesis would not imply in any way that investments in technology at the level of the firm were not productive. In very general terms, the hypothesis is that firms that do not channel sufficient financial resources to their technology budgets are destined to lose market share and profits at the expense of organisations with high levels of investment in technology.

The fourth explanation ((4) above) is that investments in technology are not actually productive at the microeconomic level of individual firms. In the literature this explanation was considered – at least up until the beginning of the nineties – to be the only one that had empirical support. Brynjolfsson (1993) argued that, notwithstanding the power of the neo-classical view of firms as agents engaged in maximising profits, it is necessary to take into consideration the possibility that certain decision-makers simply fail to act in the interest of the firm.[17] Institutional factors, regulatory restrictions, the scope for interpretation on the part of human agents, established practices and inadequate methods for evaluating strategies can all have the effect of impeding firms from obtaining benefits from investments in technology. Quite apart from these considerations, however, at the end of the day, decision-makers in firms may still encounter difficulty in transforming these benefits into overall performance (expressed in terms of "output" and "profit"), if production targets, the organisation of labour and incentive systems are not planned in an appropriate way.

3.4.2   More recent research on the productivity paradox

In the latest literature – that published after the research discussed in Brynjolfsson (1993) – further explanations have been offered for what had been identified in the earlier writing as the productivity paradox (for an overview of this literature, see Sigala, 2003):

1. The quality of the data used and analysed. Technology is characterised by an "amplifying effect", that is while the introduction of technological change in a badly managed firm does not increase productivity, positive payoffs are regularly realised in the case of investments in efficiently managed firms (Cron and Sobol, 1983; Strassmann, 1990). The inclusion of technology as an input into the production function, without specifying whether the firms in question were characterised by low or high productivity, has been a typical flaw of the research which has pointed to the existence of the productivity paradox.
2. Measures employed for the quantification of productivity. More recent advances in the relevant literature have tended to suggest that productivity measures have been capable of capturing fully the impact of technology (for example, in terms of improvements in quality or achieving competitive advantages). Within this perspective, the productivity paradox would not represent so much a *mismeasurement* of technology as a *mismanagement* of technology (Jurison, 1996), that is firms are seen as incapable of transforming the intermediate benefits of technology (such as improvements in quality) into final results (like increases in prices). Moreover, it should be noted that it is widely recognised that aggregate measures of input/output tend to obscure information while partial measures tend to highlight information, trade-offs and the complementarity of various dimensions (e.g. resources and company divisions).

3. Measures used for the quantification of technology. The value of investments in technology – as expressed in the income statement and the balance sheet[18] – is the measure most widely used for quantifying technology. This is because it is both easily obtained and reasonably objective. In spite of its reliability and validity, however, it is commonly criticised on the grounds that it does not make provision for distinguishing between hardware and software, which, by contrast, generate results and benefits of a variegated nature (Strassmann, 1990; Weill, 1992, Lucas, 1993; Gurbaxani *et al.*, 1998). In addition, this measure of investments does not take account of two important aspects of technology: the effects that the employment of technology produces and the evolution in its features and capabilities (Willcocks *et al.*, 1998) and, for this reason, it is not able to show how technology creates business value. Also, as far as standard accounting practice is concerned, in different firms the value of IT has been subject to changing accounting methods over the course of time as well as to differences in the ways that the technology is financed (consider, for example, the effects of outsourcing). Finally, even if the value of IT capital (the stock value of technology) is considered an appropriate form of measurement, there remains the problem of "how" to measure it. For every given amount of output, if the level of IT capital used is overvalued, its productivity per unit will seem less than what it really is. For example, in relation to this matter, Denison (1989) argued that the statistics relating to public entities overestimated the degree of deflation in the price of computers. The consequence of this measuring error is that a large part of the productivity improvement attributed by government bodies to the industry that produces technology should actually be attributed to the industries that use it.

4. The level of analysis at which the research on the relationship between technology and productivity is conducted. The measurement of productivity at the macroeconomic level of the industry or the country as a whole is characterised – alongside the advantages described in Section 3.2.3 – by limitations due to an inability both to capture phenomena which are manifest at the level of the firm and to show the effects of the redistribution of profits (Brynjolfsson, 1993). In relation to this, Menon (2000) maintained that the best level of analysis was that of the organisation, arguing that it made provision, on the one hand, for capturing synergies, the substitutability and complementarity of resources and the inputs and outputs of the production process and, on the other, for dealing with the analytical

difficulties present at the level of business processes (including the collection of data and the insufficient size of samples, the separation of IT effects and non-IT effects for each process and the generalisability of the results in view of the difficulty of finding analogous processes conducted by different firms with and without technology).

5. The statistical method used to correlate productivity and technology. Most studies have made recourse to regressions and the analysis of indices. The statistical technique of regression analysis is imperfect above all because it does not make provision for considering simultaneously any more than a very limited number of variables.[19] Moreover, it does not make provision for investigating the effects of a single input (or output) on multiple outputs (or multiple inputs). Finally, it does not take into consideration the existence of inefficiencies in production, which, by contrast, can be accounted for by making use of econometric techniques based on a production function (see Section 4.4.2.4). In fact, this latter technique takes into consideration multiple outputs and multiple inputs simultaneously. Given such advantages, the insistence on the use of the production function has been repeatedly emphasised in the most recent literature on the performance of technology.

3.4.3　Implications for studies on the banking industry

The problems involved in the measurement of inputs and outputs appear to have constituted the underlying reason for the emergence of the productivity paradox particularly in industries characterised by an intensive use of IT, of which the banking industry is a classic example. The speed of innovation has made the banking industry particularly susceptible to problems associated with the quantification of qualitative improvements and the evaluation of new products. In addition, it is necessary to consider the diversification in the products and the delivery channels, improvements in terms of speed and delivery times and the customisation of the services provided to clients – all additional benefits that are represented only to a very limited degree in the statistics on productivity and in accounting indices. Finally, given that information is an intangible good, increases in the implicit informational content of products and services is most probably underrepresented compared with the more evident increases in material content. It is clear, then, that this set of benefits, the so-called "soft benefits", has in all probability improved as a result of investments in technology. After all, these benefits are extremely difficult to measure using traditional accounting methods and production statistics. In fact, in the short term, traditional accounting measures do not provide an adequate measurement of soft benefits. Nonetheless, in the long term – because of the effects of the competitive process – even the traditional accounting measures should be capable of capturing improvements in the quality of outputs and the speed of delivery as well as in the customisation of services.

A few examples may serve to illustrate the problem of not being able to measure soft benefits in the banking industry. From the point of view of outputs, the convenience offered by ATMs available 24 hours a day constitutes a concrete example of an improvement in the quality of service offered to customers. It goes without saying, moreover, that this improvement is difficult to measure. For example, to what extent has this improvement contributed to strengthening the loyalty of customers? Similarly, so far as inputs are concerned, the improvements produced by computers in work procedures and conditions (the reduction of the repetitive operations of copying, tabulating and recording) do not find expression in any direct way in the accounting results and statistics relating to the labour productivity factor.

In order to overcome the wide and critical range of problems connected with the measurement of inputs and outputs, in this study we introduce X-inefficiencies as a measure of productivity along with a number of other measures of profitability traditionally put forward in the literature on information systems. X-inefficiencies measure the distance between each firm observed in the sample available and a given point on the best-practice function.[20] The reasoning underlying the adoption of such a performance measure derives from the need to resolve the traditional measuring problems in a way that not only takes account of the ubiquity of the technological function but also pays particular attention to the evaluation of the differences in the ability of managers to control costs and to maximise profits.

The interest in X-inefficiencies derives not only from a finding in the literature (X-inefficiencies account for about 20 per cent of costs in banks, while economies of scale and scope, when estimated accurately, generally constitute less than 5 per cent of costs)[21] but also – and above all – from the fact that X-inefficiences represent the distance from the efficient frontier that comes into being when the objectives of perfect rationality and complete knowledge are realised.

So far as the first of the above two considerations is concerned, it is necessary to underline immediately that differences in the capacity of managers to control costs or to maximise profits seem to be more important than the effects deriving from the choice of the scale or scope of production. As shown in a pioneering manner in the Italian literature (Fusconi, 1983, 1985), size and diversification do not always explain the differences in the efficiency of financial intermediaries. For this reason, too, then, the themes relating to the value and evolution of X-inefficiencies warrant greater attention on the part of scholars in terms of both theoretical reflection and empirical research. A similar interest in the analysis of X-inefficiencies can be seen in the research that appeared some years later in the international arena (Berger *et al.*, 1993, p. 222): "While scale and scope efficiencies have been extensively studied, primarily in the context of US financial institutions, relatively little attention has been paid to measuring what appears to be a much more important source of efficiency differences – X-inefficiencies, or deviations from the efficient frontier."

Regarding the second of the above two factors, the assumptions underlying the microeconomic theory in question, it should be underlined right from the outset that X-inefficiencies assume the existence of actors that are not perfectly rational as well as partial information and, in this way, are capable of accounting for how errors, delays, inertia and uncertainty may contribute to determining the capacity of actors to control costs or maximise profits. Basically for this reason, as will be discussed extensively in Section 4.4.2.1, X-inefficiencies constitute measures that potentially are capable of capturing those soft benefits which up to now researchers in the field of IT performance have not been able to represent in their studies. It is for this reason that in this book we seek to estimate the performance of investments in IT on the basis of X-inefficiencies.

3.5   Revisiting the productivity paradox

At the beginning of the 1990s, following on from the possible explanations of the productivity paradox offered in Brynjolfsson (1993) and later research, there emerged in the literature on information systems a renewed interest in the problem of measuring the value of technology. De Marco (1993) argued that this interest was to be attributed not just to the enormous – and growing – amounts spent on information technology but also to a greater concern for the costs and performance of technology. These latter factors account for why the interest was particularly acute in relation to the services sector.

In short, the more recent literature has provided clear empirical evidence to demonstrate that investments in technology have increased productivity and provided substantial benefits to consumers, thereby confuting the productivity paradox. On the other hand, it has not demonstrated with the same degree of certainty that there is any clear relationship between the benefits of technology and the higher company profits (this is consistent with Hitt and Brynjolfsson, 1996). It should be recognised at the outset that such findings are not contradictory, in that they are variously corroborated by the three economic theories outlined in Section 3.2.1. In what follows, we offer an overview of the theory in support of this line of reasoning.

3.5.1   The theory of production and the productivity paradox

A series of studies both at the level of individual firms and at the national level has demonstrated repeatedly (and in a consistent manner)[22] that the impact of investments in technology on the productivity of labour and on economic growth has been substantial and positive (for an exhaustive overview, see Dedrick *et al.*, 2003). The literature on information systems has essentially concluded that the productivity paradox, as it was originally formulated, has no real substance. It is clear that at the firm and industry level increased investments in technology are associated with higher growth rates in productivity.

As far as individual firms are concerned, studies on technology and productivity indicate that in the time periods taken into consideration each dollar of IT capital is associated with a substantial increase in profit (Brynjolfsson and Hitt, 1993, 1995, 1996, 1998; Dewan and Min, 1997; Malone, 1997; Bresnahan, 1999). The characteristic trait of these works is that they only take into consideration large-listed companies in the United States, making use of econometric techniques based on the economics of production. Consequently, it is necessary to recognise that their focus is on investigating the relationship between the outputs of the production process and the inputs (including labour, the stock of IT capital and the stock of non-IT capital) as well as estimating the marginal product or the elasticity of the outputs of IT capital. The sum of these studies points to a single conclusion: that technology clearly has a positive and significant impact on productivity and that, in view of this, the productivity paradox is not sustainable.

More recently, Brynjolfsson and Hitt (2000) have shown that the payoffs for investment in IT do not take the form exclusively in terms of increases in the productivity of labour but also in terms of increases in multi-factor productivity, and that the impact on the growth of multi-factor productivity reaches a peak after a lapse of time that extends from 4 to 7 years from the date in which the investment takes place. Although the benefits have been high on average, among individual firms there is a marked variation in terms of returns on investments in technology. In fact, managerial practices associated with investments in IT – like the decentralisation of the decision-making process, the redefinition of the production process (business process redesign) and total quality management – figure as critical factors in the achievement of microeconomic returns on investments in technology. Indeed, this latter consideration accounts in large part for the extensive length of the time lag identified by Brynjolfsson and Hitt (2000).

A similar picture emerges from the macroeconomic research conducted in relation to industries in respect of which the productivity paradox was originally formulated. A large number of more recent studies have shown that growth in labour productivity accelerated in a large number of industries in the period 1995–1999. The sharp growth in this period stood in contrast to what had occurred previously (Jorgenson and Stiroh, 2000; Council of Economic Advisors, 2001; Kraemer and Dedrick, 2001a; Stiroh, 2001a). This positive change in labour productivity took place in concomitance with bigger investments in technology. In fact, the studies have shown that the correlation between the two factors was even more marked in those industries where there were even higher levels of investment in IT. In a very general way, it is possible to conclude that the trend towards growth in productivity in various industries is consistent with (even if it does not prove) the idea that improvements in managerial practices and management itself as well as a more productive use of technology has played an important role in accelerating productivity.

So far as multi-factor productivity at the industry level is concerned, much of the literature shows that in the period 1995–2000 analogous increases took place both in the industries that use technology and in those that produce it (Jorgenson and Stiroh, 2000; Baily and Lawrence, 2001; Council of Economic Advisors, 2001). It should be noted, however, that Gordon (2000) did not find any evidence of an acceleration of growth in multi-factor productivity in industries other than the computer industry and some in the manufacturing sector (in the segment producing durable goods). In contrast with this controversial finding on the growth of multi-factor productivity, Triplett and Bosworth (2003) identified the following sources of improvement in labour productivity in the services sector: growth in multi-factor productivity, the strengthening (deepening) of IT capital and greater use of outsourcing. Moreover, they concluded that growth in multi-factor productivity constituted the principal factor in the acceleration of productivity in the services sector in the period after 1995, accounting for as much as half of the growth.

In the face of such findings, it has even become possible to hypothesise the existence of a new paradox, as suggested by Kraemer and Dedrick (2001b), which can be summed up as the "paradox of under-investment in IT". This new paradox presents as a big challenge to the principles of classical economic theory as it does to the original formulation of the productivity paradox. At the same time it constitutes a source of persistent concern for the managers of firms that produce technology. In fact, these managers marvel that managers of other firms do not invest in technology to an even greater extent than they do, considering that returns on investments in IT are extremely high and much greater than those on non-IT investments (Brynjolfsson, 1993, 1996; Brynjolfsson and Hitt, 1993, 1995, 1996, 1998; Lichtenberg, 1995; Bresnahan, 1999). In these studies it is held that there is considerable under-investment both at the microeconomic level of the firm and at the national level. This leads to the conclusion that the managers of firms and investors are continuing to act irrationally: that they spend too little on technology and that they are losing the opportunity to effect extremely profitable investments. On the other hand, as maintained by Kraemer and Dedrick (2001b), the assumption that there exists a massive under-investment in technology should be treated with caution. In the first place, mathematical models used for representing the production function, though useful, constitute an approach that is too simplistic for the actual nature of firms. Secondly, these models reveal a correlation but not a causal link. Moreover, the risks associated with IT investments can be greater than those associated with non-IT investments. Finally, the high rates of depreciation associated with investments in IT mean that net rates of return on investments in technology are much lower than gross rates and, thus, are presumably in line with the rates on non-IT investments.

3.5.2   The theory of strategic competition and the profitability paradox

So far as the theory of strategic competition is concerned, most of the research examines simply the statistical relationship between investments in technology and measures of profitability. Most of the research examines the statistical relationship between IT spending and operating profitability as measured by Return on Assets (Strassmann, 1985, 1990; Weill, 1992; Ahituv and Giladi, 1993; Barua *et al.*, 1995; Hitt and Brynjolfsson, 1996; Rai *et al.*, 1997; Tam, 1998; Shin, 2001) and between IT spending and Return on Equity (Alpar and Kim, 1990a,b; Hitt and Brynjolfsson, 1996; Rai *et al.*, 1997; Tam, 1998; Shin, 2001). In other studies scholars have attempted to examine correlations between

IT spending and total shareholder return, which theoretically represents the discounted value of expected cash flows (Strassmann, 1990; Dos Santos *et al.*, 1993). Finally, some studies have examined how IT influences intermediate variables of operational performance (for example, the rate of inventory turnover), which in turn impact upon profits (Barua *et al.*, 1995).

In contrast to the IT productivity paradox (investigated in the previous section), the question of whether IT contributes to profitability has not yet been clearly answered. In general terms, it can be affirmed that up until now scholars have not managed to demonstrate a link between investment in technology and profitability (expressed in any of the above measures). In fact, the evidence points to just a very limited direct correlation between the two variables. In addition, it must be said that some models are characterised by a quite low degree of explanatory power and that, in general, they do not control for the many peculiarities distinct from technology that characterise firms or industries (with the exception of the studies by Barua *et al.*, 1995; Rai *et al.*, 1997).

Neither earlier studies (Strassmann, 1990; Ahituv and Giladi, 1993; Markus and Soh, 1993) nor more recent analysis (Barua *et al.*, 1995; Hitt and Brynjolfsson, 1996; Rai *et al.*, 1997; Tam, 1998; Shin, 2001) have uncovered any clear evidence to show that technology has a positive effect on aggregate measures of profitability. In relation to intermediate profitability measures, moreover, it should be noted that Barua *et al.* (1995) estimated that investment in technology did impact on intermediate measures but, by the same token, such investment did not appear to have a significant impact in relation to aggregate measures of profitability, like ROA. Finally, Hitt and Brynjolfsson (1996), although documenting a positive impact of technology on productivity and consumer surplus, did not find any positive and significant correlation between IT spending and profitability measures. This evidence seems to suggest the existence of an IT profitability paradox.

3.5.3 The theory of the consumer and consumer surplus

In contrast to what has happened in relation to the two theoretical approaches dealt with so far, the research on the consumer surplus deriving from technology investment is not very extensive. Bresnahan (1986) made an estimate of the benefits in terms of consumer surplus that were obtained from the use of mainframe computers in the finance industry over the period between 1958 and 1972. His results suggest that the benefits to consumers during the period in question were the equivalent of at least five times the cost sustained by the firms for the hire of the computers. The evidence on the impact of technology provided in this study constitutes the only empirical evidence that is based on a sample sufficiently large and representative to be considered reliable. Similarly, Brynjolfsson (1996), employing an analogous methodology and, moreover, with reference to the entire US economy, estimated that in 1987 the employment of computers had generated a consumer surplus to the value of about US$50 billion.

3.6 The productivity paradox: A phenomenon still present in the banking industry

In view of what has been said so far, the objective of reconsidering the productivity paradox assumes particular importance in relation to the banking industry, which has been identified on several occasions as an intensive user of IT. The research to date has pointed out that an interesting variance is apparent across industries in respect of the existence of the productivity paradox (as was effectively shown by Dedrick *et al.*, 2003).

To this end, in fact, it is worthwhile recalling that, although it is clear that there has been a generally positive relationship between productivity and investment in IT in the various industries of the US economy starting from the 1990s, the banking industry has been characterised by a trend that is nowhere near as clear (nor, indeed, unidirectional). A large number of the initial studies relating to the services sector, including banks and insurance companies, pointed to weak or non-existent links between technology spending and productivity (see Franke, 1987; Earl, 1989; Child and Loveridge, 1990; Strassmann, 1990; Willcocks, 1992; Fitzgerald, 1993; Parsons *et al.*, 1993; as well as the extensive overview provided in Section 3.3).

In the face of this evidence, we might well have expected that in regard to the banking industry, too, the productivity paradox would be confuted by the more recent literature, just as in the case of the other industries of the US economy (see the discussion in the previous section). Yet the productivity paradox has not been definitively rejected even by more recent studies (Council of Economic Advisors, 2001; McKinsey Global Institute, 2001); indeed, it seems that it persists precisely in the banking industry. In fact, a good deal of the academic interest in this industry stems from the fact that more recent studies have confirmed that, even though there has been an acceleration in productivity in other industries, the productivity paradox has continued to be a feature of the US banking industry after 1995.

The Council of Economic Advisors aggregate estimates in relation to financial institutions (Council of Economic Advisors, 2001) indicate that there was an acceleration in the growth of productivity after 1995 (in line with what has been observed for the other US industries in this same period).[23] This confirms the thesis that industries that make intensive use of IT have achieved good performances. However, dividing up the overall set of financial institutions into its separate components, the evidence of an acceleration in productivity growth is confirmed only in respect of non-depository institutions and brokers. By contrast, banks and other depository institutions in the United States experienced a downturn in the growth of productivity after 1995.

A study by McKinsey Global Institute (McKinsey Global Institute, 2001) shows that 38 industries of the US economy – which account for 70 per cent of GDP – experienced a growth in productivity in the years after 1995. On the other hand, evidence relating to the US retail banking segment – including commercial banks, savings banks and credit societies – confirms the continuing existence of the productivity paradox in the years from 1995 to 1999. In spite of a substantial acceleration in investment in technology, the variation in the productivity of labour continued to be positive but decreasing. The growth rate for labour productivity in the US banking industry diminished from 5.5 per cent for the period 1987–1995 to 4.1 per cent for the period 1995–1999. At the same time growth in the intensity of IT capital increased from 11.4 per cent for the years 1987–1995 to 16.8 per cent for the period 1995–1999. These figures show by themselves that investment in technology increased by about 50 per cent over the period from 1987 to 1999. The conclusion reached in the study by McKinsey Global Institute (2001), in keeping with what emerged in the study by the Council of Economic Advisors (2001), is that, so far as the US banking industry is concerned, the existence of the productivity paradox remained a reality for the period 1995–2000, in spite of a generalised revitalisation of productivity in various other industries in the US economy.

It would appear that the only other empirical study on the impact of technology on banking industry productivity (other than that of the United States) is by the Bank of Italy (Casolaro and Gobbi, 2004). The authors point to the existence in the Italian banking industry of shifts in costs and profit functions that are strongly correlated with the accumulation of IT capital (for details on the methodological approach used, see Section 4.4.2). The study finds that the banks that have techniques involving an intensive use of IT lie closest to best practice, which, implies, all things being equal, the achievement of a higher level of efficiency. The authors regard this result as the consequence of the so-called "catching up" effects (in other words, the adoption of new technologies by "second mover" banks after a certain lapse of time in respect of the initiatives of "first mover" banks) – effects that are consistent with the pattern of diffusion of new technology.

As far as the profitability paradox is concerned, the only study on the US banking industry is that of Marcus and Soh (1993). They attempted to investigate the correlation between IT spending and profitability as measured by operating profits to operating revenues, and found that not all banks achieved clear financial benefits from IT spending. Small banks did not show a significant association between IT spending and profitability, while large banks had negative returns on their contemporaneous IT spending.

It is precisely the foregoing considerations that have given rise to our desire to investigate the performance of investments in technology in respect of the European banking industry over the period 1995–2000. In the light of the evidence confirming the productivity and profitability paradox for the US banking industry (even in respect of the second half of the 1990s), our interest lies in seeking to investigate the relationship between performance and investments in technology in respect of the same industry but in relation to Europe and within a comparative perspective. All of this also constitutes a response to what in the last few years has been felt in the field of information systems as an acute need, in that one of the major areas of future research, as has been insisted on by Dedrick *et al.* (2003), lies precisely in the direction of evaluating the performance of investments in technology in industries that make intensive use of technology.

4
The Evaluation of the Performance of IT Investments: An Empirical Analysis of the European Banking Industry

4.1 Introduction

The empirical analysis we conduct in this chapter responds to a need that has been very deeply felt over recent years: the need for an evaluation of the performance of investments in technology in an industry, like the banking industry, that makes intensive use of technology. As already indicated, our interest arises out of the fact that it has been demonstrated empirically in relation to the US banking industry that there has not been a positive relationship between productivity and investments in technology in the period following 1995. Such a situation contrasts starkly with all the other industries in the United States, where marked increases in productivity have been registered, especially in those characterised by an intensive use of technology.[1]

Although the productivity paradox is an international phenomenon, the vast majority of the empirical evidence dealing with it relates to the US economy. Remarkably, as far as we are aware, no comparative study exists on the phenomenon of the productivity paradox in the European banking industry (as evidenced by the absence of references relating to Europe in the overviews of Dedrick *et al.*, 2003 and Casolaro and Gobbi, 2004). This imbalance in scholarly attention in respect of European and US banks can presumably be explained in terms of the fact that, because of the unavailability of data relating to the relevant variables, it is difficult for researchers to adequately represent the particular nature of the production process in the European banks.[2] The comparative approach of this study in relation to Europe makes it possible not only to extend the scope of the empirical analysis to a banking system different to that of the United States but also to examine the experience of each of the European systems in relation to the productivity paradox with a view to pointing out the differences and similarities between them.

As already indicated, in order to specify the above problem in an appropriate manner, in this study we make use of a methodology based on the economic theory of strategic competition, which aims to investigate whether investment in technology improves the business profitability of banks over the short term. It follows from this that, in keeping with what has been proposed in the literature on information systems, we adopt a methodological framework that consists in empirically investigating the link between performance and investment in technology. Thus, our intention is to investigate the relationship between various measures of profitability and components of investments in technology in European banking, in order to test the existence of the so-called "profitability paradox".[3]

As far as the various issues relating to the measurement of performance are concerned (these are extensively discussed in the literature on information systems), in this study – with a view to responding to the suggestions advanced in Brynjolfsson (1996)[4] – we employ a range of performance measures that are different from the traditional accounting measures (in particular, we employ measures of financial profitability, on the one hand, and, on the other, more sophisticated measures of operating efficiency). In regard to the specification of investment in technology, instead of treating it as a monolithic entity, as has been done in a great many of the studies on the performance evaluation of technology, we conduct an empirical examination at a higher level of modularity, investigating the effects of investment in terms of separate components, namely hardware, software and IT services.

In short, in this chapter we examine data relating to performance (using traditional measures of financial performance and a global measure of operating efficiency) and to investment in technology (the overall amount and the same value broken down into its various components) in the banking industries of five European countries in order to investigate whether technology produces a significant contribution to the economic performance of the relevant banks in the course of the period in which the investments are put in place. Moreover, given that it takes time for organisations to assimilate new technology and to implement changes in business activities (DeLone and McLean, 1992), we examine whether there is a lag between the realisation of IT investments and the occurrence of potential benefits.

The chapter is organised as follows. In Section 4.2 we introduce the methodology of the analysis. In Section 4.3 we provide the comparative sample and the relevant data, while in Section 4.4 we describe the performance measures we employ in relation to the European banking industry and present the related empirical data. In Section 4.5 we deal with investment in technology (and its various components). Finally, in Section 4.6, we discuss the empirical results.

4.2 The methodology

In this chapter we propose a methodological approach for the empirical examination of the theory of strategic competition, that is, we endeavour to examine the degree to which investment in technology has contributed to an improvement in the profitability of the banking industry. The underlying economic reason for conducting such a measurement of the capacity of banks lies ultimately in the need to verify whether banks are capable of using technology to achieve competitive advantage (and thereby realise levels of profit that are higher than those that would be achieved otherwise).

The methodology we use to achieve this takes the form of a set of regressions – developed in two stages – between performance and investment in technology in the banking industry. Initially, we use a simple linear regression model that relates measures of performance (traditional accounting profitability and operating efficiency) and investment in technology in the short-to-medium term, by regressing contemporaneous and lagged bank performance on bank IT investment.[5] (See Chapter 6 for an examination of the relationship over the medium-to-long-term period.) In a second phase, we extend the model so that it is capable of including in the regression additional control variables relating to institutional or firm factors.

The first model involves examining the relationship between firm profitability and investments in technology in the banking industry. This is effected on the basis of the methodological framework traditionally proposed in the literature (Strassmann, 1985, 1990; Harris and Katz, 1989; Alpar and Kim, 1990a; Weill, 1992; Dos Santos *et al.*, 1993; Ahituv and Giladi, 1993; Markus and Soh, 1993; Barua *et al.*, 1995; Hitt and Brynjolfsson, 1996; Rai *et al.*, 1997; Tam, 1998; Shin, 2001). Although there is no single, valid approach for making an estimate of the relationship, we began by analysing simple correlations by essentially replicating the model of Strassmann (1990). We test both the non-parametric Spearman's rank correlation and the parametric Pearson's correlation.

To further examine the relationship between IT investment and bank performance, it is assumed that performance is a function of investment in technology and, in this way, a regression is estimated where the dependent variable is represented by the performance of the banking industry of each European country. The general form of the regression model can be expressed as follows:

$$P_{j,t+i} = \beta_0 + \beta_{1,jt}\mathrm{IT}_{jt} + \varepsilon_{jt} \tag{4.1}$$

where:

> $P_{j,t+i}$ = performance, calculated alternatively in terms of accounting performance ratios on an annual basis (such as return on equity and return on assets) or annual X-efficiencies (both cost efficiency and alternative profit efficiency) in respect of the banking industry of each country j at time $t+i$ (where $i = 0$ and 1);
>
> IT_{jt} = investment in information technology (IT) calculated alternatively in terms of a flow of a non-accounting nature (obtained by estimating the amounts paid by banks to the vendors of IT products and services, as will be illustrated extensively in Section 4.5) or in terms of IT ratios (investment in technology in respect of equity, investment in technology in respect of total costs or investment in technology in respect of operating costs) in respect of the banking industry of each country j for every year ending at time t;
>
> ε_{jt} = error term.

It should be noted that the performance measure used is expressed alternatively both in terms of accounting profitability (measured by way of the annual ratios ROA and ROE) and in terms of global measures of operating efficiency (estimated by way of X-inefficiencies relating both to firm costs and profit). The use of this latter measure of performance makes it possible to examine whether the new specification – never used in previous studies – improves the methodological framework for the study of the value of technology. In addition, given that it takes some time for organisations to assimilate new technology and effect the consequent changes in the activity of the enterprise, we go on to examine whether there is a time-lag between the realisation of investments in IT and the emergence of their benefits. Subsequently, with a view to investigating the occurrence of the phenomenon of assimilation, an estimate is made both of the relationship between IT investment and contemporaneous business performance (P_{jt}) and the relationship between IT investment and performance over the subsequent period ($P_{j,t+i}$). Finally, so far as the independent variable technology is concerned, in keeping with the convention that has traditionally been followed in the literature, we express it in terms of both the amount of the flow of technology investment and the values of IT ratios (in other words, the relationships between the size of the flow of technology investment and measures expressing the bank size, such as equity, total costs and operating costs).

Given the comparative perspective of this study, it is clear that it is necessary to extend the model by including in the regression additional control variables relating to institutional and firm factors. In view of the fact that the study in question relates to the banking industries in five different European countries, the above-mentioned relations are also examined aggregating all the banks into a single sample and introducing at the same time control variables for the institutional and structural characteristics of the industry in each country. This extension is of particular importance in view of the fact that traditionally the relevant literature has not controlled for the many particular, non-technological factors that characterise countries (with the exception of the work done by Barua *et al.*, 1995 and Rai *et al.*, 1997). Thus, making explicit the country factors distinct from technology, Equation (4.1) becomes:

$$P_{j,t+i} = \beta_0 + \beta_{1,jt} \mathrm{IT}_{jt} + \beta_{2,jt} \mathrm{FR} + \beta_{3,jt} \mathrm{GE} + \beta_{4,jt} \mathrm{ITA} + \beta_{5,jt} \mathrm{SP} + \varepsilon_{jt} \qquad (4.2)$$

where FR, GE, ITA, SP = the dummy variable respectively for France, Germany, Italy and Spain (the dummy is equal to 1 for the United Kingdom).

To control for risk, the standard deviation of ROA was used as a control variable. The estimated regression equation was:

$$P_{j,t+i} = \beta_0 + \beta_{1,jt} \mathrm{IT}_{jt} + \beta_{6,jt} \mathrm{St\,dev\,(ROA)}_{jt} + \varepsilon_{jt} \qquad (4.3)$$

where St dev (ROA) = standard deviation of ROA of the bank industry of country j for the annual period t.

In order to verify the impact of a size-related variable relating to the banking industry of each country, we introduce in the form of an independent control variable total balance-sheet assets. It should be noted that, given that the skewness of the curve expressing the relationship between size and technology investment is positive, we have used the natural logarithm for such variable. With a view to taking account of the size of the various national banking industries, then, Equation (4.1) takes the following form:

$$P_{j,t+i} = \beta_0 + \beta_{1,jt} \mathrm{IT}_{jt} + \beta_{7,jt} \ln(\mathrm{TA})_{jt} + \varepsilon_{jt} \qquad (4.4)$$

where $\ln(\text{TA}) =$ the natural logarithm of total assets for the banking industry of each country j for every year ending at time t.

In the final specification of the model, intended to take account of the modular nature of investment in technology, performance is taken as the dependent variable in a linear regression in respect of a set of variables that describe the various components of technology. This is done with a view to examining any possible correlation with a greater degree of precision. Expressed in symbolic form, the model is as follows:

$$P_{j,t+i} = \beta_0 + \beta_{8,jt}\text{HA}_{jt} + \beta_{9,jt}\text{SO}_{jt} + \beta_{10,jt}\text{SE}_{jt} + \varepsilon_{jt} \qquad (4.5)$$

where $\text{HA}_{jt} =$ investment in hardware by the banking industry of each country j for every year ending at time t; $\text{SO}_{jt} =$ investment in software by the banking industry of each country j for every year ending at time t; and $\text{SE}_{jt} =$ expenditure on services relating to technology by the banking industry of each country j for every year ending at time t.

A description of each of these categories is provided in Section 4.5.

In view of certain econometric considerations, this analysis, though highly indicative, cannot be viewed as conclusive. In particular, the following problems should be noted:

a) None of the variables used in the regression is completely exogenous, and the endogenous nature of the regressors may influence the estimate of their coefficients.
b) The endogenous nature of the regression means that it provides information on the correlation and not on the causality.
c) The dependent variable (X-inefficiencies) used to express performance in one of the specifications of the regression is an estimate, but its standard deviation is not taken into consideration in the regression.

In order to accommodate for issues (a) and (b), an analysis of Equation (4.1) is performed by using both ordinary least squares (OLS) regressions and two-stage least squares (TSLS) regressions. TSLS regressions are employed to correct the potential bias caused by the simultaneity problem (reverse causality): for example, instead of increased IT investments leading to an increase in profit efficiency, increased profit efficiency could be responsible for increases in IT investments. TSLS regressions are employed with the use of one-year lagged independent variables as instruments. To further investigate the existence (and direction) of causality between IT investments and performance, we use the

Granger causality Wald test based on a VAR (Vector Autoregressive) model for each banking industry under investigation (Granger and Newbold, 1986).

4.3 The comparative sample and the description of the data

The comparative European perspective developed in this chapter constitutes – as far as we are aware – the first attempt to measure the relationship between investments in technology and performance in the European banking industry.

Nonetheless, in recent times the adoption of an inter-country perspective has been becoming ever more common. Two major factors account for the growing interest in comparative studies of European countries: the process of internationalisation and the attempts to deregulate the industry. As has been emphasised by Molyneux *et al.* (1996), the achievement by the European financial industries "of overall economic gains by way of deregulation and 'free market solutions' in the allocation of resources between the various European economic systems" explains the need for empirical research of a comparative nature. In particular, many scholars have argued that the process of harmonisation, which has contributed to the creation of a more integrated and harmonised European banking market, stands out in this regard (Berg *et al.*, 1993; Fetcher and Pestieau, 1993; Bergendahl, 1995; Bukh *et al.*, 1995; Ruthenberg and Elias, 1996; European Commission, 1997; Pastor *et al.*, 1997; Inzerillo *et al.*, 2000).

The underlying assumption of this work is that an understanding of the reasons for the differences between the various national industries is crucial for evaluating the changes introduced and for developing appropriate strategies for investment in technology. Thus, the comparative perspective is important not only because it provides information about the degree of the impact of technology investment on the performance of the institutions operating in the various countries, but also because it makes it possible to understand the reasons for the existence of any empirical data pointing to variations in the technology investment strategies of the different national industries.

The decision to use financial statement data to measure performance has been determined not only by the significance that they assume in a description of the production process of banks but also by the fact that alternative sources are not available to external researchers. The careful examination that we have conducted of the composition of the variables

Table 4.1 The composition of the sample – number of banks

Year	France	Germany	Italy	Spain	UK	Panel
2000	117	156	86	72	66	497
1999	145	177	92	65	74	553
1998	165	194	91	72	79	601
1997	171	197	87	78	74	607
1996	186	194	85	77	71	613
1995	192	189	74	73	57	585
1994	200	184	74	65	40	563
1993	171	127	63	17	17	395
Total	1347	1418	652	519	478	4414

The table shows the number of banks that make up the sample for each country and the panel data in respect of each year in the period under investigation (1993–2000).
Source: Data elaborated by author.

used in this analysis makes it possible to assume that it is indeed possible to compare them.

The empirical analysis relates to a sample of 737 banks operating in the five major banking markets of the European Union (France, Germany, Italy, Spain and the United Kingdom). The panel data deals with the period 1993–2000 (it includes the data available for all or for some of the banks examined in each of the years in question), and it involves a total of 4414 observations. The data was drawn from two databases that contain information in electronic form derived from the balance sheets and the income statements of European banks: Bankscope and Financial Analysis Made Easy (FAME), both of which are edited by Bureau van Dijk.

Table 4.1 shows the number of banks that make up the sample for each country and the panel data for every year in the period under investigation.

4.4 Performance measures for the European banking industry

Regarding the definition of performance – the dependent variable involved in the regressions specified in the section 4.2 – our intention in this study is to complement and extend what has been proposed up to date in the relevant literature. The definition of performance constitutes a key step that deeply influences the accuracy of results as well as the capacity of such results to confirm or confute the profitability paradox. Performance measures can be vitiated by errors in the identification of the appropriate variables and in the definition of the problems of economic theory to which it is intended to offer a response. Although the choice of appropriate measures of performance is complex and problematic, the joint use of a range of definitions makes it possible to broaden the validity in respect of which the theme of the value of technology is investigated empirically. Our immediate objective, then, is to investigate to what extent different sets of performance measures are suitable for representing the value of technology in the banking industry.

Previous studies in the field have generally concentrated on accounting measures of profitability – in terms of ROE and ROA – with a view to revealing the performance of individual banks. In contrast with this excessive focus on financial issues, however, technology leads to – or, at least, in the light of the hypothesis of positive payoffs, should lead to – improvements in organisational capacities, in the variety and the quality of the products and services offered and in client satisfaction – not to mention a simplification in administrative processes and increases in the productivity of labour and management. The acceptance of the existence of such technology-driven effects necessarily implies the use of a measure of performance that encompasses the entire firm. Thus, an appropriate performance measure – one which expresses the effect of technology on the business entity as a whole – must be capable of quantifying the concept of "IT impacts" (as proposed by Sambamurthy and Zmud, 1994),[6] which takes one (or more) of the following forms:

1) the development of new products and services, which in their turn generate a rage of outcomes for the bank, including an increase in customer satisfaction;
2) the redesign of productive processes so as to increase efficacy and efficiency, to which are tied outcomes like an increase in productivity and an increase in the satisfaction of staff;
3) improvements in decision-making processes in terms of a more comprehensive understanding of the input markets and the clients, with which are associated outcomes such as a better provision of inputs and a better specification of the features of products and services;
4) greater organisational flexibility between the members of the organisation and with the clients, which in its turn produces outcomes such as a reduction in production/delivery times (and an

increase in the flexibility of delivery), and, presumably, an expansion in market share.

Note that the intuition as to the existence of these so-called IT impacts seems to be connected to the "soft-benefits" associated with investments in technology and originally identified by Brynjolfsson (1993) as one of the reasons for the existence of the productivity paradox.

For technology to have a positive impact on the performance of a bank as a whole, however, it is necessary for the performance of the technology itself to be positive in its own right. Thus, it is necessary to take into consideration the concept of "appropriate use" (as defined by Trice and Treacy, 1986; Lucas, 1993) and the conversion of IT investments into IT goods ("IT conversion", as in the expression proposed by Weill, 1992).[7] It would appear clear that suitable performance measures for appropriate use and IT conversion generally constitute performance measures of the technology itself and not of the actual firm. In other words, even if the performance of technology, as measured with reference to these factors, is positive, this does not necessarily imply that the performance of the technology is positive for the firm as a whole. The absence of such an overlap is due precisely to the need to take into account IT impacts. We believe that basically it is possible to affirm that a positive performance associated with appropriate use and IT conversion is a condition that should favour – but that does not necessarily imply – the realisation of a positive performance for the firm as a whole. By way of example, it is enough to think of the introduction of an ATM system by a bank. This involves a positive performance in terms of IT conversion and appropriate use (the best available technology for the execution of withdrawal/enquiry operations and the use of the technology in an appropriate manner), but, if the bank is not capable of applying a price premium in relation to the increase in the quality of the service generated for the client by way of the adoption of the new technology, performance at the level of the firm will not improve.

The three dimensions through which the impact of technology unfolds (IT impacts, appropriate use and IT conversion) do not necessarily take the form of improvements in accounting measures of profitability. In fact, these benefits can be redistributed within a single organisation or between different organisations as well as transferred to consumers. Thus, it is necessary to identify a measure of performance capable of capturing the above-mentioned implications; in other words, a measure that expresses the capacity of the bank to supply itself with scarce resources and transform these productively into outputs that have value.

In view of the matters discussed up to this point, in this study we use a global measure of operating productivity, the so-called "X-inefficiencies" (Leibenstein, 1966), which make it possible to overcome the limitations of the measures that are traditionally employed in the literature in the field. Taking account of delays, errors, distance and disturbance in respect of a situation of equilibrium on the managerial best practice frontier, X-inefficiencies capture the extent to which investments in IT, contribute, among other factors, to increasing (or decreasing) the efficiency of banks. Essentially, they make it possible to examine whether IT impacts, appropriate use and IT conversion ultimately take the form of increases (or decreases) in operating productivity. The object is to determine whether the relation with investment in technology remains negative even in the case of a measure of productivity that is more sophisticated and better able to capture the various dimensions of the impact of technology. This would result in a confirmation of the validity of the profitability paradox in respect of the banking industry, thanks to the use of a performance measure that overcomes many of the limits of the accounting measures that have been used traditionally.

It should also be noted that it is widely acknowledged in the literature that the measures of X-inefficiencies – estimated by way of parametric and/or non-parametric approaches – are characterised by a series of clear advantages compared with traditional accounting indices of profitability: frontier analysis provides an overall, objectively determined, numerical efficiency value and ranking of firms that is not otherwise available (cf., by way of just one example, Berger and Humphrey, 1997). In the first place, these measures make provision for making an estimate of productivity that takes account of the many different inputs and outputs that play a role in the productive process. Secondly, the results are more objective and all inclusive (to use the expression employed in Thanassoulis *et al.*, 1996).

Notwithstanding the advantages of the measures of X-inefficiencies (tied to the capacity, on the one hand, to capture the various dimensions of the impact of technology and, on the other, to take into consideration the production process in its entirety, incorporating the multiplicity of factors that impact upon it), no study, as far as we are aware, has yet made use of X-inefficiencies to analyse the perspective of strategic competition in the relationship between technology and performance.

The reason for this surprising omission is presumably to be found in the fact that, while X-inefficiencies are the object of extensive analysis in the literature on banking, this is not the case in the literature on information systems, where, by contrast, interest has centred primarily around the accounting performance of investments in IT from the perspective of strategic competition. With a view to overcoming this gap, in this study, use is made of four different specifications of the concept of performance, which can, in turn, be divided into two overriding categories:

1) Traditional accounting measures of profitability:

   a) return on assets (ROA);
   b) return on equity (ROE);

2) Alternative measures of operating efficiency:

   a) profit operating efficiency (alternative profit X-inefficiencies);
   b) cost operating efficiency (cost X-inefficiencies).

In the following sections, we will deal with each of these measures as well as with the corresponding values that have been estimated for the banking industry of each European country under investigation.

4.4.1 Traditional accounting measures of profitability

The traditional accounting measures of profitability may be defined as follows:

1) Return on Assets (ROA), which measures the efficacy with which a bank uses existing assets to generate profits. As such, it constitutes an index of the efficacy of investments put in place by the banks, which does not, however, include the joint effects of financial leverage.[8] The studies in which this measure has already been used include Cron and Sobol (1983), Strassmann (1990, 1985), Weill (1992), Ahituv and Giladi (1993), Barua *et al.* (1995), Hitt and Brynjolfsson (1996), Rai *et al.* (1997), Tam (1998) and Shin (2001);
2) Return on Equity (ROE), which provides an alternative measure of the efficacy with which a bank uses shareholders' equity and which indicates the efficacy with which management manages the resources invested by shareholders. This measure of profitability has been employed in a relatively limited number of studies, amongst which it is worth citing Alpar and Kim (1990a), Hitt and Brynjolfsson (1996), Rai *et al.* (1997), Tam (1998) and Shin (2001).

It should be emphasised at the outset that these accounting measures of profitability can be difficult to interpret on account of the complexity of the accounting procedures that are involved. In addition, it should be recognised that, when using comparative data, it is necessary to take a great deal of care in assembling the material so as to be able to take into consideration the differences in the standards and conventions of different countries; from the comparative perspective, such differences are to be found in the accounting principles, accounting practices and fiscal legislation of the various countries (Nobes and Parker, 1988).

Such cautionary remarks apart, the evaluation of the evolution of the profitability indices of the European banking industry reveals a positive trend in average profitability over the course of the years 1994–2000 (as can be seen in Table 4.2, where the profitability indices are listed for the banks in each country included in the sample). In terms of ROE, the increase in the index was a feature of the banking industries of all the

Table 4.2 Profitability indices (ROA and ROE) for each European banking industry

	France	Germany	Italy	Spain	UK
ROA					
2000	0.50	0.35	0.88	0.76	0.94
1999	0.35	0.21	0.81	0.71	1.00
1998	0.37	0.60	0.53	0.70	1.00
1997	0.11	0.26	−0.10	0.53	0.76
1996	0.02	0.29	0.16	0.51	0.78
1995	0.10	0.31	−0.06	0.45	0.50
1994	−0.29	0.33	−0.10	0.45	0.46
ROE					
2000	13.64	7.53	12.75	10.53	16.51
1999	7.09	5.40	11.29	12.04	17.21
1998	10.04	14.43	7.64	11.69	19.08
1997	3.33	6.13	−1.69	9.56	15.60
1996	0.71	6.45	2.56	8.50	15.94
1995	2.77	6.39	−1.06	7.51	9.65
1994	−8.64	6.81	−1.72	6.95	9.17

The table shows the average value in percentage terms of the profitability indices (ROE (Return on Equity) and ROA (Return on Assets) in respect of the European banks of each country in each year over the course of the period 1994–2000.
Source: Data elaborated by author on the basis of the *London-based International Bank Credit Analysis Ltd., Bankscope* database and the *Financial Analysis Made Easy, FAME* database.

countries in question. In 2000, the UK banking industry was characterised by the highest average value of ROE (16.51 per cent) at the European level, while the lowest value (7.53 per cent) was registered in respect of German banks. The upward trend is particularly marked in relation to the Italian banking industry. By way of example, it is instructive to compare the trends in ROE for Italy and the United Kingdom (the country characterised by the highest ROE). In particular, such a comparison reveals that, while the average values for the two countries are similar in 2000 (12.75 per cent versus 16.51 per cent), the Italian banks reached this figure after having set out in 1994 with an ROE value of −1.72 per cent. By contrast, the British industry, setting out in 1994 with a value of 9.17 per cent, effectively achieved what was a more limited (but anyhow large) increase.

The alternative measure of profitability – that relating to total assets – shows a similar positive trend for the period 1994–2000. In this case too, although the trend is positive throughout the European countries in question, it is particularly so in respect of Italy. Moreover, just as was observed in relation to ROE, the two countries with the highest and lowest levels of ROA in 2000 were, respectively, the United Kingdom (0.94 per cent) and Germany (0.35 per cent).

These figures can be interpreted in terms of the process of liberalisation brought about in the European Union by the Single Market Programme (SMP) together with the introduction in 1986 of the Single European Act. In the last decade, the effect of the pressures of competition appears to have led the banks in strategic terms to concentrate increasingly on generating profits for shareholders, in particular, by acting both on costs and revenues (Goddard *et al.*, 2001; Beccalli *et al.*, 2006).

4.4.2 X-inefficiencies as an alternative measure of performance

4.4.2.1 Some reflections on the utility of X-inefficiencies in studies on the value of technology

With a view to overcoming the exclusive use of accounting measures of profitability as traditionally practised in the literature on the value of technology, we proceed to an estimate of productive efficiency (otherwise known as operating efficiency or X-inefficiencies), aiming, in particular, at capturing the various dimensions of the impact of technology on the creation of business value (IT impact, IT use and IT conversion).

The capacity of actors (management or firm staff) to control costs or maximise profits – that is, measured by X-inefficiencies – can be explained by factors like errors, delays in the decision to invest and in the realisation of the investment, inertia in human behaviour, distortions in communication and uncertainty – in respect of a situation of equilibrium on the best practice frontier.[9] These considerations clearly demonstrate that X-inefficiencies are capable of capturing the degree to which technology impacts on operating productivity. They are, in other words, measures of the impact of IT (improvements/deterioration in organisational capacities, in the quality and variety of the products and services offered, in the speed and flexibility of delivery, in the simplification of administrative processes and in the productivity of labour), of IT use (the adequacy of the use of the technology) and of IT conversion (the capacity to transform IT investment into IT goods).

If this interpretative approach is correct, an increase in investment in technology that is accompanied by lower operating efficiency may be an expression of errors, delays and inertia in relation to the IT investment. And this would constitute a confirmation of the paradox.

To capture the impact of technology on performance, then, greater attention needs to be given to the pressures on the decision-making process and on the discretionary power of management. The efficient frontier presupposes the existence of perfectly rational actors who, having access to information on prices and the relevant technology, set in place production plans without delays and with full information. Because of uncertainty and partial information, however, the actual situation is quite different from that involving a rational perspective.[10] Delays and difficulties in communication – together with the principal–agent problem – mean that the actions of each actor are influenced by an interpretative process that is based on a variety of factors, such as power and position in the organisation.[11]

As well as proposing a range of determinants of the distance from the situation of equilibrium that relate to the scope for interpretation on the part of actors, the microeconomic literature on productivity sets out a number of determinants that relate to institutional conditions and structural factors.[12] In particular, the main sources of inefficiency in banks feature the following: ownership, organisational form, the scale of the firm, market power, environmental conditions, bad luck and regulatory factors, as well as – obviously – bad management (cf. Mester, 1997; DeYoung, 1998).

The distance of the resulting position of equilibrium of each firm from the optimal operating efficiency identifies the so-called X-inefficiencies. A bank that has a greater operating efficiency (as in the formulation originally introduced by Farrell, 1957) may be characterised by one of the following forms of efficiency:

1) Profit efficiency, which provides a measure of how close a bank is to the realisation of the maximum level of profit given its level of outputs (generally known as alternative profit X-inefficiencies). Thus, a bank is said to be profit maximising when it produces a greater quantity of outputs given the amount of inputs employed; in other words, this term indicates that the bank produces more outputs (or outputs of a higher quality) using the same amount of inputs and, thus, is able to apply a price premium. This measure has never been used before to examine the relationship between performance and technology. Yet, its advantages are very clear. In the case that the client of a bank is willing to pay a higher price to obtain increases in the quality of the products and services or in the speed and convenience of the delivery, this measure of profit efficiency is able to reflect part of the increase in the intangible value of the production. It goes without saying that this improvement does not appear in any way in the accounting measures of profitability (at least over the short term). Moreover, part of the value of the investments in technology put in place by banks is transferred to consumers by way of competition. Once again, even though it cannot be observed, profit efficiency captures part of this intangible value;

2) Cost efficiency, which provides a measure of how close a bank is to the cost sustained by the best practice bank to produce a given mix of outputs (assuming that the banks are operating under the same conditions). A bank is said to be cost minimising when it consumes a lower quantity of inputs for the production of a given amount of outputs or, in other words, produces the same amount of outputs using less inputs and, in this way, enjoys a cost advantage. This provides indications about the effects of technology on the cost function, avoiding the inconveniences associated with the estimate of technical change (which will be discussed in Chapter 5).

In short, the economic reason for focusing this analysis on the X-inefficiencies (both profit and cost) of banks stems from two essential factors: on the one hand, the opportunity they provide to investigate the production process in its entirety, taking into consideration the multiplicity of factors that impact upon it and, on the other, the need to capture the various dimensions of the impact of technology (IT impact, IT use and IT conversion).

4.4.2.2 The method of measuring X-inefficiencies: The stochastic frontier

The first methodological problem associated with measuring X-inefficiencies lies in the choice of approach. In this study, we employ a parametric technique,[13] in particular, the Stochastic Frontier Approach (SFA)[14] in the version presented independently by Aigner *et al.* (1977) and Meeusen and Van den Broeck (1977).

Specifically, we have chosen to adopt the model advanced by Battese and Coelli (1992), the so-called "technical effects model": a (non-weighted) stochastic frontier function for panel data with firm effects which are assumed to be distributed as truncated normal random variables[15] and are also permitted to vary systematically over time (for more detail on the methodology of SFA, see Coelli *et al.*, 1998). The level of cost for a firm in a given moment is taken to be equal to the true minimal cost frontier, account being taken of the inefficiency term (u) and the noise component (v). Following Coelli (1996), the model can be expressed as follows:

$$\mathrm{TC}_{it} = x_{it}\,\beta + v_{it} + u_{it} \qquad (4.6)$$

with $i = 1, \ldots, N$ and $t = 1, \ldots, T$. In Equation (4.6), TC_{it} is the logarithm of the total cost for the ith firm in the tth period; x_{it} is a $K \times 1$ vector of the transformation of the input and output prices of the ith firm in the tth period; β is a vector of unknown parameters. These parameters can be calculated using the maximum likelihood method (Olson *et al.*, 1980; Coelli *et al.*, 1998), which requires the numerical maximisation of the probability function.[16] The v_i are assumed to be independently and identically distributed, and the u_i are assumed to be distributed independently of the v_i.[17]

In particular, we use a time-varying model for the technical inefficiency effects in the stochastic frontier function for panel data (Battese and Coelli, 1992). The variation in inefficiency over time follows the following law:

$$u_{it} = u \exp\left[-\eta\,(t - T)\right] \qquad (4.7)$$

where η is a parameter to estimate. Inefficiency decreases over time when $\eta > 0$, increases if $\eta < 0$ and is constant when $\eta = 0$.[18]

The alternative profit function has the same specification as the above Equation (4.6), the only difference being that the dependent variable is replaced with profits (π), as specified in Berger and Mester (1997).

Nevertheless, because we are maximising profits (as opposed to minimising costs), the inefficiency term, u, is subtracted from the estimated residuals. π represents the profits of the bank, proxied by net income before taxes (with the relevant adjustments to exclude negative values) as done in Altunbas *et al.* (2001).

4.4.2.3 Cost X-inefficiencies versus profit X-inefficiencies

A bank is said to be inefficient if its costs (profits) are higher (lower) than those estimated for an efficient bank that produces the same combination of inputs and outputs, and if the difference cannot be explained in terms of statistical noise.

In the cost function, costs depend upon the prices of the inputs, the quantities of the outputs, every fixed input or output, environmental factors, random error and efficiency (Berger and Mester, 1997). Thus, the function takes as given the quantities of outputs (and not the prices of the outputs). The form of the cost function is as follows:

$$C = C\,(y, w, z, v, u_{c}, \varepsilon_{c}) \tag{4.8}$$

where C expresses variable costs, w is the vector of the prices of the inputs, y the quantity of outputs and z the quantities of every fixed *netput* (input or output); v describes a set of external variables impacting upon performance. The inefficiency factor u_{c} (where c stands for firm costs) incorporates both allocative inefficiency (the non-optimal reaction to the relative prices of inputs) and technical inefficiency (an excessive quantity of inputs for the production of a given output y). ε_{c} indicates random error (which incorporates measuring errors and temporary good/bad fortune as factors that impact positively or negatively on costs).

With a view to rewriting Equation (4.8) in a form that is more immediately comprehensible, u_{c} and ε_{c} are assumed to be multiplicatively separable from the rest of the cost function and both sides of the equation are expressed in the form of a natural logarithm (Aigner *et al.*, 1977):

$$\ln C = f\,(y, w, z, v) + \ln u_{c} + \ln \varepsilon_{c} \tag{4.9}$$

where f indicates the functional form of the production function. The disentanglement of the composite form, $\ln u_{c} + \ln \varepsilon_{\pi}$, into its two components (inefficiency and random error) differentiates between the various measuring techniques.

The cost efficiency of a bank is calculated as the cost necessary for the production of the output vector of bank b in the case that the bank is as efficient as the best practice institution in the sample (in the face of the same set of exogenous variables) divided by the actual cost sustained by bank b:

$$\text{CostEFF}^{b} = \frac{\hat{C}^{\min}}{\hat{C}^{b}} = \frac{\left\{\exp\left[\hat{f}\left(y^{b}, w^{b}, z^{b}, v^{b}\right)\right]\cdot\exp\left(\ln\hat{u}_{c}^{\min}\right)\right\}}{\left\{\exp\left[\hat{f}\left(y^{b}, w^{b}, z^{b}, v^{b}\right)\right]\cdot\exp\left(\ln\hat{u}_{c}^{b}\right)\right\}} = \frac{\hat{u}_{c}^{\min}}{\hat{u}_{c}^{b}} \quad (4.10)$$

where b stands for bank and $\hat{u}_{c}^{\min}$ represents the minimum $\hat{u}_{c}^{b}$ amongst all the banks in the sample. Equation (4.10), whose values vary between (0,1), measures the proportion of the costs that are used efficiently: a value of 80 per cent indicates that the firm is efficient to the order of 80 per cent (or, looked at from the opposite end, wastes 20 per cent of its costs) in respect of the best practice firm.

The standard profit function specifies variable profits and takes variable output prices as given (exogenous parameters). Profits depend on both output and input mix. The expression of the standard profit function, in log form, is:

$$\ln\left(\pi + \theta\right) = f\left(p, w, z, v\right) + \ln u_{\pi} + \ln \varepsilon_{\pi} \quad (4.11)$$

where π represents the profit of the bank (revenues earned on outputs minus costs, C, of the cost function); θ is a constant added to the profit of each firm with a view to obtaining a positive value for the logarithm; p is the vector of prices of the variable outputs, ε_{π} expresses the random error, and u_{π} represents the inefficiencies that reduce profits.

An interesting recent development in the efficiency analysis is the concept of alternative profit efficiency, which measures the distance of a firm from the maximum profit, given the level of its outputs as opposed to the prices of those outputs, as in the standard profit function (cf. Berger *et al.*, 1996 for an empirical application).[19] This function involves the same dependent variable as the standard profit function (firm profit) and the same independent variables as the cost function. The quantities of the outputs are constant while the prices of the outputs may vary. The alternative profit function is expressed in the following formula:

$$\ln\left(\pi + \theta\right) = f\left(y, w, z, v\right) + \ln u_{a\pi} + \ln \varepsilon_{a\pi} \quad (4.12)$$

where y stands for the quantities of the outputs; and u_{π} expresses random error of the alternative profit. In comparison to Equation (4.11), here y replaces p.

The alternative profit efficiency makes explicit the relationship between estimated actual profits and estimated maximum profits for the best practice bank in the sample:

$$a\pi\, \mathrm{EFF}^b = \frac{a\hat{\pi}^b}{a\hat{\pi}^{\max}}$$

$$= \frac{\left\{\exp\left[\hat{f}\left(y^b, w^b, z^b, v^b\right)\right]\cdot\exp\left(\ln\hat{u}^b_{a\pi}\right)\right\} - \theta}{\left\{\exp\left[\hat{f}\left(y^b, w^b, z^b, v^b\right)\right]\cdot\exp\left(\ln\hat{u}^{\max}_{a\pi}\right)\right\} - \theta} \qquad (4.13)$$

where $\hat{u}^{\max}_{\pi}$ is the maximum value of $\hat{u}^b_{\pi}$ in the sample. Equation (4.13) indicates the proportion of maximum profits that are actually realised: a ratio equal to 80 per cent means that the bank is losing 20 per cent of potential profit in respect of the best practice bank. The ratio may be negative and its maximum value is equal to 1.

4.4.2.4 The form of the function: The Fourier flexible

The choice of the functional form constitutes a further critical methodological step that profoundly influences the estimates of X-inefficiencies (Berger *et al.*, 1993; McAllister and McManus, 1993).[20] After a careful examination of the limits and advantages associated with each form, the function we selected for the cost frontier was the Fourier flexible (FF), which represents the specification that has been increasingly appreciated and adopted in the studies on bank efficiency, thanks to the fact that it is able to better approximate the underlying cost structure of the phenomenon under investigation.[21]

In particular, the Fourier flexible cost function is recognised as the global approximation that dominates the conventional translog form. The function combines the stability of the translog specification around the average of the sample and the flexibility of the Fourier specification for the observations that are far from the average. The characteristic of global approximation is particularly important in the case of the banking industry, because the scale of banks, the diversification of their products and services and the levels of their inefficiency are often heterogeneous.

The Fourier flexible function includes a standard translog function and all first- and second-order trigonometric terms as well as a two-component error term estimated using the maximum likelihood method.[22] Expressed in symbolic form, the function is as follows:

$$\ln TC = \alpha_0 + \sum_{i=1}^{3}\alpha_i \ln Q_i + \sum_{j=1}^{3}\beta_j \ln P_j + \tau_1 T + \lambda_1 \ln E$$

$$+ \frac{1}{2}\left[\sum_{i=1}^{3}\sum_{j=1}^{3}\delta_{ij}\ln Q_i \ln Q_j + \sum_{i=1}^{3}\sum_{j=1}^{3}\gamma_{ij}\ln P_i \ln P_j + \phi_{11}\ln E \ln E + \tau_{11}T^2 \right]$$

$$+ \sum_{i=1}^{3}\sum_{j=1}^{3}\rho_{ij}\ln Q_i \ln P_j + \sum_{j=1}^{3}\kappa_{j1}\ln P_j \ln E + \sum_{i=1}^{3}\varsigma_{i1}\ln Q_i \ln E$$

$$+ \sum_{i=1}^{3}\psi_i T \ln Q_i + \sum_{j=1}^{3}\theta_j T \ln P_j + \sum_{i=1}^{3}[a_i \cos(z_i) + b_i \sin(z_i)]$$

$$+ \sum\sum [a_{ij}\cos(z_i + z_j) + b_{ij}\sin(z_i + z_j)] + \varepsilon \tag{4.14}$$

where TC is a measure of the total cost of production (which includes operating costs and interests paid on deposits). Bank outputs (with 1.0 added to avoid taking the log of zero) are $Q_1 = $ total loans; $Q_2 = $ securities; $Q_3 = $ off-balance sheet business. Bank input prices for labour, loanable funds and physical capital, respectively, are $P_1 = $ personnel expenses/total assets; $P_2 = $ depreciation and other capital expenses/fixed assets; $P_3 = $ interest expenses/total funds. E is the financial capital variable. t is a time variable which is assumed to have a linear trend. ε is the two-component stochastic error term $\epsilon_i = u_i + v_i$. z_i are the adjusted values of the log output $\ln Q_i$ such that they span the interval $[0.1 \times 2\pi, 0.9 \times 2\pi]$. $\alpha, \beta, \delta, \gamma, \tau, \lambda, \phi, \rho, \kappa, \varsigma, \psi, \theta$ are parameters to be estimated.

The alternative profit function has the same specification as the above, the only difference being that the dependent variable is replaced with ln profits (ln π), as specified in Berger and Mester (1997).

In this empirical analysis, we chose to apply the Fourier terms only to the output variables, leaving the specification of the effects of the prices of inputs to be expressed entirely in transcendental translog terms (in this regard, see the arguments put forward in Berger *et al.*, 1997 and Altunbas *et al.*, 1999). The primary aim is to maintain the limited number of Fourier terms for describing the scale and inefficiency measures associated with differences in bank size. The traditional input price homogeneity restrictions are imposed, as will by shown, on the logarithmic price terms; these, however, cannot be easily imposed on trigonometric terms.[23] Finally, it is to be noted that the term standing for financial capital (E) is fully interactive with the output (Q) and input (P) variables but is not included in the Fourier terms.[24]

Moreover, the scaled log-output quantities, z_i, are calculated as $z_i = \mu_i (\ln Q_i + w_i)$, where $\ln Q_i$ represents the unscaled log-output quantities; μ_i and w_i are scaled factors, calculated – before the application of the Fourier flexible methodology – as the periodic sine and cosine trigonometric functions within one period length, 2π (cf. Gallant, 1981). The values of μ_i are chosen in such a way as to render the maximum value of each scaled log-output variable as close as possible to 2π, while w_i are restricted to assume a minimum value as close as possible to 0. Just as in Berger *et al.* (1997), in this study the values z_i have been set to lie in the interval $[0.1 \times 2\pi, 0.9 \times 2\pi]$ to reduce approximation problems near the endpoints of the interval, as theorised by Gallant (1981) and practised in an empirical analysis by Mitchell and Onvural (1996).

In order to respect standard symmetry conditions (Jorgenson, 1986), it is necessary to impose the following restrictions on the second-order parameters of the function given as (4.14):

$$
\begin{aligned}
\delta_{ij} &= \delta_{ji} \quad \text{for } 1 < i < 3 \text{ and } 1 < j < 3 \\
\gamma_{ij} &= \gamma_{ji} \quad \text{for } 1 < i < 3 \text{ and } 1 < j < 3
\end{aligned}
\tag{4.15}
$$

In addition, the one-degree homogeneity of the input prices in the total cost function TC makes it necessary to impose the following restrictions on the parameters:

$$
\sum_{j=1}^{3} \beta_j = 1 \quad \sum_{i=1}^{3} \gamma_{ij} = 0 \quad \sum_{j=1}^{3} \rho_{ij} = 0 \quad \delta_{ij} = \delta_{ji} \quad \gamma_{ij} = \gamma_{ji}
\tag{4.16}
$$

The imposition of the restriction of linear homogeneity in the prices means that it is correct to adopt – as we do below – the procedure of normalising TC, P_1 and P_3, in respect of the price of financial capital, P_2. In addition, we judged it appropriate to extend the calculation procedure typically adopted in the literature on technical change (see Section 5.3) or, in other words, to express in real terms the values for TC, Q_i and E, an approach that, in practice, takes the form of using deflators based on the Gross National Product (GNP) pertaining to each of the countries under investigation. The year 1995 was chosen as the point of reference for the deflator. In fact, in the context of an extended period of observation it becomes particularly important to identify a calculation procedure that makes it possible to exclude the effects of the nominal variation in the value of money.

4.4.2.5   The definition of inputs and outputs

The definition of inputs and outputs in the specification of the stochastic frontier for the analysis of X-inefficiencies has a profound influence on the accuracy of the estimates, and it constitutes a particularly controversial issue for the banking industry. In fact, measures of efficiency can be vitiated by errors in the identification of the correct variables and in the definition of the economic objectives of a productive unit.

In the light of the critical factors connected with the choice of an approach for the definition and measurement of the productive process of banks,[25] in this study the definition of inputs and outputs is based on what is proposed in the Approach to Intermediation in the original formulation by Sealey and Lindley (1977), where inputs (labour, physical capital and deposits) are used to produce outputs (including bank loans).

The definition of the input variables is based on what has been proposed in previous studies on the banking industry. Thus, the inputs are identified in the form of labour, physical capital and financial capital, whose prices are defined as follows:

a) the price of labour, in terms of the average unit price of personnel, is given by the total cost of labour divided by total assets;
b) the price of physical capital is calculated as the relationship between operating expenses (minus the cost of labour and interest expenses) and total fixed assets (including both tangible and intangible assets);
c) the price of financial capital measured in terms of interest expenses on total funds.

With a view to capturing the true nature of the production process, the definition of outputs in the model in question takes the form of a specification of the activities carried on by banks:[26] the value of total loans, the value of securities and the value of off-balance sheet items. The first two of these classes of outputs typically constitute earning assets for the bank. Although off-balance sheet items do not constitute income-generating activities in the strict sense, they do represent an ever more significant source of revenue for the bank. Thus, in keeping with the predominant orientation in the recent literature, we have included them as a class of outputs, so as to avoid underestimating the total level of bank production (in this regard, see the detailed discussion in Jagtiani and Khanthavit, 1996).

There are a range of different reasons why the three categories of activity constitute outputs of particular importance in the study of the impact of technology on performance in the banking industry. First of all, the huge increases in the volumes of these outputs have been made possible precisely by technology. In fact, the first consequence of technology is of an exquisitely quantitative (in the sense of size) nature. Secondly, the outputs in question involve an intensive use of information, both in the case that they are viewed as products offered on the market and in the case that reference is made to the process of producing them. On the one hand, investments in IT make it possible to improve the characteristics of the outputs of the bank understood as products offered to the clients and to produce a greater level of suitability to the needs of the market. As far as loans are concerned, one evident improvement relates to the issue of risk which, as a consequence of the adoption of IT infrastructures, should not only be more contained in terms of size but also more appropriate in respect of the specific needs of the bank and its clients. In regard to asset management services offered to clients (an off-balance sheet item), IT makes it possible to perfect the features of the products, which correspond ever more closely to the return, risk and liquidity requirements of the investors. On the other hand, investments in IT impact on the production process of all these outputs, resulting in a rationalisation of the process itself and, thereby, a higher level of operating adequacy. It is enough to think of the importance of IT in the collection, elaboration and management of information relating to entering into and administering of a mortgage/loan contract or, alternatively, of the impact on the asset allocation and securities selection relating to the financial instruments to be inserted by a given bank into its own portfolio and, in a later phase, on the management of the portfolio itself. Finally, one need only think of the implications of the automation of services relating to the safeguarding and administering of investments, or the arranging of deals in investments for customers (typically included among off-balance sheet items).

The variable relating to financial capital (E) is included in the specification of the model with a view to taking into consideration the differences in the risk preferences of the banks (Hughes and Mester, 1993; Mester, 1996).

See Table 4.3 for a detailed specification of the variables used in the model. Table 4.4, on the other hand, shows the descriptive statistics for inputs, outputs and the control variable in nominal terms in respect of 2000.

4.4.2.6   *X-inefficiencies: Empirical results*

In this study, the functional form used for the specification of the frontier is a Fourier flexible, as illustrated in Equation (4.17).[27] We use a time-varying model for the estimate of the effects of technical inefficiency, adopting the Stochastic Frontier Approach for a sample relating to the various years (panel data) as developed methodologically by Battese and Coelli (1992).

Table 4.5 presents the estimates of the average annual value and the standard deviation of the cost and profit X-efficiencies for each of the banking industries in the countries under investigation over the period

Table 4.3 Definitions of the variables used in the model

Variable	Name of variable	Definition
TC	Total costs	Cost of labour, depreciation, other operating expenses, other administrative expenses, interest expenses.
π	Total profits	Income statement value of net income.
Q_1	Total loans	Value of total loans as shown in the balance sheet.
Q_2	Securities	Value of securities as shown in the balance sheet.
Q_3	Off-balance sheet items	The value of off-balance sheet items as shown in the balance sheet.
P_1	Price of labour	The average cost of personnel (personnel expenses divided by total assets).
P_2	Price of financial capital	Interest expenses on total funds (deposits).
P_3	Price of physical capital	Operating expenses (depreciation and other capital expenditures) on total fixed assets.
E	Equity	The value of equity as shown in the balance sheet.

The table presents the definitions of the output, input and risk variables used in the stochastic cost frontier.

1994–2000. The average levels of cost efficiency are between 58.61 per cent (United Kingdom) and 76.78 per cent (Italy) for the year 2000. The majority of the banks seem to be characterised by levels of cost inefficiency to the order of about 25 per cent. In terms of the trend over the course of the period 1994–2000, cost productivity worsened in two countries (Germany and Italy), while it improved in the other three European countries in question (France, Spain and the United Kingdom).

The estimate of the average value of cost efficiency is slightly lower than that suggested in the recent literature on the European banking industry.[28] In this regard, see Altunbas *et al.*, 2001, the only study, as far as we are aware, that investigates – though only in terms of cost efficiency – the totality of the banking industries in Europe.[29] As reported in Altunbas *et al.* (2001), it appears that on average the banks in the United Kingdom have been relatively inefficient if compared with the

Table 4.4 Statistical results for total costs, output, input and risk control variables

	Average	Median	Min	Max	St dev
France					
TC	785,345	54,202	2,791	31,611,907	3,552,285
Q_1	4,562,591	419,795	3,257	163,011,659	19,274,275
Q_2	982,352	61,164	279	29,650,411	3,939,035
Q_3	6,491,154	334,189	4,653	265,391,880	32,162,418
P_1	0.0181	0.0146	0.0001	0.2153	0.0227
P_2	0.0743	0.0475	0.0141	0.9481	0.1086
P_3	6.6673	2.3538	0.2645	168.0914	20.0954
E	468,836	68,764	5,583	16,837,879	1,896,816
Germany					
TC	300,446	30,846	744	16,026,017	1,642,459
Q_1	3,534,534	284,454	1	181,567,708	18,722,021
Q_2	1,136,531	59,691	1	68,669,105	6,948,515
Q_3	1,122,557	30,846	1	60,648,187	6,848,579
P_1	0.0200	0.0140	0.0005	0.2667	0.0285
P_2	0.0478	0.0398	0.0080	0.3971	0.0398
P_3	0.9472	0.4445	0.0025	29.0108	2.6606
E	297,841	42,989	837	16,990,016	1,576,915
Italy					
TC	509,955	61,041	3,350	6,315,774	1,177,894
Q_1	6,199,707	777,527	1	83,335,848	14,466,331
Q_2	1,432,762	173,911	1,489	16,710,959	3,228,079
Q_3	4,013,126	143,297	1	71,983,549	11,761,540
P_1	0.0218	0.0167	0.0059	0.1506	0.0229
P_2	0.2638	0.0408	0.0062	15.5108	1.6534
P_3	0.7730	0.2272	0.2530	16.9218	2.3632
E	772,990	107,752	16,749	10,585,006	1,736,756
Spain					
TC	335,594	34,382	1,116	8,383,813	1,334,975
Q_1	3,655,590	468,368	1	85,509,215	13,019,218
Q_2	1,060,080	18,982	1	33,406,563	4,583,885
Q_3	1,410,616	60,390	1	42,705,243	6,296,161
P_1	0.0178	0.0139	0.0008	0.1017	0.0189
P_2	0.1274	0.0322	0.0023	6.5054	0.7626
P_3	0.2730	0.1894	0.0250	2.0837	0.3190
E	533,407	68,066	6,327	15,840,475	2,174,261
United Kingdom					
TC	1,887,739	119,061	1,687	20,805,244	4,352,264
Q_1	16,527,947	772,814	1	241,114,593	39,206,102
Q_2	4,296,457	124,568	35	84,949,269	13,720,903
Q_3	10,576,696	108,813	89	191,644,285	34,009,092

P_1	0.0198	0.0182	0.0010	0.1598	0.0206
P_2	0.0735	0.0625	0.0078	0.3459	0.0481
P_3	1.0171	0.6635	0.0317	9.9403	1.6055
E	1,619,105	251,072	8,057	22,056,103	3,875,752

The table summarises the nominal values for outputs, inputs and risk control variables – specified as in Table 4.3 – used in the stochastic cost frontier expressed in thousands of US$ in respect of the year 2000.
Source: Data elaborated by author on the basis of the *London-based International Bank Credit Analysis Ltd., Bankscope* database and the *Financial Analysis Made Easy, FAME* database.

Table 4.5   Estimates of the X-efficiency values of the European banks

	France		Germany		Italy		Spain		UK	
	Mean	St dev	Mean	St dev	Mean	St dev	Mean	St dev	Mean	St dev
Cost										
2000	0.6419	0.1640	0.7105	0.1538	0.7678	0.1338	0.6643	0.1888	0.5861	0.2124
1999	0.6309	0.1709	0.7207	0.1486	0.7763	0.1275	0.6590	0.1897	0.5654	0.2121
1998	0.6310	0.1774	0.7363	0.1412	0.7766	0.1247	0.6660	0.1886	0.5635	0.2011
1997	0.6208	0.1821	0.7457	0.1398	0.7839	0.1115	0.6630	0.1851	0.5398	0.2021
1996	0.6135	0.1812	0.7537	0.1361	0.7881	0.1052	0.6569	0.1880	0.5524	0.1993
1995	0.6091	0.1836	0.7631	0.1313	0.7919	0.1035	0.6449	0.1907	0.5247	0.1956
1994	0.6024	0.1904	0.7714	0.1288	0.7980	0.1011	0.6445	0.1736	0.5085	0.1874
Profit										
2000	0.4679	0.2147	0.4729	0.2344	0.5039	0.2229	0.4747	0.2423	0.4705	0.2167
1999	0.4819	0.2106	0.4784	0.2284	0.5535	0.1970	0.5347	0.2352	0.5126	0.2038
1998	0.4818	0.2121	0.4750	0.2340	0.5449	0.2137	0.5213	0.2416	0.5529	0.1965
1997	0.4820	0.2157	0.4608	0.2433	0.5527	0.2132	0.5289	0.2307	0.5810	0.1880
1996	0.4770	0.2208	0.4453	0.2374	0.5397	0.2129	0.5302	0.2259	0.6191	0.1729
1995	0.4806	0.2213	0.4245	0.2457	0.5653	0.2167	0.5421	0.2242	0.6121	0.1716
1994	0.4814	0.2048	0.4354	0.2367	0.6245	0.1931	0.5971	0.2090	0.6592	0.1367

The table presents the estimates of the X-efficiency values (cost and profit) calculated by using the error components model (Battese and Coelli, 1992). The estimates relate to the banks of each European country investigated in respect of the period 1994–2000.
Source: Data elaborated by author.

institutions in the other European countries. Likewise, the banks in Italy and Germany have been the most efficient.

In regard to profit X-inefficiencies – presented in the second part of Table 4.5 in terms of alternative profit X-inefficiencies – it appears that there was a downward trend in the European countries over the period 1994–2000 (although the trend was not linear). The only exception to this is represented by Germany, where efficiency increased from 43.54 per cent (1994) to 47.29 per cent (2000). Nonetheless, it should be noted that in 2000 profit efficiency worsened in the banking industry in all five European countries.

A comparison of the profit and cost efficiency trends results in a finding that is particularly interesting and to a certain extent unexpected. In the European banking industries where cost efficiency increased over the course of the period 1994–2000, profit efficiency, by contrast, diminished (Spain, France and the United Kingdom). In the countries where, on the other hand, cost efficiency decreased, profit efficiency increased (Germany). The only exception to this was the Italian banking industry, where there was a decrease in both cost and profit efficiency. Cost efficiency may improve but this may not be reflected in higher profit efficiency if revenues also decline. For example, banks may cut costs that reduce service quality/product range that reduces revenue and also may reduce profit efficiency, although cost efficiency improves. Cost inefficient banks may employ more costly staff and systems, but this may generate more revenue boosting profit efficiency.

4.5   The measures of IT investment for the European banking industry

In dealing with measures of IT investment, it is very important to recognise that European banks are not under any obligation – whether in terms of national accounting principles or in terms of banking legislation – to publish in their balance sheets any information about investment in IT (or its related costs). Thus, there is no source of an accounting nature that can provide in a comprehensive and systematic manner data relating to the IT investment of individual European banks. Consequently, so far as IT activity is concerned, the only form of disclosure pertaining to bank financial statements is of a voluntary nature, and the actual content of such disclosure is neither extensive, nor detailed, nor uniform. The reason for this limited degree of disclosure is presumably to be found in a perception, on the part of banks, that IT activity constitutes a possible source of competitive advantage. Indeed, the fact that it is costly to acquire this information explains the existence of organisations like Financial Insights – IDC (International Data Corporation) and Convenzione Interbancaria per i Problemi dell'Automazione (CIPA) (The Inter-bank Convention on Problems of Automation) that provide – the first commercially at an international level, the second at the institutional level in Italy – proxies for investments in IT.

In this study, then, the investments in technology effected by European banks in the period 1995–2005[30] are expressed in terms of estimated real values. The estimates employed – calculated on the basis of the price (including channel mark-up) paid to the vendors of the technology – are provided by Financial Insights – IDC (2006). IDC monitors sales in the IT market and calculates – on the basis of the turnover of the vendors – a flow of a non-accounting nature relating to expenditure on IT in the banking industry.[31] Thus, given that it is not possible to make use of financial statement values but rather, only of estimates of sums paid by banks to acquire IT products and services, in this study the term "IT investment" loses any sense of an accounting nature[32] and refers exclusively to a flow obtained by estimating the turnovers of vendors of IT in respect of the banking industry. This flow, moreover, is not influenced either by policies of depreciation (in fact, generally accelerated) or by the withdrawal of technology that may become obsolete over time.

An ideal solution would be to incorporate all the components that can be defined as technology into a single measure to be used to define investment in technology. A broad definition would include hardware (computers, telecommunications equipment, peripherals), software (produced in house or acquired), costs tied to support services and even investment in related activity of an organisational nature (such as expenditure on training staff and the operating costs for the design and implementation of business processes). It should be noted that the literature – including that on the US economy – generally involves a set of information on IT investment that is considerably more limited and that is capable of capturing only a part of the investment in technology (for an extensive discussion of the impact of IT investment that is not taken into consideration, see Brynjolfsson and Hitt, 1996).

The novel and interesting features of the database used in this study – characteristics that are not often found in other studies on the value of technology[33] – lie precisely in the fact that it makes available data in relation to all the above-mentioned components. In particular, as listed below, there emerge three macro-categories in terms of which to divide investments in technology (as specified by Financial Insights – IDC, 2006):

1) Hardware (HA): commercial systems (CPUs (central processing units) and peripheral equipment, including data storage devices, terminals, memory and peripherals), single-user systems (including personal computers and workstations), and data-communication systems (LAN hardware, WAN hardware, analog modems and digital access).
2) Software (SO): standard commercial applications (packaged software), application solutions software, application tools and systems

infrastructure software. Packaged software consists in programmes offered commercially (for sale or lease) by the systems vendors or by independent software vendors. The estimated value includes the fees of the packaged software itself as well as additional non-consulting costs (charges for maintenance and support). Application solutions software includes consumer, commercial and technical programmes designed to provide packaged solutions for particular problems inhering to functions in a firm or industry. Cross-industry applications address problems that are not unique to a particular industry. Examples of applications solutions software common to various industries include software applications for office automation, accounting, the management of human resources, payroll, project management and word processing. On the other hand, vertical industry applications address problems that are unique to a particular industry. An example of an application solutions software pertaining specifically to the banking industry is one employed for dealing with loan processing. Application tools are divided into information access tools (instruments geared towards the final user with facilities for ad hoc data access, analysis and reporting) and developers development tools (software products that support professional programmers in the design, development and implementation of a range of software systems and solutions).[34] Finally, systems infrastructure software is divided into four main categories: system management software (used for managing the entire range of computing resources in a firm), middleware (independent software and services systems used in geographically dispersed businesses to share computing resources among heterogeneous technologies), serverware (products that deliver housekeeping capabilities used for co-ordinating resources between the different servers in the network) and system-level software (products that jointly make it possible to run the hardware platforms and communications networks on which business applications are based);

3) IT services (SE): consulting services, implementation services, operations management services (including services provided in the form of outsourcing), training and staff development services, and support services. Consulting services include services in support of the formulation of strategies for information systems, the planning of IT and networks, the evaluation of technological architectures, the operational analysis of information systems, the design of technical systems and networks, the evaluation of IT suppliers and the planning of maintenance services.[35] Implementation services

include activities aimed at constructing technical and business solutions (implementation activity begins at the moment when an IT project evolves from a concept to an actual system prototype).[36] Like consulting services, implementation services can be supplied either as standalone activities or packaged with larger offering (e.g. systems integration projects).[37] Operating services (known as operations management) are aimed at taking responsibility for the management of the various components of the information system infrastructures in a bank (such as help desks or network management) or even, as in the case of outsourcing, of the information system as a whole.[38] Given that most outsourcing contracts are of a multi-year nature, the expenses captured in this category represents an annual fee – in the context of the multi-period contract – paid to the external supplier who assumes responsibility for managing an operation or process. Training and staff development services include educational activity aimed at promoting a general knowledge of IT as well as extending practical IT skills. These services are intended to promote the acquisition of new behaviours, skills and actions to be used in the realisation of specific tasks or in the achievement of an improvement in the performance of labour.[39] Support services include all the activities that are designed to guarantee that IT products and services function adequately.[40]

Table 4.6 shows the amount of investment in IT for the European banking industry in the course of each year from 1995 to 2005. In particular, figures are provided for the values pertaining to each of the banking industries investigated in the study, the aggregate value for the five countries in question and the overall value for investment in Western Europe. The total amount of IT investment in the banking industry in Western Europe more than doubled between 1995 and 2005 (from US$21,872 million to US$49,191 million). A very similar trend can be seen in respect of the average value of the investments in the five countries investigated in this study (from US$16,026 million to US$36,311 million) according to Financial Insights – IDC (2006). Note that although the trend is continuously upward, the increase in IT investments has been more pronounced in the period 1995–2001 than in 2002–2005. A further reduction in the growth rate of IT investments for Western European banks is expected for 2006–2007, when total IT investments are forecasted to grow by about 10 per cent in comparison to 2005.

Table 4.6 Investment in IT by European banks

Year	1995	1996	1997	1998	1999	2000	2001	2002	2003	2004	2005
Nominal amount	**US\$ (millions)**										
Western Europe	21,872	23,468	26,707	30,686	34,277	38,870	42,287	42,889	44,234	46,628	49,191
France	3,299	3,473	3,946	4,589	4,998	5,687	6,269	6,338	6,464	6,662	6,900
Germany	3,350	3,639	4,319	5,066	5,730	6,440	6,946	7,015	7,269	7,791	8,297
Italy	2,854	3,031	3,359	3,795	4,221	4,773	5,239	5,287	5,375	5,550	5,728
Spain	1,115	1,207	1,402	1,610	1,777	2,063	2,265	2,302	2,377	2,502	2,635
UK	5,408	5,792	6,586	7,541	8,483	9,722	10,563	10,757	11,197	11,926	12,749
The 5 EU countries	16,026	17,143	19,612	22,601	25,209	28,687	31,282	31,698	32,683	34,430	36,311
Ratio	**Banking System IT Investment/Western Europe IT Investment (%)**										
France	15.08	14.80	14.77	14.95	14.58	14.63	14.82	14.78	14.61	14.29	14.03
Germany	15.32	15.50	16.17	16.51	16.72	16.57	16.43	16.36	16.43	16.71	16.87
Italy	13.05	12.92	12.58	12.37	12.31	12.28	12.39	12.33	12.15	11.90	11.65
Spain	5.10	5.14	5.25	5.25	5.19	5.31	5.36	5.37	5.37	5.37	5.36
UK	24.73	24.68	24.66	24.57	24.75	25.01	24.98	25.08	25.31	25.58	25.92

The table presents the estimated real values of investment in technology (hardware, software and services) effected by European banks in the period 1995–2005. The estimates – expressed in terms of price paid to the vendors of the technology, including the channel mark-up – have been provided by International Data Corporation (Financial Insights – IDC, 2006). The values are expressed in millions of US\$. The table also shows the relationship (expressed as a ratio) between the total amount of investment in technology by the banking industry of each of the European countries investigated and the total amount of investment in technology by the banking industry in Western Europe as a whole. Western Europe include Austria, Belgium, Denmark, Finland, France, Germany, Greece, Ireland, Italy, Netherlands, Norway, Portugal, Spain, Sweden, Switzerland and the United Kingdom.
Source: Financial Insights – IDC (2006).

The banking industry in the United Kingdom accounted for the highest proportion of the IT investment made by the Western European countries as a whole (25.92 per cent in 2005). Spain, on the other hand, accounted for the lowest proportion (5.36 per cent in 2005). The banking industries in France and Germany each accounted for 14.03 per cent and 16.87 per cent of the overall amount of investment in IT in Western Europe, whereas the proportion of Italian banks was 11.65 per cent in 2005. The Italian banking industry accounted for a decreasing proportion over the last years. The greatest increase in IT investment was registered by the German banks (+147.64 per cent between 1995 and 2005), while the lowest is to be ascribed to the Italian banks (+100.73 per cent, nonetheless, over the same period.)

In order to arrive at a fully comprehensive description of investment in technology, it has been stressed that, rather than deal with investment as a monolithic entity – as was done in the original studies – it would be more opportune to tease out the different components of IT investment in terms of how they contribute to business value. In fact, there is little doubt that the manner in which IT investments are allocated among the various components of technology (hardware, software and services) should be investigated jointly with the aggregate amount of those investments. In accordance with this consideration, in this study we have undertaken an analysis of a higher level of complexity, engaging in an examination of the composition of total IT investment.[41]

Table 4.7 shows a detailed breakdown of the components making up the total of IT investments, providing figures for the three categories: hardware, software and IT services. It can be seen that on average, investment by the European banks in the period 1995–2005 (expressed as a proportion of total investment in IT) stood at 24.60 per cent for hardware, 16.75 per cent for software and 58.65 per cent for IT services (Financial Insights – IDC, 2006). The trend in this period clearly shows an increase in the amount of resources dedicated to IT services (from 46.68 per cent in 1995 to 58.65 per cent in 2005) and a reduction in the investment in hardware (from 37.64 per cent in 1995 to 24.60 per cent in 2005). Investment in software, on the other hand, remained stable. This trend is especially pronounced for the UK banks.

An examination of the relative weight of the three components in respect of the banking industries of the various European countries investigated reveals that on the European level the banks in the United Kingdom allocated the highest proportion of their resources to IT services (64.21 per cent in 2005 in comparison to 53.86 per cent of their total IT investment in 2000) and the lowest proportion to hardware

Table 4.7 Investment in IT by European banks according to the categories: hardware, software and services

	1995	1996	1997	1998	1999	2000	2001	2002	2003	2004	2005
	Western Europe (IT asset categories investments/Total IT investment, %)										
Hardware	37.64	37.32	36.77	35.87	34.78	33.86	31.58	0.3002	0.2849	0.2665	0.2460
Software	15.68	16.35	16.15	15.78	16.07	16.35	16.99	0.1699	0.1681	0.1682	0.1675
Services	46.68	46.33	47.09	48.35	49.16	49.79	51.43	0.5299	0.5471	0.5652	0.5865
	France (IT asset categories investments/Total IT investment, %)										
Hardware	34.80	34.90	33.46	31.44	30.66	29.53	27.54	0.2667	0.2603	0.2532	0.2449
Software	17.13	17.75	17.23	17.07	17.38	17.29	17.83	0.1766	0.1735	0.1693	0.1643
Services	48.07	47.35	49.31	51.49	51.95	53.18	54.63	0.5567	0.5662	0.5775	0.5908
	Germany (IT asset categories investments/Total IT investment, %)										
Hardware	42.67	41.69	40.53	40.74	39.80	38.45	36.02	0.3438	0.3250	0.3023	0.2761
Software	14.50	15.59	15.57	14.84	15.29	15.72	16.45	0.1653	0.1654	0.1693	0.1713
Services	42.83	42.73	43.90	44.42	44.91	45.82	47.53	0.4910	0.5096	0.5284	0.5526
	Italy (IT asset categories investments/Total IT investment, %)										
Hardware	37.95	37.27	36.19	34.78	33.88	34.18	32.21	0.3132	0.3047	0.2937	0.2814
Software	17.63	17.82	17.36	16.91	16.62	16.23	16.81	0.1699	0.1709	0.1747	0.1781
Services	44.43	44.91	46.45	48.30	49.50	49.60	50.98	0.5169	0.5244	0.5316	0.5406

			Spain (IT asset categories investments/Total IT investment, %)								
Hardware	39.79	39.68	39.24	38.93	38.54	39.08	37.36	0.3561	0.3392	0.3188	0.2943
Software	12.88	13.38	13.11	12.92	14.01	13.92	14.55	0.1444	0.1411	0.1375	0.1337
Services	47.32	46.93	47.65	48.14	47.44	47.01	48.09	0.4995	0.5197	0.5437	0.5720
			UK (IT asset categories investments/Total IT investment, %)								
Hardware	32.36	32.45	32.39	31.40	29.84	28.87	26.50	0.2464	0.2293	0.2098	0.1864
Software	15.90	16.35	16.59	16.22	16.85	17.26	17.83	0.1778	0.1749	0.1737	0.1715
Services	51.74	51.20	51.02	52.38	53.31	53.86	55.67	0.5758	0.5958	0.6165	0.6421

The table indicates the categories of investment in IT as specified by Financial Insights – IDC (2006). The products/services that make up each of the three categories are as follows:

1. Hardware (HA): commercial systems, single-user systems and data-communication systems;
2. Software (SO): packaged software, application solutions software, application tools and systems infrastructure software;
3. IT Services (SE): consulting services, implementation services, operations management services, training and staff development services and support services.

The values in the table are given in terms of the ratio between the value of each category and the total value of investments in IT in respect of each country for each of the years in the period under investigation (1995–2005).
Source: Financial Insights – IDC (2006).

(18.64 per cent in 2005 in comparison to 28.87 per cent in 2001). On the contrary, the very opposite picture can be seen in the Italian banks, which have traditionally invested less in IT services (54.06 per cent in 2005) and more in hardware (28.14 per cent). It is interesting to note that the allocation of resources on the part of the French and German banks shows the same characteristics that have been encountered in relation to, respectively, the United Kingdom and Italy. The allocation put in place by the Spanish banks, on the other hand, stood at very high levels for hardware (29.43 per cent in 2005) and very low for software (13.37 per cent).

To better illustrate the tie between investments in technology and the structural characteristics of the banking industry, we have also made estimates of the so-called "IT indices", as has traditionally been proposed in the literature as a way of examining the relationship between investments in technology and performance. The measures that are generally used relate to the size of the firm and are defined in terms of the number of employees, revenues, equity and total costs. The choice of a denominator for the IT index should not influence the results to any great degree. Nonetheless, there is the possibility of a negative bias in the case that the denominator refers to revenue; independently of the contribution of technology, an unexpected increase in the value of revenues increases profits but reduces the value of the IT index, producing a negative coefficient. The use of other size measures as a denominator – such as the number of employees, equity or total costs – avoids this complication. Because of the lack of data on the number of employees, we do not use this value as a denominator for the index. In this study, we calculate the ratios of IT total investment – and its components – as a proportion of equity, total costs and operating costs.[42]

Table 4.8 shows the IT ratios or, more particularly, IT investments as a proportion of equity, total costs and operating costs in relation to each European banking industry over the period 1995–2000. By way of an overview, it can be seen that in 2000, the average Italian bank spent on IT as much as 0.94 per cent of its total costs (6.19 per cent of its operating costs),[43] while French, Spanish and the UK banks spent, respectively, 0.72, 0.61 and 0.51 per cent of their total costs (7.27, 6.08 and 5.33 per cent of their operating costs).[44] German banks spent a much higher proportion than banks in other EU countries (2.14 per cent of their total costs in 2000, 10.80 per cent of their operating costs). The UK banking industry shows the lowest percentage of IT investments over total costs (and operating costs). In regard to the trend over the period 1995–2000, it is important to underline the considerable increase

Table 4.8 Ratios of IT investment in European banking

	Ratio of IT investments to equity (%)					Ratio of IT investments to total costs (%)					Ratio of IT investments to operat. costs (%)				
	France	Germany	Italy	Spain	UK	France	Germany	Italy	Spain	UK	France	Germany	Italy	Spain	UK
2000	1.21	2.16	0.62	0.38	0.60	0.72	2.14	0.94	0.61	0.51	7.27	10.80	6.19	6.08	5.33
1999	1.10	1.39	0.60	0.57	0.65	0.97	1.24	1.03	0.80	0.51	7.98	6.80	6.16	6.33	5.69
1998	1.49	1.27	0.47	0.49	0.55	0.79	1.13	0.59	0.60	0.37	7.67	6.93	5.25	5.78	3.08
1997	1.63	1.10	0.58	0.53	0.62	0.83	0.96	0.54	0.51	0.26	7.87	6.62	5.29	5.56	3.75
1996	1.39	1.07	0.52	0.40	0.59	0.73	0.90	0.42	0.31	0.27	6.67	6.42	5.11	4.68	2.85
1995	1.32	0.93	0.50	0.34	0.64	0.63	0.79	0.36	0.26	0.36	6.19	5.65	4.75	4.29	3.24

The table presents the ratios of IT investments in respect of equity, total costs and operating costs for the banking industry of each country in respect of each of the years in the period 1995–2000.
Source: Data elaborated by author on the basis of Financial Insights – IDC (2006) data.

registered in 1999 in most of the European banking industries: note, for example, the jump that took place in the Italian industry – from 0.59 per cent in 1998 to 1.03 per cent in 1999. The reasons for this growth are to be attributed principally to the adjustments required for Year 2000 and to the adoption of the single European currency (the Euro). The same observations can be made in relation to the IT indices relating to equity – as might well be expected, moreover, in view of the analyses advanced in the earlier literature on the US economy.

With a view to specifying the incidence on total IT investment in its various asset categories (hardware, software and IT services), Table 4.9 shows the values relating to each European banking industry in each

Table 4.9 Ratios of IT asset categories in European banking

	1995	1996	1997	1998	1999	2000
Ratio of hardware investments to equity (%)						
France	0.46	0.48	0.54	0.47	0.34	0.36
Germany	0.40	0.45	0.45	0.52	0.55	0.83
Italy	0.19	0.19	0.21	0.16	0.20	0.21
Spain	0.14	0.16	0.21	0.19	0.22	0.15
UK	0.21	0.19	0.20	0.17	0.19	0.17
Ratio of hardware investments to total costs (%)						
France	0.22	0.26	0.28	0.25	0.30	0.21
Germany	0.34	0.39	0.39	0.46	0.50	0.82
Italy	0.14	0.16	0.20	0.20	0.35	0.32
Spain	0.10	0.12	0.20	0.23	0.31	0.24
UK	0.12	0.09	0.08	0.11	0.15	0.15
Ratio of hardware investments to operating costs (%)						
France	2.16	2.32	2.63	2.41	2.45	2.15
Germany	2.41	2.68	2.68	2.82	2.71	4.15
Italy	1.04	1.16	1.19	1.13	1.41	1.43
Spain	0.91	1.06	1.40	1.47	1.67	1.59
UK	1.05	0.93	1.21	0.97	1.70	1.54
Ratio of software investments to equity (%)						
France	0.23	0.25	0.28	0.25	0.19	0.21
Germany	0.13	0.17	0.17	0.19	0.21	0.34
Italy	0.09	0.09	0.10	0.08	0.10	0.10
Spain	0.04	0.05	0.07	0.06	0.08	0.05
UK	0.10	0.10	0.10	0.09	0.11	0.10
Ratio of software investments to total costs (%)						
France	0.11	0.13	0.14	0.13	0.17	0.12
Germany	0.11	0.15	0.15	0.17	0.19	0.34

Italy	0.06	0.07	0.09	0.10	0.17	0.15
Spain	0.03	0.04	0.07	0.08	0.11	0.09
UK	0.06	0.04	0.04	0.06	0.09	0.09
Ratio of software investments to operating costs (%)						
France	1.06	1.18	1.36	1.31	1.39	1.26
Germany	0.82	1.00	1.03	1.03	1.04	1.70
Italy	0.48	0.55	0.57	0.55	0.69	0.68
Spain	0.29	0.36	0.47	0.49	0.61	0.57
UK	0.51	0.47	0.62	0.50	0.96	0.92
Ratio of IT services to equity (%)						
France	0.64	0.66	0.80	0.77	0.57	0.64
Germany	0.40	0.46	0.48	0.57	0.62	0.99
Italy	0.22	0.23	0.27	0.23	0.30	0.31
Spain	0.16	0.19	0.25	0.24	0.27	0.18
UK	0.33	0.30	0.31	0.29	0.35	0.32
Ratio of IT services to total costs (%)						
France	0.30	0.35	0.41	0.41	0.51	0.38
Germany	0.34	0.40	0.42	0.50	0.56	0.98
Italy	0.16	0.19	0.25	0.28	0.51	0.46
Spain	0.12	0.15	0.24	0.29	0.38	0.29
UK	0.19	0.14	0.13	0.19	0.27	0.28
Ratio of IT services to operating costs (%)						
France	2.98	3.15	3.88	3.95	4.15	3.90
Germany	2.42	2.74	2.90	3.08	3.05	4.90
Italy	1.22	1.40	1.53	1.57	2.06	2.08
Spain	1.08	1.26	1.70	1.82	2.05	1.92
UK	1.67	1.46	1.91	1.61	3.03	2.87

The table presents the ratios of each IT asset category (hardware, software and IT services) in respect of equity, total costs and operating costs for the banking industry of each country in respect of each of the years in the period 1995–2000.
Source: Data elaborated by author on the basis of Financial Insights – IDC (2006) data.

year over the period 1995–2000. The figures for 2000 confirm the finding that emerged in Table 4.7 or, in other words, that the component with the biggest incidence – even on total costs – is represented by investment in IT services, followed by investment in hardware and, finally, investment in software.

4.6   The empirical results

To embark upon the analysis of the relationship between investment in technology and performance in the European banking industry, it is first necessary to define the correlation between the variables under investigation. Table 4.10 presents the matrix of the correlations (expressed in terms of both the non-parametric Spearman's rank correlation and the parametric Pearson's correlation) relating to the sample, obtained by aggregating the data for all the national banking industries. The correlated variables are as follows: total investment in technology (IT), investment in hardware (HA), investment in software (SO) and expenditure on technology-related services (SE). Investment in technology is expressed both in terms of flow of capital invested in technology and the IT ratios (investment in IT as a proportion of equity, total costs and operating costs).

Adopting this framework, there emerge the following empirical results. First of all, while there is a positive correlation (and statistically significant at 0.01) between profit efficiency and ROA, there is a negative correlation (again statistically significant) between cost efficiency and accounting measures of profitability (both ROA and ROE). This finding is consistent with the theoretical hypotheses at the basis of the theory of productivity and constitutes an empirical confirmation of it. Secondly, and, for our purposes, more interestingly, the correlation between profit efficiency and investment in technology is negative and statistically significant. This finding holds true both with nominal values of IT investments (significance at 0.05) and when IT investments are calculated as ratios to equity, to total costs and to operating costs (significance at 0.01). Note that throughout the analysis the actual choice of the denominator for the IT ratio does not affect the results substantially. In addition, it should be noted that the negative (and statistically significant) correlation persists even when we consider separately the three components of IT investment (hardware, software and IT services). Thirdly, in regard to accounting measures of profitability, it can be observed that the sign of the correlation between ROA and the IT ratios is negative and statistically significant, while the sign of the correlation between ROE and investment in IT is positive and statistically significant. This finding represents an initial piece of empirical evidence that is of considerable importance for our investigation of the profitability paradox in relation to the European banking industry. In the face of a significant negative relationship between investment in technology and an alternative performance measure like that identified in operating profit efficiency, when reference is made to traditional accounting measures of profitability, the relationship with investment in technology is either positive or negative. It would appear that the performance measure used for the first time in this study makes it possible to investigate the relation in question in a more appropriate manner than has been allowed by traditional accounting measures. In

Table 4.10 Correlation matrix

Spearman / Pearson	HA	SO	SE	IT	ROA	ROE	Profit Eff	Cost Eff
HA	1.000	0.938***	0.930***	0.974***	0.139	0.440**	−0.163	−0.314*
SO	0.940***	1.000	0.994***	0.989***	0.185	0.469***	−0.23	−0.445**
SE	0.925***	0.993***	1.000	0.986***	0.224	0.496***	−0.18	−0.486**
IT	0.965***	0.994***	0.992***	1.000	0.201	0.487***	−0.55	−0.425**
ROA	0.095	0.173	0.257	0.198	1.000	0.836***	0.339**	−0.267
ROE	0.425***	0.475***	0.562***	0.515***	0.796***	1.000	0.147	−0.460**
Profit Eff	−0.113	−0.018	0.013	−0.030*	0.396***	0.167	1.000	−0.112
Cost Eff	−0.237	−0.386**	−0.453**	−0.384**	−0.318*	−0.507***	0.269	1.000

Spearman / Pearson	ln(HA/E)	ln(SO/E)	ln(SE/E)	ln(IT/E)	ROA	ROE	Profit Eff	Cost Eff
ln(HA/E)	1.000	0.866***	0.873***	0.917***	−0.498***	−0.357*	−0.518***	0.053
ln(SO/E)	0.933***	1.000	0.977***	0.981***	−0.494***	−0.241	−0.538***	−0.190
ln(SE/E)	0.936***	0.985***	1.000	0.987***	−0.382**	−0.119	−0.551***	−0.286
ln(IT/E)	0.974***	0.985***	0.991***	1.000	−0.429**	−0.188	−0.521***	−0.199
ROA	−0.570***	−0.514***	−0.442**	−0.508***	1.000	0.836***	0.339*	−0.267
ROE	−0.330*	−0.253	−0.153	−0.236	0.796**	1.000	0.147	−0.460**
Profit Eff	−0.631***	−0.527***	−0.546***	−0.584***	0.396**	0.167	1.000	−0.112
Cost Eff	0.126	−0.010	−0.104	−0.006	−0.318*	−0.507***	−0.269	1.000

Spearman / Pearson	ln(HA/TC)	ln(SO/TC)	ln(SE/TC)	ln(IT/TC)	ROA	ROE	Profit Eff	Cost Eff
ln(HA/TC)	1.000	0.926***	0.936***	0.974***	−0.332*	−0.273	−0.676***	0.468***
ln(SO/TC)	0.935***	1.000	0.979***	0.977***	−0.340*	−0.224	−0.613***	0.355*

Table 4.10 (Continued)

Spearman Pearson	ln(HA/TC)	ln(SO/TC)	ln(SE/TC)	ln(IT/TC)	ROA	ROE	Profit Eff	Cost Eff
ln(SE/TC)	0.947***	0.982***	1.000	0.986***	−0.247	−0.130	−0.630***	0.293
ln(IT/TC)	0.979***	0.981***	0.992***	1.000	−0.301*	−0.206	−0.652***	0.366**
ROA	−0.342*	−0.343*	−0.242	−0.303	1.000	0.836***	0.339*	−0.267
ROE	−0.263	−0.223	−0.111	−0.189	0.796***	1.000	0.147	−0.460**
Profit Eff	−0.699***	−0.664***	−0.667***	−0.697***	0.396**	0.167	1.000	0.112
Cost Eff	0.534***	0.425**	0.360*	0.441**	−0.318*	−0.507***	−0.269	1.000

Spearman Pearson	ln(HA/OC)	ln(SO/OC)	ln(SE/OC)	ln(IT/OC)	ROA	ROE	Profit Eff	Cost Eff
ln(HA/OC)	1.000	0.870***	0.889***	0.937***	−0.290	−0.186	−0.819***	0.099
ln(SO/OC)	0.900***	1.000	0.955***	0.961***	−0.310	−0.171	−0.661***	−0.082
ln(SE/OC)	0.907***	0.975***	1.000	0.984***	−0.128	0.014	−0.693***	−0.196
ln(IT/OC)	0.962***	0.976***	0.987***	1.000	−0.225	−0.085	−0.730***	−0.067
ROA	−0.308	−0.248	−0.114	−0.208	1.000	0.944***	0.209	−0.332
ROE	−0.177	−0.100	0.038	−0.061	0.945***	1.000	0.140	−0.468***
Profit Eff	−0.825***	−0.692***	−0.707***	−0.767***	0.224	0.163	1.000	−0.130
Cost Eff	0.166	−0.002	−0.116	0.002	−0.404**	−0.508**	−0.269	1.000

The table presents the correlation matrix relating to the sample obtained by aggregating all the data pertaining to all the national banking industries under investigation. The horizontal axis of each block shows the non-parametric Spearman's rank correlation, while the vertical axis shows the parametric Pearson's correlation. The correlated variables are as follows: IT = total investment in technology, HA = investment in hardware, SO = investment in software and SE = expenditure on technology-related services. Investment in technology is expressed both in terms of the flow of investment in technology and the IT ratios (investment in IT as a proportion of equity, total costs and operating costs). The symbols *, ** and *** indicate a significant correlation, respectively, at 10%, 5% and 1% (two-tailed).

Source: Data elaborated by author.

fact, with it there emerges – be it simply in terms of a correlation between values – a clear confirmation of the profitability paradox: greater investment in technology does not correspond to an increase in operating productivity or, in other words, there is no evidence of a positive correlation between the amount of investment in technology and the capacity of a bank to apply a price premium in consequence of a higher quality in the outputs produced for a given input mix employed. Finally, turning attention to costs, while the sign of the correlation between cost efficiency and IT ratios is negative and statistically significant, the sign of the correlation between cost efficiency and investment in IT is positive and statistically significant. The relationship on the costs side, then, calls for further investigation aimed at overcoming the statistical limits of an analysis of simple correlations.

In order to assess better the relationships described above, we proceed to examine the results in relation to the models proposed in Section 4.2. In regard to Equation (4.1), which regress investment in technology on a series of contemporaneous performance measures (respectively ROA, ROE, profit efficiency and cost efficiency), the results of the estimates – using the Ordinary Least Square (OLS) method – are reported in Table 4.11. Regarding the use of the measure of profit efficiency as a dependent variable, the coefficient in respect of the IT ratios (both in respect of equity, total costs and operating costs) is negative and significant at 0.01,[45] as expected in the light of the findings reported in the correlation matrix. The magnitude of the coefficient is extremely high. This indicates that variations in investment in technology have a significant impact on profit efficiency. For example, an increase of 10 per cent in the IT ratio to operating costs implies a reduction of 0.905 per cent in profit efficiency.

The results of the TSLS regression are similar to the results of the OLS regression analysis here above, suggesting that there is no causality bias. Such non-causality is confirmed by the Granger causality Wald test. The null hypothesis of non-causality (i.e. IT investments do not cause profit efficiency) can be rejected at the 1 per cent level for all countries (with the exception of the UK where it can be rejected at the 10 per cent level). Contrarily, the null hypothesis that profit efficiency do not cause IT investments cannot be rejected at the level of 1 per cent for all countries (with the exception of Spain).

The empirical results presented up to now suggest that the impact of investments in IT on the performance of banks is negative on the side of profit efficiency: profit X-efficiencies do not improve with an increase in investment in IT. This represents a confirmation of the

Table 4.11 Regression between technology and contemporaneous performance (OLS regression)

Equation (4.1)	Dependent variable	Contemporaneous ROA				Contemporaneous ROE			
	Parameters	IT	ln(IT/E)	ln(IT/TC)	ln(IT/OC)	IT	ln(IT/E)	ln(IT/TC)	ln(IT/OC)
β_0	CONSTANT	0.003 (0.002)	0.0203 (0.008)	−0.0999 (0.009)	−0.0001 (0.004)	0.0336 (0.020)	−0.0371 (0.1)	−0.0122 (0.102)	0.0651 (0.077)
$\beta_{1,jt}$	IT	0.000 (0.000)	–	–	–	0.0001** (0.000)	–	–	–
	ln(IT/E)	–	0.0052** (0.002)	–	–	–	−0.0262 (0.02)	–	–
	ln(IT/TC)	–	–	−0.0030 (0.002)	–	–	–	−0.0203 (0.020)	–
	ln(IT/OC)	–	–	–	−0.0016 (0.001)	–	–	–	−0.0081 (0.025)
Diagnostic tests	R	0.198	0.508	0.303	0.208	0.515	0.236	0.189	0.061
	R^2	0.039	0.258	0.092	0.043	0.265	0.056	0.036	0.004
	Adjusted R^2	0.005	0.231	0.059	0.009	0.239	0.022	0.001	−0.032

Equation (4.1)	Dependent variable	Contemporaneous profit efficiency				Contemporaneous cost efficiency			
	Parameters	IT	ln(IT/E)	ln(IT/TC)	ln(IT/OC)	IT	ln(IT/E)	ln(IT/TC)	ln(IT/OC)
β_0	CONSTANT	0.514*** (0.020)	0.234** (0.073)	0.178* (0.065)	0.235*** (0.044)	0.736*** (0.033)	0.666*** (0.158)	1.039*** (0.142)	0.673*** (0.119)
$\beta_{1,jt}$	IT	−0.001 (0.000)	–	–	–	−0.0001 (0.000)	–	–	–
	ln(IT/E)	–	−0.0569*** (0.015)	–	–	–	−0.0010 (0.032)	–	–
	ln(IT/TC)	–	–	−0.0655*** (0.013)	–	–	–	0.0725 (0.028)	–
	ln(IT/OC)	–	–	–	0.0905** (0.014)	–	–	–	0.0004 (0.038)
Diagnostic tests	R	0.030	0.584	0.697	0.767	0.384	0.006	0.441	0.002
	R^2	0.001	0.341	0.486	0.588	0.147	0.000	0.195	0.000
	Adjusted R^2	−0.035	0.318	0.468	0.573	0.117	−0.036	0.166	−0.036

The table presents the results of the regression analysis of the model as expressed in Equation (4.1) when the dependant variable is codified respectively in terms of contemporaneous return on assets (ROA), contemporaneous return on equity (ROE), contemporaneous profit efficiency and contemporaneous cost efficiency. The symbols *, ** and *** indicate a significant correlation respectively at 10%, 5% and 1%.
Source: Data elaborated by author.

profitability paradox. For this reason, it would seem that the paradigm in IT adoption is not related to production process rationalisation, but mainly to operational and market adequacy (or rather the ability of management to accept the variability of demand and to provide the consequent variety in products and delivery channels that this brings about in terms of quality, convenience, flexibility and time-to-market).[46] In such a context, it becomes important not just to rationalise production by lowering unit costs but also to produce appropriate products and services when, how and where they are required by the market (so to be able to boost revenue). In this way, one passes from a use of technology on the basis of a paradigm involving the rationalisation of the processes of production to a paradigm founded on operational and market adequacy.

It seems, then, that banks do not invest in technology so as to be able to apply a premium price given the higher quality of their outputs. On the contrary, it appears more plausible to maintain – adopting the perspective pertaining to strategic competition, as discussed above – that technology represents a strategic necessity and not a variable capable of generating competitive advantage. The adoption by banks of ever more expensive IT infrastructure seems to be a structural component of the competition in the industry. In essence, these investments in technology seem more and more to take the form of a requirement to enter (or to remain in) the industry – in other words, a commodity – as opposed to an element of differentiation underpinning a competitive advantage. And from this stems the incapacity of banks to benefit from technology in terms of profit operating efficiency. If this assumption is accepted, it follows that banks should seek to reduce the costs arising from the customisation of technology, accepting that certain systems are standard systems for the industry and that these can be developed conjointly with their competitors and shared with them. In fact, it is evident that this is already happening in some cases within banking groups as well as in certain common structures (such as CRIF and CDB Software).[47] One cautionary note, however, should be sounded in this regard. If, in fact, there is no leader operating impartially and at a national level (like, for example, the central banks in respect of the establishment of the infrastructures relating to payment systems), it is unlikely that individual banks will reach agreement and develop common projects, given that, in consequence of the presumed importance for competition of technology, they tend to act autonomously.

Regarding the relationship between cost efficiency and IT ratios, some values for the coefficients are positive (investment in technology on total costs and on operating costs), while others are negative (investment in technology on equity), but none are significant. Therefore, in terms of cost efficiency over the short term, although there is no clear evidence, it appears that improvements in efficiency as a result of successive investments in IT requires an accumulation of competencies and periods for learning and adapting arising from cumulative IT investments. This finding seems to indicate that aggregate investment in technology has begun to reach a critical mass that can influence the profitability of the capital invested, but this critical mass has not been realised in all the European banking industries. Such a finding is fully consistent with what has been advanced in the past in the context of the theory on management productivity. In this regard, it is worth drawing attention to Strassmann (1988), where the following line of reasoning is advanced with great clarity: "in the first place, computers do not render a badly managed company better; moreover, expenditure on computerisation that results – as a consequence of the computers themselves – in increased organisational rigidity in all probability hastens the decline of incompetent management".

Viewed in terms of accounting measures of profitability, the relation between investment in IT and performance is not so clear or unambiguous. The association between ROA and IT ratios is negative but only in terms of the specification in respect of total costs and operating costs (nor, moreover, is this significant). On the other hand, the relationship is positive and significant in terms of the IT ratios relating to equity. Finally, the regression coefficient is null in relation to the nominal value of total investments in IT. The absence of a clear association between total investment in technology and the accounting measures of profitability is consistent with what has been shown in previous studies (Hitt and Brynjolfsson, 1996; Rai *et al.*, 1997; Shin, 2001). Previous studies use several reasons to explain this result. They refer to the capacity of IT either to lower or increase entry barriers, and thus either to intensify or reduce competitive rivalry. They also cite the equivocal effect of IT on competitive strategy and industry structure.[48] Our results offer a better view on this ambiguity, which seems mainly attributable to the methodological framework used to measure performance. In fact, whereas the effect of IT investments on financial profitability measures is ambiguous, there is significant evidence that IT investments have a negative effect on banks' profit efficiency.

Regarding the explanatory power of Equation (4.1), when the dependent variable is profit efficiency, the IT ratios – relating to equity, total costs and operating costs – explain 34.1 per cent, 48.6 per cent and 58.8 per cent of the variation of estimates of the European banks' profit efficiency ($R^2 = 0.341$ when IT to equity is the dependent variable, $R^2 = 0.486$ when IT to total costs is used, and $R^2 = 0.588$ when IT to operating costs is employed). On the other hand, the model seems to lose its explanatory power when the regression employs as independent variables the accounting measures of profitability, $R^2 = 0.036$, 0.004 and 0.056, respectively for the IT ratios relating to total costs, operating costs and equity, when performance is measured by ROE and R^2 at 0.092, 0.043 and 0.258 in respect of ROA.

On the basis of what we said previously about the explanatory power of the model, it is interesting to note that the value of the statistical parameter R^2 relating to profit efficiency – a measure of the adaptability of the function to the data – is much higher than the value traditionally found in the previous studies where accounting measures of profitability were employed (about 3 per cent in Hitt and Brynjolfsson, 1996).[49] This suggests that investments in IT are not reflected in the accounting measures of profitability (ROE and ROA) to the same extent that this occurs in relation to the estimates of profit efficiency. From this point of view too, then, it seems that it is particularly appropriate to use profit X-efficiencies as a measure of performance. In keeping with what has already been extensively discussed from a theoretical point of view, our empirical investigation supports the arguments in relation to the superiority of this measure – in terms of its capacity to capture the IT impacts associated with technology – over the traditional accounting measures.

To take into account the lag between the occurrence of IT investments and their impact on bank performance, or rather to test the relationship for non-contemporaneous influences, the results derived from Equation (4.1) are reported in Table 4.12. Interestingly, our results are similar to contemporaneous effects – the profitability paradox is still apparent over time when we take into account short-term assimilation, learning and adjustment factors.

With a view to investigating the influence of the geographical location of banks on the impact of investment in technology in respect of performance, the results deriving from the estimate pertaining to Equation (4.2) are reported in Table 4.13. On average, the geographical location of the European banks has a significant influence on the explanation of business performance. The German, French and Italian banks are characterised by values for ROA, ROE and profit efficiency that are constantly (and significantly) inferior to the coefficient pertaining to the United Kingdom.[50] To relate the impact of geographical location on IT investments, we also calculated the correlation between IT investments

Table 4.12 Regression between technology and lagged performance (OLS regression)

Equation (4.1)	Dependent variable	Lagged ROA				Lagged ROE			
	Parameters	IT	$\ln(IT/E)$	$\ln(IT/TC)$	$\ln(IT/OC)$	IT	$\ln(IT/E)$	$\ln(IT/TC)$	$\ln(IT/OC)$
β_0	CONSTANT	0.005**	−0.0286**	−0.01548	−0.0028	0.0435**	−0.0575	−0.0487	0.0377
		(0.002)	(0.008)	(0.010)	(0.005)	(0.023)	(0.115)	(0.116)	(0.087)
$\beta_{1,jt+s}$	IT	0.000	–	–	–	0.0000	–	–	–
		(0.000)				(0.000)			
	$\ln(IT/E)$	–	−0.0071***	–	–	–	−0.0318	–	–
			(0.002)				(0.023)		
	$\ln(IT/TC)$	–	–	−0.0042	–	–	–	−0.0286	–
				(0.002)				(0.022)	
	$\ln(IT/OC)$	–	–	–	−0.0026	–	–	–	−0.0193
					(0.002)				(0.028)
Diagnostic tests	R	0.055	0.652	0.405	0.328	0.483	0.272	0.257	0.144
	R^2	0.003	0.425	0.164	0.108	0.233	0.074	0.066	0.021
	Adjusted R^2	−0.040	0.400	0.128	0.069	0.200	0.034	0.025	−0.022

Table 4.12 (Continued)

Equation (4.1)	Dependent variable	Lagged profit efficiency				Lagged cost efficiency			
	Parameters	IT	ln(IT/E)	ln(IT/TC)	ln(IT/OC)	IT	ln(IT/E)	ln(IT/TC)	ln(IT/OC)
β_0	CONSTANT	0.512*** (0.020)	0.228** (0.073)	0.175* (0.063)	0.248*** (0.044)	0.743*** (0.035)	0.610** (0.177)	1.015*** (0.162)	0.666*** (0.130)
$\beta_{1,jt+s}$	IT	−0.000 (0.000)	–	–	–	−0.00001 (0.000)	–	–	–
	ln(IT/E)	–	−0.0575*** (0.015)	–	–	–	−0.0128 (0.036)	–	–
	ln(IT/TC)	–	–	−0.0648*** (0.012)	–	–	–	0.0666 (0.031)	–
	ln(IT/OC)	–	–	–	−0.0843*** (0.014)	–	–	–	0.0022*** (0.041)
Diagnostic tests	R	0.035	0.628	0.744	0.782	0.419	0.074	0.405	0.011
	R^2	0.001	0.394	0.554	0.611	0.175	0.005	0.164	0.000
	Adjusted R^2	−0.042	0.368	0.534	0.594	0.139	−0.038	0.128	−0.043

The table presents the results of the regression analysis of the model as expressed in Equation (4.1) when the dependent variable is codified, respectively, in terms of lagged return on assets (ROA), lagged return on equity (ROE), lagged profit efficiency and lagged cost efficiency. The symbols *, ** and *** indicate a significant correlation, respectively, at 10%, 5% and 1%.
Source: Data elaborated by author.

(and categories) and business performance (ROA, ROE, profit and cost X-efficiency) for each country of our sample (as shown in Table 4.17). The negative and statistically significant relationship between profit efficiency and IT investment is confirmed in four national banking industries. The only exception is Germany, where the relationship is positive and significant at 0.05. The association between cost efficiency and IT investment is heterogeneous across countries: while it is significantly positive in France and the UK, it is significantly negative in Germany and Italy. This may explain the mixed evidence on cost efficiency obtained by pooling all the countries together. One possible explanation of this result is to be found in the fact that the Anglo-Saxon banks are typically more oriented towards wholesale and international activity, whereas the continental European banks have a focus on the retail segment and their national markets.

To take into account the risk of banks' activities, the results derived from Equation (4.3) are reported in Table 4.14. Interestingly, these results confirm the evidence with no control variable for risk. In particular, when profit efficiency is used as a dependent variable, and a proxy for risk is included, the explanatory power of the regression remains high, and the coefficient of profit efficiency remains significantly negative.

The weighting for the incidence of the various differences in size of the European banks, realised methodologically by way of the inclusion in Equation (4.4) of another independent variable (i.e. the natural logarithm of total assets) does not increase significantly the explanatory power of the model when profit efficiency is the dependent variable, as shown in Table 4.15 (R^2 equal to 0.410 when the IT index in respect of equity is the independent variable, and R^2 equal to 0.496 when the IT index in respect of total costs is used). This indicates that total assets do not seem to contribute significantly to accounting for the relationship between profit efficiency and investment in IT. In the face of this result, which seems to confirm the capacity of profit efficiency to capture even certain structural features tied to size, we can see that the models explanatory power increases notably when ROE and ROA are used as independent variables (R^2 at 0.320 and 0.285 when ROE is used; R^2 at 0.362 and 0.173 when ROA is used). This indicates that technology investments alone are not capable of explaining the values of the accounting profitability, while the variable expressing bank size is much more strongly related to these same accounting measures of performance.

Table 4.13 Regression between technology, performance and the country dummies

Equation (4.2)	Dependent variable	ROA			ROE		
	Parameters	IT	ln(IT/E)	ln(IT/TC)	IT	ln(IT/E)	ln(IT/TC)
β_0	CONSTANT	0.0024 (0.005)	0.0243 (0.023)	0.0381** (0.012)	−0.0059 (0.049)	0.259 (0.240)	0.476*** (0.142)
$\beta_{1,jt}$	IT	−0.0001 (0.000)	–	–	0.0001** (0.000)	–	–
	ln(IT/E)	–	0.0028 (0.004)	–	–	−0.0197 (0.047)	–
	ln(IT/TC)	–	–	0.0051 (0.002)	–	–	0.0567 (0.028)
$\beta_{2,j}$FR	DUMMY FRANCE	−0.0044 (0.003)	−0.0106 (0.004)	−0.0121*** (0.003)	−0.0289 (0.028)	−0.1110 (0.045)	−0.1370*** (0.037)
$\beta_{3,j}$GE	DUMMY GERMANY	−0.0050 (0.003)	−0.0104 (0.004)	−0.140*** (0.003)	−0.0268 (0.026)	−0.0978 (0.042)	−0.1480*** (0.038)
$\beta_{4,j}$ITA	DUMMY ITALY	−0.0002 (0.003)	−0.0047* (0.002)	−0.0075** (0.002)	−0.0239 (0.031)	−0.1030*** (0.025)	−0.1330*** (0.037)
$\beta_{5,jt}$SP	DUMMY SPAIN	−0.0060 (0.005)	−0.0008 (0.003)	−0.0030 (0.002)	0.0746 (0.042)	−0.0490 (0.028)	−0.0704** (0.045)

Diagnostic tests		Profit efficiency			Cost efficiency		
	R	0.731	0.688	0.751	0.815	0.706	0.777
	R^2	0.534	0.473	0.564	0.665	0.499	0.604
	Adjusted R^2	0.436	0.363	0.473	0.595	0.394	0.522

Equation (4.2)	Dependent variable	Profit efficiency			Cost efficiency		
	Parameters	IT	$\ln(\mathrm{IT}/E)$	$\ln(\mathrm{IT/TC})$	IT	$\ln(\mathrm{IT}/E)$	$\ln(\mathrm{IT/TC})$
β_0	CONSTANT	0.680***	0.688***	0.368***	0.526***	0.377***	0.549***
		(0.038)	(0.183)	(0.100)	(0.022)	(0.084)	(0.053)
$\beta_{1,jt}$	IT	−0.0001**	–	–	0.0000	–	–
		(0.000)			(0.000)		
	$\ln(\mathrm{IT}/E)$	–	0.0258	–	–	−0.0348	–
			(0.036)			(0.016)	
	$\ln(\mathrm{IT}/TC)$	–	–	−0.0337	–	–	−0.0010
				(0.018)			(0.009)
$\beta_{2,j}$FR	DUMMY FRANCE	−0.128***	−0.0989*	−0.0532	0.0799***	0.0960***	0.0691***
		(0.021)	(0.034)	(0.022)	(0.012)	(0.016)	(0.012)

Table 4.13 (Continued)

Equation (4.2)	Dependent variable	Profit efficiency			Cost efficiency		
	Parameters	IT	ln(IT/E)	ln(IT/TC)	IT	ln(IT/E)	ln(IT/TC)
$\beta_{3,j}$GE	DUMMY GERMANY	−0.139*** (0.020)	−0.116*** (0.032)	−0.0585 (0.027)	0.193*** (0.012)	0.209*** (0.015)	0.184*** (0.014)
$\beta_{4,j}$ITA	DUMMY ITALY	−0.0759** (0.024)	−0.0123 (0.019)	0.0017 (0.020)	0.241*** (0.014)	0.223*** (0.009)	0.227*** (0.010)
$\beta_{5,j}$SP	DUMMY SPAIN	−0.134*** (0.033)	−0.0288 (0.022)	−0.0275 (0.018)	0.126*** (0.019)	0.0927*** (0.010)	0.104*** (0.010)
Diagnostic tests	R	0.859	0.788	0.814	0.985	0.987	0.984
	R^2	0.737	0.621	0.663	0.971	0.974	0.969
	Adjusted R^2	0.683	0.0542	0.593	0.965	0.968	0.962

The table presents the results of the regression analysis of the model as expressed in Equation (4.2) when the dependent variable is codified respectively in terms of return on assets (ROA), return on equity (ROE), profit efficiency and cost efficiency. The independent variables, on the other hand, are technology (respectively, investment in IT and IT ratios) and the country dummies (France, Germany, Italy and Spain). The symbols *, ** and *** indicate a significant correlation at respectively 10%, 5% and 1%.

Source: Data elaborated by author.

Table 4.14 Regression between technology, performance and the risk variable

Equation (4.3)	Dependent variable	ROA				ROE			
	Parameters	IT	ln(IT/E)	ln(IT/TC)	ln(IT/OC)	IT	ln(IT/E)	ln(IT/TC)	ln(IT/OC)
β_0	CONSTANT	0.003 (0.002)	−0.01999 (0.008)	−0.0087 (0.009)	0.0007 (0.004)	0.0353 (0.020)	−0.030 (0.094)	0.0252 (0.098)	0.0825 (0.072)
$\beta_{1,jt}$	IT	0.0000 (0.000)	–	–	–	0.000 (0.000)	–	–	–
	ln(IT/E)	–	−0.0051** (0.002)	–	–	–	−0.0222 (0.019)	–	–
	ln(IT/TC)	–	–	−0.0027 (0.002)	–	–	–	−0.0104 (0.019)	–
	ln(IT/OC)	–	–	–	−0.0011 (0.001)	–	–	–	0.0020 (0.024)
$\beta_{6,jt}$St dev ROA	St dev ROA	0.0097 (0.012)	0.00987 (0.010)	0.0088 (0.011)	0.0128 (0.007)	0.164 (0.111)	0.250 (0.112)	0.247 (0.117)	0.267 (0.115)
Diagnostic tests	R	0.248	0.533	0.334	0.397	0.566	0.450	0.414	0.412
	R^2	0.062	0.284	0.111	0.157	0.320	0.202	0.172	0.169
	Adjusted R^2	0.008	0.231	0.046	0.095	0.270	0.143	0.110	0.108

Table 4.14 (Continued)

Equation (4.3)	Dependent variable	Profit efficiency				Cost efficiency			
	Parameters	IT	ln(IT/E)	ln(IT/TC)	ln(IT/OC)	IT	ln(IT/E)	ln(IT/TC)	ln(IT/OC)
β_0	CONSTANT	0.515*** (0.020)	0.235** (0.074)	0.178 (0.067)	0.237*** (0.045)	0.733*** (0.032)	0.656*** (0.148)	0.994*** (0.139)	0.648*** (0.112)
$\beta_{1,jt}$	IT	−0.00002 (0.000)	–	–	–	−0.00001 (0.000)	–	–	–
	ln(IT/E)	–	−0.0559*** (0.015)	–	–	–	−0.0072 (0.030)	–	–
	ln(IT/TC)	–	–	0.0655*** (0.013)	–	–	–	0.0607 (0.028)	–
	ln(IT/OC)	–	–	–	−0.0897*** (0.015)	–	–	–	−0.0143 (0.037)
$\beta_{6,jt}$ St dev ROA	St dev ROA	0.118 (0.115)	0.0654 (0.088)	0.0003 (0.081)	0.0221 (0.072)	−0.286 (0.182)	−0.388 (0.177)	−0.296 (0.167)	−0.388 (0.178)
Diagnostic tests	R	0.195	0.595	0.697	0.768	0.468	0.389	0.528	0.387
	R^2	0.038	0.355	0.486	0.589	0.219	0.152	0.278	0.150
	Adjusted R^2	0.033	0.307	0.448	0.559	0.161	0.089	0.225	0.087

The table presents the results of the regression analysis of the model as expressed in Equation (4.3) when the dependent variable is codified respectively in terms of return on assets (ROA), return on equity (ROE), profit efficiency and cost efficiency. The independent variables, on the other hand, are technology (respectively, investment in IT and IT ratios) and the bank risk (standard deviation of ROA). The symbols *, ** and *** indicate a significant correlation at respectively 10%, 5% and 1%.

Source: Data elaborated by author.

Table 4.15 Regression between technology, performance and the size variable

Equation (4.4)	Dependent variable	ROA			ROE		
	Parameters	IT	ln(IT/E)	ln(IT/TC)	IT	ln(IT/E)	ln(IT/TC)
β_0	CONSTANT	−0.116 (0.054)	−0.0725* (0.026)	−0.0550 (0.029)	−0.556 (0.54)	−0.934** (0.290)	−0.8600** (0.290)
$\beta_{1,jt}$	IT	0.0000 (0.000)	–	–	0.0000 (0.000)	–	–
	ln(IT/E)	–	−0.0050** (0.002)	–	–	−0.0212 (0.018)	–
	ln(IT/TC)	–	–	−0.0021 (0.002)	–	–	−0.0026 (0.018)
$\beta_{7,jt} \ln TA$	LN TOTAL ASSETS	0.0079 (0.004)	0.0033 (0.002)	−0.0031 (0.002)	0.0387 (0.035)	0.0573** (0.018)	0.0582** (0.019)
Diagnostic tests	R	0.433	0.602	0.416	0.544	0.566	0.534
	R^2	0.188	0.362	0.173	0.296	0.320	0.285
	Adjusted R^2	0.127	0.315	0.112	0.244	0.270	0.232

Table 4.15 (Continued)

Equation (4.4)	Dependent variable	Profit efficiency			Cost efficiency		
	Parameters	IT	ln(IT/E)	ln(IT/TC)	IT	ln(IT/E)	ln(IT/TC)
β_0	CONSTANT	−1.444***	−0.166	0.0325	1.474	1.750***	1.767***
		(0.420)	(0.237)	(0.214)	(0.899)	(0.492)	(0.448)
$\beta_{1,jt}$	IT	−0.0001***	–	–	−0.0001	–	–
		(0.000)			(0.000)		
	ln(IT/E)	–	−0.0547***	–	–	−0.0070	–
			(0.014)			(0.030)	
	ln(IT/TC)	–	–	−0.0625***	–	–	0.0573
				(0.014)			(0.028)
$\beta_{7,jt}$ ln TA	LN TOTAL ASSETS	0.129***	0.0255	0.0100	−0.0484	−0.0692	−0.0500
		(0.028)	(0.014)	(0.014)	(0.059)	(0.030)	(0.029)
Diagnostic tests	R	0.669	0.640	0.704	0.410	0.406	0.523
	R^2	0.447	0.410	0.496	0.168	0.165	0.273
	Adjusted R^2	0.406	0.366	0.458	0.106	0.103	0.219

The table presents the results of the regression analysis of the model as expressed in Equation (4.4) when the dependent variable is codified respectively in terms of return on assets (ROA), return on equity (ROE), profit efficiency and cost efficiency. The independent variables, on the other hand, are technology (respectively, investment in IT and IT ratios) and the bank size (natural logarithm of total assets). The symbols *, ** and *** indicate a significant correlation at respectively 10%, 5% and 1%.
Source: Data elaborated by author.

The differentiation between the components of the IT portfolio (hardware, software and IT services) makes it possible to specify the previous equations breaking down the value relating to the sum of investment in IT. This is vital in order to explain empirically how strategic decisions relating to technology itself impact upon performance. In this way, it is possible to provide useful guidance to the managers responsible for information systems. The estimate of Equation (4.5) – whose results are reported in Table 4.16 – indicates that, when the categories of technology investment are used as independent variables, the impact of each of the categories on the accounting measures of profitability (ROE and ROA) and on profit efficiency is mixed. The sign of the coefficients relating to hardware and software is negative (and statistically significant), while the coefficient for IT services is positive. While IT services received from external suppliers (consulting services, implementation services, operations management services, staff-development and training services and support services) impact positively on the accounting profitability of banks, the acquisition of hardware and software have a negative impact on the profitability of banks. The same observations can be made if the variable expressing performance is profit efficiency.

Note also that the explanatory power of the model referred to IT components strongly increases in comparison to the explanatory power of the model related to IT investment as a single entity, particularly when accounting performance ratios are used, with a value for R^2 that rises to as much as 69.5 per cent when the dependent variable is profit efficiency, 54.2 per cent when ROE is employed and 54.5 per cent when ROA is used (and IT to operating costs is the dependent variable).[51]

On the basis of what has been observed up to now, it is possible to draw some conclusions that help to delineate the profitability paradox in relation to the European banking industry. In fact, the paradox does not seem to relate to all the components of investment in technology but, rather, just to some. This seems to suggest that the opportunities associated with the acquisition of hardware and software can be fully exploited when they take place conjointly with the acquisition of IT services from external suppliers. If we accept the hypothesis that the positive potential of hardware and software can be exploited fully conjointly with IT services, the implication is that an increase in expenditure on IT services will increase profitability and productivity. It goes without saying that this should induce firms to increase the amount of resources they allocate to IT services (on the total of the investment in technology). It is interesting to note that such a tendency

Table 4.16 Regression between the components of technology and performance

Equation (4.5)	Dependent variable	ROA				ROE			
	Parameters	HA SO SE	ln(HA/E) ln(SO/E) ln(SE/E)	ln(HA/TC) ln(SO/TC) ln(SE/T)	ln(HA/OC) ln(SO/OC) ln(SE/OC)	HA SO SE	ln(HA/E) ln(SO/E) ln(SE/E)	ln(HA/TC) ln(SO/TC) ln(SE/TC)	ln(HA/OC) ln(SO/OC) ln(SE/OC)
β_0	CONSTANT	0.0059*** (0.002)	−0.0401*** (0.009)	−0.0315* (0.011)	−0.0185** (0.005)	0.0547*** (0.013)	−0.2750* (0.098)	−0.237 (0.101)	−0.235 (0.094)
$\beta_{8,jt}$	HA	−0.000001 (0.000)	–	–	–	0.00003 (0.000)	–	–	–
$\beta_{9,jt}$	SO	−0.00007*** (0.000)	–	–	–	−0.0009*** (0.000)	–	–	–
$\beta_{10,jt}$	SE	0.00003*** (0.000)	–	–	–	0.0003*** (0.000)	–	–	–
	ln(HA/E)	–	−0.0108* (0.004)	–	–	–	−0.136** (0.042)	–	–
	ln(SO/E)	–	−0.0208* (0.007)	–	–	–	−0.294*** (0.078)	–	–
	ln(SE/E)	–	0.0282** (0.008)	–	–	–	0.431*** (0.088)	–	–
	ln(HA/TC)	–	–	−0.0090 (0.004)	–	–	–	0.1410** (0.040)	–
	ln(SO/TC)	–	–	−0.0271*** (0.007)	–	–	–	−0.3100*** (0.070)	–
	ln(SE/TC)	–	–	0.0354*** (0.009)	–	–	–	0.4610*** (0.083)	–

ln(HA/OC)	–	–	–	−0.0070*	–	–	–	−0.127**
				(0.002)				(0.042)
ln(SO/OC)	–	–	–	−0.0175***	–	–	–	−0.298***
				(0.004)				(0.074)
ln(SE/OC)	–	–	–	0.0241***	–	–	–	0.437***
				(0.005)				(0.083)
Diagnostic tests	R	0.737	0.731	0.680	0.738	0.895	0.741	0.758	0.736
	R^2	0.543	0.534	0.463	0.545	0.801	0.549	0.574	0.542
	Adjusted R^2	0.490	0.480	0.401	0.493	0.778	0.496	0.525	0.489

Equation (4.5)	Dependent variable	Profit efficiency				Cost efficiency			
	Parameters	HA SO SE	ln(HA/E) ln(SO/E) ln(SE/E)	ln(HA/TC) ln(SO/TC) ln(SE/TC)	ln(HA/OC) ln(SO/OC) ln(SE/OC)	HA SO SE	ln(HA/E) ln(SO/E) ln(SE/E)	ln(HA/TC) ln(SO/TC) ln(SE/TC)	ln(HA/OC) ln(SO/OC) ln(SE/OC)
β_0	CONSTANT	0.5360***	0.199	0.134	0.147	0.6750***	0.973***	1.2610***	1.053***
		(0.024)	(0.096)	(0.096)	(0.068)	(0.029)	(0.142)	(0.149)	(0.137)
$\beta_{8,jt}$	HA	−0.00005	–	–	–	0.0001	–	–	–
		(0.000)				(0.000)			
$\beta_{9,jt}$	SO	−0.00014	–	–	–	0.0007	–	–	–
		(0.000)				(0.000)			
$\beta_{10,jt}$	SE	0.00007	–	–	–	−0.0003***	–	–	–
		(0.000)				(0.000)			
	ln(HA/E)	–	−0.0995	–	–	–	0.265***	–	–
			(0.041)				(0.061)		
	ln(SO/E)	–	0.0665	–	–	–	0.384**	–	–
			(0.077)				(0.114)		

Table 4.16   (Continued)

Equation (4.5)	Dependent variable	Profit efficiency				Cost efficiency			
	Parameters	HA SO SE	ln(HA/*E*) ln(SO/*E*) ln(SE/*E*)	ln(HA/TC) ln(SO/TC) ln(SE/*T*)	ln(HA/OC) ln(SO/OC) ln(SE/OC)	HA SO SE	ln(HA/*E*) ln(SO/*E*) ln(SE/*E*)	ln(HA/TC) ln(SO/TC) ln(SE/TC)	ln(HA/OC) ln(SO/OC) ln(SE/OC)
	ln(SE/*E*)	–	0.0305 (0.086)	–	–	–	−0.686*** (0.128)	–	–
	ln(HA/TC)	–	–	0.0499 (0.038)	–	–	–	0.2770*** (0.059)	–
	ln(SO/TC)	–	–	0.0081 (0.067)	–	–	–	0.2790 (0.104)	–
	ln(SE/TC)	–	–	0.0221 (0.080)	–	–	–	−0.5210*** (0.123)	–
	ln(HA/OC)	–	–	–	−0.124*** (0.030)	–	–	–	0.274*** (0.061)
	ln(SO/OC)	–	–	–	−0.032 (0.053)	–	–	–	0.335** (0.108)
	ln(SE/OC)	–	–	–	0.0037 (0.060)	–	–	–	0.629*** (0.121)
Diagnostic tests	R	0.348	0.657	0.701	0.834	0.741	0.770	0.777	0.763
	R^2	0.121	0.431	0.491	0.695	0.550	0.592	0.603	0.582
	Adjusted R^2	0.019	0.366	0.432	0.660	0.498	0.545	0.557	0.534

The table presents the results of the analysis of regression of the model as expressed in Equation (4.5) when the dependent variable is codified respectively in terms of return on assets (ROA), return on equity (ROE), profit efficiency and cost efficiency. The independent variables, on the other hand, are the components of investment in IT, i.e. hardware, software and IT services, expressed both in terms of investment in IT and IT ratios. The symbols *, ** and *** indicate a significant correlation respectively at 10%, 5% and 1%.

Source: Data elaborated by author.

towards an increase in the resources dedicated to IT services is precisely what has been observed over recent years in the banking industries in all the European countries and, in particular, in the United Kingdom.

Although it does not seem possible to identify a technical relationship of proportionality – at an aggregate level – between the three categories (hardware, software and IT services), nonetheless, by shifting attention to the particular components that make up each category, we can observe some technical relationships between them. Although we are not aware of any analytical studies in this regard, the following are examples of such technical relationships: between hardware and basic packaged software (such as, for example, operating systems), between application solutions software (such as accounting and human resources management programmes) and database systems and between customer relationship management systems (in their hardware and software components) and implementation services or services available in outsourcing.

At this point, there comes into play the economic concept of bundling (as defined by Varian *et al.*, 2004 and Shapiro and Varian, 1999), which refers to the practice of selling two or more distinct IT products/services jointly at a single price (the classical example of this phenomenon is Microsoft Office, a software product that unites a word processor, a spreadsheet, a database and a presentation tool with the possibility, moreover, that any of the components may be sold separately). Given that the marginal cost of the sale of an additional product in the bundle is minimal – especially in the IT industry – the practice involves three major characteristics. First of all, all the components in the package are technically integrated and, therefore, are capable of working together and communicating with each other. Secondly, the price of the bundle is generally lower than the sum of the prices of its components, that is, it is possible to buy additional components at an incremental price that is lower than the price on an individual basis. Finally, bundling involves an increase in the supply of IT products and services as a consequence of the so-called "option value": the customer does not use all the components of the bundle at the moment of purchase but, once the bundle has been acquired, he is in the position of being able to use these components at any moment at an incremental cost of zero.

Regarding the relationship between cost efficiency and the components of investment in technology (be these expressed in terms of nominal value or IT ratios), a very interesting result emerges: while the coefficient of hardware and software is positive and statistically significant, the coefficient of IT services is negative (as reported in Table 4.16).

The relationship between investment in hardware and software and cost efficiency indicates the existence of positive effects on the cost function over the short term (both in terms of contemporaneous and lagged effects). This is fully consistent with the results obtained by way of an alternative methodology oriented towards the quantification of technical change: reduction of the real cost of production to the order of about 3.1 per cent per annum in terms of a medium-to-long-term time span (see Chapter 5 for an empirical examination conducted in relation to the same sample). This confirmation of the results obtained by the measurement of the technical change makes it possible to place a lower emphasis on the cautionary warnings – in respect of the measurement of investment in technology by way of a single time variable T – expressed in relation to the same concept of technical change.

Finally, given the comparative nature of this study, and taking account of the composition of the sample investigated, it is important to take into consideration the correlation between investment in technology (and its components) and measures of performance (ROA, ROE, profit efficiency and cost efficiency) for the banking industry of each country in the sample. Table 4.17 confirms the negative – and statistically significant – relationship between profit efficiency and IT investment for all the countries investigated. The only exception is represented by

Table 4.17 Correlations matrix for the banking industries of the various countries

Spearman / Pearson	HA	SO	SE	IT	ROA	ROE	Profit Eff	Cost Eff
France								
HA	1.000	1.000***	1.000***	1.000***	0.655	0.841**	−0.655	0.971***
SO	0.998***	1.000	1.000***	1.000***	0.655	0.841**	−0.655	0.971***
SE	0.997***	0.997***	1.000	1.000***	0.655	0.841**	−0.655	0.971***
IT	0.998***	0.998***	1.000***	1.000	0.655	0.841**	−0.655	0.971***
ROA	0.708	0.720*	0.717*	0.716	1.000	0.664	−1.000***	0.674
ROE	0.901**	0.899**	0.924***	0.916**	0.756*	1.000	−0.664	0.940***
Profit Eff	−0.708	−0.720	−0.717	−0.716*	−1.000***	−0.756*	1.000	−0.674
Cost Eff	0.983***	0.974***	0.986***	0.984***	0.678	0.942***	−0.674	1.000
Germany								
HA	1.000	1.000***	1.000***	1.000***	0.131	0.213	0.812**	−0.986***
SO	0.989***	1.000	1.000***	1.000***	0.131	0.213	0.812**	−0.986***
SE	0.997***	0.996***	1.000	1.000***	0.131	0.213	0.812**	−0.986***
IT	0.998***	0.995***	1.000***	1.000	0.131	0.213	0.812**	−0.986***
ROA	0.167	0.061	0.116	0.125	1.000	0.696	0.531	−0.133
ROE	0.271	0.189	0.238	0.242	0.956***	1.000	0.185	−0.216
Profit Eff	0.816**	0.789*	0.786*	0.798*	0.430	0.421	1.000	−0.794
Cost Eff	−0.962***	−0.976***	−0.970***	−0.969***	0.042	−0.077	−0.723*	1.000

Table 4.17   (Continued)

Spearman / Pearson	HA	SO	SE	IT	ROA	ROE	Profit Eff	Cost Eff
				Italy				
HA	1.000	1.000***	1.000***	1.000***	0.878**	0.829**	−0.618	−0.926***
SO	0.994***	1.000	1.000***	1.000***	0.878**	0.829**	−0.618	−0.926***
SE	0.993***	0.998***	1.000	1.000***	0.878**	0.829**	−0.618	−0.926***
IT	0.996***	0.999***	0.999***	1.000	0.878**	0.829**	−0.618	−0.926***
ROA	0.849**	0.877**	0.893**	0.880**	1.000	0.878**	−0.503	−0.738*
ROE	0.888**	0.904**	0.906**	0.902**	0.930***	1.000	−0.647	−0.617
Profit Eff	−0.814**	−0.784*	−0.756*	−0.777*	−0.552	−0.705	1.000	0.556
Cost Eff	−0.933***	−0.923***	−0.918***	−0.924***	−0.728*	−0.691	0.784*	1.000
				Spain				
HA	1.000	1.000***	1.000***	1.000***	0.655	0.812**	−0.820**	0.507
SO	0.994***	1.000	1.000***	1.000***	0.655	0.812**	−0.820**	0.507
SE	0.998***	0.990***	1.000	1.000***	0.655	0.812**	−0.820**	0.507
IT	0.999***	0.995***	0.999***	1.000	0.655	0.812**	−0.820**	0.507
ROA	0.559	0.557	0.570	0.565	1.000	0.664	−0.696	0.775*
ROE	0.782*	0.769*	0.819**	0.799*	0.700	1.000	−0.647	0.772*
Profit Eff	−0.833**	−0.805*	−0.800*	−0.815**	−0.387	−0.387	1.000	−0.718*
Cost Eff	0.506	0.472	0.533	0.515	0.914**	0.789*	−0.322	1.000
				UK				
HA	1.000	1.000***	1.000***	1.000***	–	0.794*	−0.943***	0.943***
SO	0.989***	1.000	1.000***	1.000***	–	0.794*	−0.943***	0.943***
SE	0.990***	0.997***	1.000	1.000***	–	0.794*	−0.943***	0.943***
IT	0.994***	0.998***	0.999***	1.000	–	0.794*	−0.943***	0.943***
ROA	–	–	–	–	–	–	–	–
ROE	0.682	0.599	0.594	0.618	–	1.000	−0.706	0.794*
Profit Eff	−0.980***	−0.988***	−0.993***	−0.991***	–	−0.528	1.000	−0.892**
Cost Eff	0.932***	0.939***	0.935***	0.937***	–	0.740*	−0.886**	1.000

The table presents the matrix of the correlations relating to each national banking industry investigated in the study (France, Germany, Italy, Spain and the United Kingdom). The horizontal axis of each block shows the non-parametric Spearman's rank correlation, while the vertical axis shows Pearson's parametric correlation. The correlated variables are as follows: IT = total investment in technology, HA = investment in hardware, SO = investment in software and SE = expenditure on technology-related services. The symbols *, ** and *** indicate a significant correlation at respectively 10%, 5% and 1% (two-tailed).
Source: Data elaborated by author.

Germany, where the coefficient has a positive sign (significant at 0.05). On the other hand, breaking down the sample on the basis of the nationality of the banks, the traditional accounting measures of profitability (ROE and ROA) reveal a positive association (though not always significant) with investment in IT. On a national level, we see a substantial confirmation of the results (in respect of the relationship between investment in technology and traditional and alternative measures of profitability) already discussed in relation to the entire sample on an aggregate basis.[52] The association between cost efficiency and investment in IT, on the other hand, varies between the banking industries of the individual countries. While it is significantly positive in France and the United Kingdom, it is significantly negative in Germany and Italy. This makes it possible to explain the absence of a clear direction in the coefficient of cost efficiency observed previously in respect of the aggregate sample.

These results clearly show that, in evaluating the possible explanations of the existence of the productivity paradox in respect of the European banking industry, it is necessary to pay attention to the variegated nature of the impact of investment in technology on performance, in particular, analysing it in terms of the distinctive characteristics of the different components of the investment itself. To this end, in Chapter 6 we will illustrate the variegated nature of investment in technology and the various objectives associated with it, together with the obstacles to their successful realisation. The specification of the peculiarities of the activities exercised by the banks will make it possible to show more precisely the reasons for our empirical enquiry into the existence of the profitability paradox.

5
Technical Change in the European Banking Industry: Methodological Problems and Empirical Results

5.1   Introduction

After analysing in the previous chapter the (contemporaneous and lagged) impact of IT investments on performance in the short-to-medium term, we now proceed to an examination of its effects in the medium-to-long term. More precisely, after confirming the existence of the profitability paradox in the European banking industry in respect of the short term, the next step is to evaluate the impact of technology investments on performance over the medium-to-long term or, in other words, to proceed to measure the so-called "technical change".

From a theoretical point of view, it is necessary to recognise at the outset that the concept of technical change cannot be defined as a single-faceted phenomenon. This derives from the fact that it depends strictly on the presence of a dual nature (technical and human) in the very definition of technology (Orlikowski, 1992. See Chapter 1 for an extensive discussion). The simultaneous presence of technical and human components makes it necessary above all to consider the manifold nature of the technological applications that have constituted fundamental steps in technical change.[1] This dual nature, moreover, makes it extremely difficult to measure the economic effects of technical change: in fact, the marked variability in the degrees of interpretative flexibility associated with the use of technology reduces the possibility of forecasting returns on investments in IT (both in the short term and in the medium-to-long term).

Notwithstanding the complexity of the concept, however, the literature on banking clearly recognises that it is necessary to endeavour to evaluate empirically the impact of technical change both on the characteristics of production and on the cost structure in the banking industry over the medium-to-long term. This interest comes about basically for two reasons. In the first place, technical change is widely recognised as one of the major sources of change in the industry (among others, see Fusconi, 1996). Secondly, only a very limited number of studies have offered estimates of the extent to which technical change impacts on factors like the costs of providing banking services or the impact it has on the size or input mix of banks (Goddard *et al.*, 2001).

The empirical investigation we conduct in this chapter makes it possible to take into consideration the above-mentioned interests as well as to respond to the need to estimate – within a comparative perspective – the extent of technical change on the European banking industry.

5.2   The concept of technical change: theoretical problems

The issues that it is necessary to examine in relation to the evaluation of the impact of IT on costs and revenues in the medium-to-long term have generally been dealt within the literature – at least form an analytical point of view – in terms of the specification of a methodological approach for measuring technical change. Up to now, two approaches in particular have been adopted with considerable success in much of the empirical research: econometric estimates and index numbers (Baltagi and Griffin, 1998; Fox, 1998). The econometric approach involves the inclusion of a deterministic time variable T in the estimate of the production function, be it in relation to total costs or profit. This variable can be linear or non-linear and its specification can make provision for interactions between time and other independent variables. The coefficients of the time variable T are interpreted as measures of technical change. The alternative approach based on index numbers involves a direct comparison between the rate of growth of output and input indexes, with any difference attributed to technical change.

In both approaches, however, the perception of the impact of IT on the cost/profit function involves the adoption of the time variable T as an index of technical change. Because of the high degree of complexity involved in the phenomenon of technical change discussed here, it is necessary to give voice to a few cautionary words. In particular, the approaches outlined above have two major conceptual limits. In the first place, the time variable T may capture phenomena emerging over time that are different from technical change. This measure does not just represent the pure effect of IT on the production function

(Hunter and Timme, 1991). Although the use of the time variable T captures technical change that takes place in a given period of time, unfortunately it does not reveal in a direct and unambiguous manner the sources of that change. Being a residual index, the time variable does not express only innovations in production but may also capture the impact of other environmental factors such as (de)regulation and financial innovation. For this reason, when measuring technical change, the coefficients of the time variable T must be interpreted with extreme care.[2]

Moreover, the large number and the importance of the variables involved in the deployment of technology in a bank's production process mean that it is necessary to interpret the cost/profit function no longer as an implicit and secondary factor but rather as a structural function in a context of focused strategies. "In this context, it becomes important to specify the impact of technical change no longer in relation to the simple time factor with which to compare the variations in a bank's production function – and implicitly, in its total costs, maintaining unchanged the mix of production factors used – but rather as a complex variable whose configuration is such as to necessarily involve the very nature of the production function" (Fusconi, 1996, pp. 480–481).

In essence, the type of procedure put forward in this chapter – which is based on the adoption of a standard econometric approach with the inclusion of a time variable T – allows us to construct a model for estimating technical change that can be regarded as being of a general nature. This model emerges inductively from the adoption of T as an index of technical change. With a view to overcoming any limits that might emerge from such a standard approach, one possible extension of the literature on the subject might take the form of the design of a new model for evaluating the impact of IT on the production function of individual banks and the industry as a whole over the medium-to-long term as well as for measuring its economic consequences. In fact, according to Fusconi (1996), it is possible to specify theoretically an IT cost function, expressed as a function of the determinants of investments in technology themselves (including the following: level of diffusion of technology, speed of innovation in technology, ability to use technology, degree of labour inter-changeability, level of adequacy to market needs, level of maintenance costs, degree of security needs, level of institutional adequacy and implied costs). Attempts to empirically develop this IT cost function deserve further attention.

5.3 Review of the literature on technical change in the banking industry

Although issues tied to technical progress are widely recognised as one of the major sources of change in the financial services industry (Cecchini, 1988; Andersen, 1993; Fusconi, 1996; European Commission, 1997; Altunbas *et al.*, 1999; Bank for International Settlements, 1999; European Central Bank, 1999), up until now they have received very little attention in the literature. This consideration suggests that it is necessary to dedicate more attention to the measurement of the impact of technical change on the costs of providing financial services and, in particular, banking services. Many of the studies on technical change relate to the banking industry in the United States and only a limited amount of the research views the banks from a comparative perspective. In this chapter we intend to go some way towards filling the gap in attention dedicated to the measurement of technical change in relation to the European banking industry, endeavouring to quantify the effect of such change on the cost function of banks.

The first work done on the measurement of technical change was conducted by Hunter and Timme (1991) in relation to large American commercial banks. Their empirical results, which related to the period 1980–1986, showed a reduction in the real costs of production of about 1 per cent a year, with the bigger banks enjoying a more substantial reduction than the smaller ones. A further study relating to the measurement of technical change was undertaken a year later by Berger and Humphrey (1992). In contrast to the previous study, the authors of this study, using the Thick-Frontier Approach (TFA)[3] in their estimate of the cost frontier, quantified technical change and productivity. Their analysis revealed a limited variation in such measures over the course of the 1980s. In a more recent study, Berger and DeYoung (2002) analysed the effects of technical change on geographical expansion, dealing with a sample of American banks in relation to the period 1985–1998. Their empirical results support the view that technical progress has facilitated geographical expansion in the banking industry. It is to be noted, furthermore, that a study conducted by McKillop *et al.* (1996) showed that technical change has had an analogous impact on the Japanese banking industry.

In contrast to previous studies, the empirical results of the work of Humphrey (1993) showed that technical change has had a negative impact on the costs of American banks and that this has come about as a result of the deregulation that has taken place within the US banking industry. The panel data (similar to the sample used by Hunter and Timme, 1991) included 683 banks characterised by the following three features: they had assets of more than 100 million dollars, they operated in states that permit banking activity through branches and they did business continuously over the period 1977–1988. The estimates were obtained by making use of a simple measure for the time trend, a specific time index, and the annual variations in cost functions. The three methodologies produced very similar results. The changes in the cost functions revealed an average increase in costs between 0.8 and 1.4 per cent per year. The smaller banks (those with assets of between \$100 and \$200 million) were characterised by average increases that were higher than those of the big banks. A great deal of the reduction in cost efficiency was attributed to the deregulation of interest rates on deposits, an initiative, it might be noted, which has led to benefits in favour of deposit holders. Like Humphrey (1993), Bauer *et al.* (1993), using data relating to the same period (1977–1988), made use of both the stochastic frontier approach and the thick frontier approach with a view to estimating a global productivity factor by way of a cost function model. Their estimates showed a variation in productivity between −3.55 and 0.16 per cent per year.

Only two studies have been conducted on the impact of technical change on the costs of the banking industry in the pan-European zone. In the first of these, Altunbas *et al.* (1999) measured the impact of technical change on the costs of the banking industry in 15 European countries using a stochastic cost frontier. Their estimates showed an acceleration in the reduction of costs in the course of the period 1989–1996, which culminated in 1996 with a cumulated diminution of 3.6 per cent. Consistently with the results obtained by Hunter and Timme (1991) for the US banking industry, the estimates of Altunbas *et al.* (1999) showed that the bigger banks seem to have benefited to a greater extent than the smaller ones from the reduction in costs brought about by technical change. In a more recent study, the same authors (Altunbas *et al.*, 2001) were able to confirm the previous result: that the impact of technical progress on the reduction of the costs of banks increases systematically with the increase in the dimensions of the bank. The biggest European banks extract the greatest profit from technical change, even though they do not appear to enjoy any economy of scale advantages vis-à-vis their smaller counterparts.

By way of concluding this overview of research on the impact of technical change on banks, we mention some studies relating to savings banks. Wagenvoort and Schure (1999) made an estimate of technical progress in terms of a shift in the efficient cost frontier. Their study, which involved a sample of about 2000 banks, related to the same 15 countries dealt with in the study by Altunbas *et al.* (1999), but it covered the period 1993–1997. Moreover, Wagenvoort and Schure (1999) made a distinction between commercial banks and savings banks. Although the authors did not find any evidence to suggest that the efficient cost frontier shifted in the course of the relevant period either in respect of the entire sample or in respect of the commercial banks, they did identify a shift in respect of the savings banks. Their findings suggested that for efficient savings banks costs fell by about 2 per cent per annum as a result of technical change. Like Wagenvoort and Schure (1999), Williams and Gardener (2003) made an estimate of the rate of technical change in respect of a sample of large European savings banks in relation to the period 1989–1997. Their empirical results showed that on average technical change reduced the total costs of savings banks by about 3.4 per cent per annum, although the reductions in costs diminished over the course of the period taken into consideration. As in the case of the studies on commercial banks, the empirical evidence showed that technical change had a greater cost reduction impact in relation to bigger savings banks.

Finally, some European studies have been conducted at the level of national banking industries. Maudos *et al.* (1996) analysed the savings bank segment in Spain in relation to the period 1985–1994. Their results confirm that on average technical change reduced running costs. Similarly, Lang and Welzel (1996) showed that in Germany smaller co-operative banks have benefited from technical change to a greater extent than bigger banks. Thus, while Maudos *et al.* (1996) showed that bigger Spanish savings banks seem to have obtained greater benefits from technical change than smaller ones, Lang and Welzel (1996) came up with the opposite result in respect of the German co-operative banking industry.

5.4 The methodology

5.4.1 The method of measuring technical change: the econometric estimates

After carefully considering the methodological problem of measuring technical change and, in particular, the major limits that the theoretical debates have thrown up in relation to the approaches so far adopted (in other words, the adoption of an approach based on econometric estimates as opposed to number indexes), we have chosen in this study to adopt the methodology that is most widely applied in the literature (see, for example, Lang and Welzel, 1996; McKillop *et al.*, 1996; Altunbas *et al.*, 1999, 2001): the estimate of the movements in the cost function of a bank over the course of time. To this end a time variable T is used as a proxy for technical change. Viewed in this light, technical change allows a bank to produce a given output at cost levels that become lower with the passing of time, all the time maintaining at the same level the price of the inputs and the effects of environmental factors. In addition, technical change, in keeping with an extended sense that also makes reference to changes in the human and organisational phenomena associated with technical innovation, manifests itself in the possibility of realising a more efficient use of existing inputs. Once again, however, it should be noted that this temporal measurement of trends has a significant limit in that it represents a variable that captures not just the effects of technical progress but also the effects produced by other factors, such as changes in environmental conditions (Nelson, 1984; Baltagi and Griffin, 1988).

5.4.2   The estimate of technical change

To arrive at an evaluation of the economic impact of technical change, it is necessary to calculate the variation in average cost due to a given change in technology. The first methodological problem associated with the adoption of an econometric estimate of technical change relates to the choice of an approach for measuring X-efficiencies, as is made clear in Section 4.4.2.

It follows that, given the specification – outlined above – of the bank cost function that underlies the measurement of X-efficiencies, technical change can be measured by way of the partial derivative of the cost function in respect of the time variable (T). The resulting equation is given by

$$\frac{\partial \ln TC}{\partial T} = \tau_1 + \tau_{11} T + \sum_{j=1}^{3} \theta_j \ln P_j + \sum_{i=1}^{3} \psi_i \ln Q_i \qquad (5.1)$$

where the terms are defined as in Equation (4.14).

In the context of the theory of technical change – as originally advanced by Baltagi and Griffin (1988) – it is customary to analyse Equation 5.1 (the expression of technical change in its totality) into the following three components:

i) pure technical change, $\tau_1 + \tau_{11}T$ – this component expresses the reduction in total costs that can be achieved maintaining unaltered both the scale of efficient production necessary to produce any particular combination of outputs and the incidence of each class of inputs on total costs;

ii) scale augmenting technical change, $\sum_{i=1}^{3} \psi_i \ln Q_i$ – this reflects changes in the sensitivity of total costs to variations in the scale of efficient production; when $\psi_i < 0$ for every i, the scale of production that minimises average costs for a given output mix increases over time;

iii) non-neutral technical change, $\sum_{j=1}^{3} \theta_j \ln P_j$ – this expresses the sensitivity of total costs to variations in the prices of inputs; if $\theta_j < 0$, the incidence of the costs of a class of inputs on total costs decreases over time.

5.4.3   The comparative sample and the description of the data

The adoption of a comparative perspective in this study constitutes an attempt to add to the limited number of analogous studies that have appeared in the literature on the banking industry. As has already been noted, only two studies (Altunbas *et al.*, 1999, 2001) have offered an estimate of technical change in banks in a panel of European countries. The majority of studies deal with the industry essentially in terms of single nations. To a significant extent this orientation has come about as a consequence of the difficulties involved in conducting and interpreting estimates at the cross-country level.

Our empirical analysis of technical change relates to the same sample of banks – 737 banks operating in the 5 major banking markets in the EU – that was used to evaluate the impact of IT spending on bank performance (see Table 4.1). Moreover, the observations made in relation to the need to compare input and output values in real terms – a procedure that requires the specification of a deflator – finds confirmation in the fact that these values make provision not only for removing the effects of inflation but also for expressing changes in quality.[4] In fact, many of the problems involved in measurement are due to the difficulty of developing price deflators that take account of quality (Brynjolfsson, 1993). The data used in the model are all expressed in real terms using deflators based on the GDP pertaining to each country taken into consideration (the figures relating to 1995).

5.5   Empirical results

5.5.1   Estimate of the parameters of the cost frontier

As described in the previous chapter, the parameters of the stochastic frontier – defined by Equation (4.14) – can be evaluated by way of the maximum likelihood method which requires the maximisation of the probability function, using the technical effect model (Battese and Coelli, 1992). Table 5.1 shows the estimates of the parameters and other statistics obtained by using the stochastic cost frontier in relation to the pooled sample, as specified in Table 4.1.

In regard to the parameters relating to pure technical change (τ), it is apparent that the coefficient τ_1 is negative, while τ_{11} is positive. In terms of parameters tied to the estimate of scale augmenting technical change (ψ), both ψ_1 and ψ_3 are positive, while the co-efficient ψ_2 is negative (where, however, neither of the coefficients is significant). This means that the scale of efficient production for outputs in terms of bank securities portfolios has increased in the course of the 1990s, while it has decreased in relation to loans and off-balance sheet items. The hypothesis advanced by Altunbas *et al.* (1999) to explain the value of the coefficient relating to off-balance sheet items turns around the fact that at the beginning of the relevant period the kinds of activity that took the form of off-balance sheet items were undertaken mainly by the big banks while at the end banks of all sizes engaged in such activity. In regard to the parameters relating to the measurement of non-neutral technical change (θ), θ_2 is negative, but not significant. On the contrary, θ_1 is positive and significant, which, in fact, points to an increase in the share of the cost of labour on total costs. Although this increase in the incidence of the labour factor is partly a corollary of the reduction in banking costs due to the component of interest costs (which is itself a consequence of the phenomenon produced by the general downward movement of national interest rates that took place during the nineties), it also shows that attempts to achieve cost savings in relation to the labour component have contributed only in a secondary manner to the realisation of overall cost savings. To some extent this has been caused by the rigidity of the EU labour market and it stands as evidence of such rigidity.

5.5.2   Estimates of technical change

When we consider the estimate of the reduction in total costs that can be attributed to technical change, as illustrated in Table 5.2, it emerges that technical change has had a positive effect at the level of the European

Table 5.1 Estimates of the parameters of the stochastic frontier in European banks

Variable	Parameter	Coefficient	Standard-error	t-ratio	Variable	Parameter	Coefficient	Standard-error	t-ratio
$\ln q_1$	a_1	−0.8593	0.4553	−1.8871	T	τ_1	−0.0356	0.0168	−2.1270
$\ln q_2$	a_2	0.3567	0.0489	7.3027	T^*T	τ_{11}	0.0030	0.0012	2.4850
$\ln q_3$	a_3	0.1661	0.3312	0.5014	$T\ln p_1$	θ_1	0.0133	0.0020	6.5541
$\ln p_1$	β_1	0.8560	0.0383	22.3504	$T\ln p_2$	θ_2	−0.0017	0.0018	−0.9810
$\ln p_2$	β_2	0.1724	0.0402	4.2864	$T\ln q_1$	ψ_1	0.0019	0.0014	1.3050
$\ln q_1\ln q_1$	d_{11}	0.0921	0.0235	3.9188	$T\ln q_2$	ψ_2	−0.0010	0.0010	−0.9869
$\ln q_1\ln q_2$	d_{12}	−0.0228	0.0017	−13.7555	$T\ln q_3$	ψ_3	0.0001	0.0012	0.0426
$\ln q_1\ln q_3$	d_{13}	−0.0034	0.0016	−2.0817	$\cos(z_1)$	a_1	−2.9952	1.2502	−2.3959
$\ln q_2\ln q_2$	d_{22}	−0.0033	0.0045	−0.1935	$\cos(z_2)$	a_2	1.3163	0.0886	14.8556
$\ln q_2\ln q_3$	d_{23}	−0.0027	0.0013	−2.0905	$\cos(z_3)$	a_3	0.0077	0.9137	0.0085
$\ln q_3\ln q_3$	d_{33}	0.0077	0.0173	0.4443	$\sin(z_1)$	b_1	0.0605	0.2571	0.2354
$\ln p_1\ln p_1$	γ_{11}	0.0342	0.0014	25.0108	$\sin(z_2)$	b_2	−0.3845	0.2714	−1.4170
$\ln p_1\ln p_2$	γ_{12}	−0.0417	0.0023	−18.4983	$\sin(z_3)$	b_3	0.4039	0.1980	2.0400
$\ln p_2\ln p_2$	γ_{22}	0.0143	0.0020	7.0378	$\cos(z_1+z_1)$	a_{11}	−0.5144	0.1640	−3.1365
$\ln p_1\ln q_1$	ρ_{11}	−0.0051	0.0027	−1.8844	$\cos(z_1+z_2)$	a_{12}	−0.2180	0.0549	−3.9746
$\ln p_1\ln q_2$	ρ_{12}	−0.0019	0.0022	−0.8758	$\cos(z_1+z_3)$	a_{13}	−0.0023	0.0431	−0.0527
$\ln p_1\ln q_3$	ρ_{13}	0.0036	0.0024	1.4986	$\cos(z_2+z_2)$	a_{22}	0.3092	0.0540	5.7300
$\ln p_2\ln q_1$	ρ_{21}	−0.0152	0.0023	−6.5881	$\cos(z_2+z_3)$	a_{23}	−0.1815	0.0391	−4.6429
$\ln p_2\ln q_2$	ρ_{22}	−0.0081	0.0017	−4.7857	$\cos(z_3+z_3)$	a_{33}	0.1225	0.1229	0.9968
$\ln p_2\ln q_3$	ρ_{23}	−0.0111	0.0022	−4.9236	$\sin(z_1+z_1)$	b_{11}	−0.2662	0.0839	−3.1727
$\ln E$	λ_1	0.2620	0.0435	6.0191	$\sin(z_1+z_2)$	b_{12}	0.6084	0.0544	11.1741
$\ln E\ln E$	F_{11}	0.0167	0.0012	13.8560	$\sin(z_1+z_3)$	b_{13}	−0.0467	0.0528	−0.8845
$\ln E\ln q_1$	ς_{11}	−0.0284	0.0033	−8.4970	$\sin(z_2+z_2)$	b_{22}	−0.5712	0.0700	−8.1625
$\ln E\ln q_2$	ς_{21}	−0.0036	0.0027	−1.3084	$\sin(z_2+z_3)$	b_{23}	0.0595	0.0428	1.3890
$\ln E\ln q_3$	ς_{31}	−0.0104	0.0028	−3.6558	$\sin(z_3+z_3)$	b_{33}	0.0414	0.0612	0.6768
$\ln p_1\ln E$	κ_{11}	−0.0210	0.0033	−6.3794					
$\ln p_2\ln E$	κ_{21}	0.0173	0.0038	4.5073					

The table shows the values of the estimate of maximum likelihood conducted in relation to the parameters included in the specified stochastic cost function using the Fourier flexible function in respect of the panel sample (See Table 4.1).
Source: Author own estimates.

Table 5.2 Estimates of technical change (and of its components) in European banks

Country	Pure technical change	Non-neutral technical change	Scale augmenting technical change	Total technical change
France	−0.0215	−0.0278	0.0142	−0.0350
Germany	−0.0225	−0.0203	0.0141	−0.0286
Italy	−0.0230	−0.0199	0.0140	−0.0288
Spain	−0.0234	−0.0188	0.0150	−0.0272
UK	−0.0241	−0.0249	0.0139	−0.0350
Panel	−0.0225	−0.0228	0.0142	−0.0311

The table shows pure technical change, scale augmenting technical change, non-neutral technical change and total technical change (obtained by way of the sum of the previous three measures) in European banks (for each country) during the period 1993–2000. *Source*: Author own estimates.

banking industry (understood in terms of the specification of a single cost function for the five countries in question): in empirical terms, it has accounted for a reduction in the real cost of production of about 3.1 per cent per annum.

These results are consistent with the average measures of technical change from the other two comparative studies relating to European banks (Altunbas *et al.*, 1999, 2001). These previous studies applied a model equivalent to the one we have adopted here, and estimated that the impact of technical change in the period 1989–1997[5] implied a reduction in total costs of about 3 per cent per annum.

This measurement of the positive overall impact of technical change makes it necessary to differentiate between the different components of technical change, as specified in Section 5.4.2, and to estimate their economic effects. The phenomenon of the reduction in total costs is to be attributed partly to pure technical change (−2.25 per cent) and partly to non-neutral technical change (−2.28 per cent). On the other hand, it seems clear that scale augmenting technical change has led to an increase in the level of total banking costs (+1.42 per cent).

If we adopt a comparative perspective breaking down the average figures for Europe in terms of the individual countries in which the banks operate, we find that the banking industries in France and the United Kingdom have enjoyed greater reductions in costs as a result of technical change. The average of the reduction in total costs for these two countries is about 3.50 per cent per annum. The lowest figure for such cost reduction is that of Spain (−2.72 per cent).

Table 5.3 Estimates of technical change in European banks

	France	Germany	Italy	Spain	UK	Average
2000	−0.0449	−0.0380	−0.0360	−0.0328	−0.0423	−0.0391
1999	0.0369	−0.0338	−0.0302	−0.0264	−0.0410	−0.0341
1998	−0.0389	−0.0323	−0.0322	−0.0297	−0.0394	−0.0347
1997	−0.0346	−0.0293	−0.0322	−0.0273	−0.0316	−0.0313
1996	−0.0325	−0.0266	−0.0301	−0.0283	−0.0359	−0.0302
1995	−0.0341	−0.0241	−0.0249	−0.0251	−0.0269	−0.0279
1994	−0.0318	−0.0227	−0.0207	−0.0213	−0.0252	−0.0257
1993	−0.0308	−0.0217	−0.0202	−0.0220	−0.0214	−0.0254
Δ2000–1993	−0.0141	−0.0163	−0.01583	−0.0108	−0.0209	−0.0137

The table shows total technical change in European banks (for each country and for each year) during the period 1993–2000.
Source: Author own estimates.

In regard to the evolution in the importance of technical change over the course of the period in question, Table 5.3 shows that the impact in terms of a systematic reduction in total costs has progressively increased, the figure passing from −2.54 per cent in 1993 to −3.91 per cent in 2000. This result too is consistent with the positive trend that Altunbas *et al.* (1999, 2001) identified in the reduction of costs brought about by technical change at the European level.

In comparative terms, once again it is the United Kingdom that benefited to the greatest extent from the effects of technical change. In fact, not only did technical change impact positively on the cost structure of UK banks in a more marked manner than in other European countries, but the trend also registered an increase in the period 1993–2000. By contrast, the Spanish banking industry has constantly been characterised by a figure below the European average.

If we put the two dimensions of the analysis – the geographic and the temporal – together, as in Table 5.4, we see that pure technical change and non-neutral technical change were both characterised by negative values in each year in question and in every country under investigation. By contrast, scale augmenting technical change was characterised by positive values in both intra-temporal and intra-country terms. It is clear that the general trend registered at the level of the entire European banking industry (as detailed in Table 5.2) reappears with the same characteristics at the level of the individual countries studied. Thus, in regard to the breakdown of the various components of technical change, the investments in technology put in place by banks in the various

Table 5.4 Estimates of the components of technological change in European banks

	France			Germany			Italy		
	$\tau_1 + \tau_{11}\,T$	$\sum_{j=1}^{3}\theta_j \ln P_j$	$\sum_{i=1}^{3}\psi_i \ln Q_i$	$\tau_1 + \tau_{11}\,T$	$\sum_{j=1}^{3}\theta_j \ln P_j$	$\sum_{i=1}^{3}\psi_i \ln Q_i$	$\tau_1 + \tau_{11}\,T$	$\sum_{j=1}^{3}\theta_j \ln P_j$	$\sum_{i=1}^{3}\psi_i \ln Q_i$
2000	−0.0327	−0.0268	0.0146	−0.0327	−0.0193	0.0139	−0.0327	−0.0170	0.0137
1999	−0.0297	−0.0212	0.0140	−0.0297	−0.0181	0.0140	−0.0297	−0.0146	0.0141
1998	−0.0267	−0.0259	0.0138	−0.0267	−0.0195	0.0139	−0.0267	−0.0193	0.0139
1997	−0.0238	−0.0247	0.0139	−0.0238	−0.0200	0.0144	−0.0238	−0.0224	0.0140
1996	−0.0208	−0.0259	0.0142	−0.0208	−0.0203	0.0146	−0.0208	−0.0233	0.0141
1995	−0.0178	−0.0307	0.0145	−0.0178	−0.0204	0.0142	−0.0178	−0.0213	0.0142
1994	−0.0149	−0.0311	0.0141	−0.0149	−0.0218	0.0140	−0.0149	−0.0200	0.0142
1993	−0.0119	−0.0335	0.0146	−0.0119	−0.0237	0.0140	−0.0119	−0.0223	0.0141

Table 5.4 (Continued)

	Spain			UK			Average		
	$\tau_1 + \tau_{11}\, T$	$\sum_{j=1}^{3} \theta_j \ln P_j$	$\sum_{i=1}^{3} \psi_i \ln Q_i$	$\tau_1 + \tau_{11}\, T$	$\sum_{j=1}^{3} \theta_j \ln P_j$	$\sum_{i=1}^{3} \psi_i \ln Q_i$	$\tau_1 + \tau_{11}\, T$	$\sum_{j=1}^{3} \theta_j \ln P_j$	$\sum_{i=1}^{3} \psi_i \ln Q_i$
2000	−0.0327	−0.0169	0.0168	−0.0327	−0.0236	0.0140	−0.0327	−0.0209	0.0145
1999	−0.0297	−0.0121	0.0153	−0.0297	−0.0251	0.0138	−0.0297	−0.0185	0.0141
1998	−0.0267	−0.0180	0.0150	−0.0267	−0.0266	0.0140	−0.0267	−0.0220	0.0140
1997	−0.0238	−0.0185	0.0150	−0.0238	−0.0217	0.0138	−0.0238	−0.0217	0.0142
1996	−0.0208	−0.0219	0.0144	−0.0208	−0.0289	0.0138	−0.0208	−0.0236	0.0143
1995	−0.0178	−0.0214	0.0142	−0.0178	−0.0232	0.0142	−0.0178	−0.0243	0.0143
1994	−0.0149	−0.0210	0.0146	−0.0149	−0.0247	0.0144	−0.0149	−0.0249	0.0142
1993	−0.0119	−0.0248	0.0147	−0.0119	−0.0227	0.0132	−0.0119	−0.0277	0.0143

The table shows the components of total technical change in European banks (according to country and year) over the years 1993–2000: pure technical change, $\tau_1 + \tau_{11}\, T$; non-neutral technical change, $\sum_{j=1}^{3} \theta_j \ln P_j$; and scale augmenting technical change, $\sum_{i=1}^{3} \psi_i \ln Q_i$.

Source: data elaborated by author.

individual European countries involved an impact on the cost function analogous to what has been observed for the European industry as a whole.

In conclusion, European banks have benefited from reductions in costs consequent upon technical change at an increasing rate over the period 1993–2000. Moreover, if we distinguish between the components of change defined above, it emerges that the impact of technological innovations has been characterised by considerable variation in respect of inputs, outputs and a pure temporal variable.

5.5.3   Technical change and the size of banks

With a view to offering a comparative perspective on the relationship between technical change and bank size, the raw figures of bank assets, taken as a measure of the size of firms, are presented in Table 5.5. Two features are immediately apparent. First, there is a general tendency in all European countries towards an increase in the size of banks, and this is accompanied by a decrease in their number. This phenomenon, which is particularly evident in respect of the latter part of the period analysed, is to be attributed principally to the considerable impact of the merger and acquisition activity that has taken place in the European banking industry (as discussed in Chapter 2). Secondly, there are significant variations in the dimensions of the banks present in the various countries. In particular, the banks in continental Europe are smaller than those in the United Kingdom. In fact, the UK operators are characterised by a combination of a more marked uniformity of size and a larger scale of operations. In the period 1993–2000 the average total assets for the UK banking industry were US$22,596 million, compared with a figure of US$5988 million for the Spanish industry, US$7393 for the French banks, US$8114 million for the German and US$9963 for the Italian banks.

This variation suggests that it is necessary to investigate the relationship between the size of banks and the level of technical change with a view to examining whether different structural configurations are associated with different levels of cost savings. In this way it is possible to examine the effectiveness – in respect of investments in technology – of the decisions taken in recent years by the major operators to expand the scale of their operations. The theme is particularly interesting in view of the future development of the financial industry: the interest lies in establishing whether structural changes in the scale of the operations of banks can have a positive effect on the cost structure of banks with regard to investments in technology.

Table 5.5 The size of European banks

Country	1993	1994	1995	1996	1997	1998	1999	2000	1993–2000
Number of banks									
France	171	200	192	186	171	165	145	117	1347
Germany	127	184	189	194	197	194	177	156	1418
Italy	63	74	74	85	87	91	92	86	652
Spain	17	65	73	77	78	72	65	72	519
UK	17	40	57	71	74	79	74	66	478
Average bank size (total assets)									
France	2,778,225	6,069,185	7,128,924	7,175,615	7,541,945	8,329,768	9,280,090	12,691,172	7,392,948
Germany	6,068,351	6,471,744	7,512,259	7,799,985	9,273,175	9,616,774	10,475,054	6,416,851	8,114,090
Italy	7,787,157	9,452,725	9,849,641	9,515,320	9,524,085	11,673,233	9,829,468	11,221,587	9,963,345
Spain	10,931,236	5,080,642	5,395,448	5,096,258	4,774,265	5,390,285	5,288,734	7,418,447	5,988,343
UK	17,834,194	22,399,214	16,228,419	20,260,275	21,983,066	25,727,105	22,326,398	28,298,457	22,596,437

The table shows the number of banks in the banking industry in each of the countries studied and the average value of their total assets (figures expressed in thousands of US$) in relation to each year in the period 1993–2000 and in relation to the entire period.
Source: Author own estimates.

With a view to examining the effect of bank size on technical change, the sample was divided into seven classes in accordance with the total value of assets (as shown in Table 5.6).

The investigation of the relationship from a comparative perspective shows that the situation in the banking industries of the various European countries varies substantially. In addition, within each of the national banking industries there is a marked variety in the size of banks. In each country the difference in size between the first and the seventh class is very marked; on the other hand, there is an even distribution of banks between the various classes identified. In the UK banking industry, however, the number of big banks (the seventh class) is much higher than in every other European country. In fact, if we consider just the banks with assets of more than US$10 billion, the UK banking sector included 41 operators of that size over the period 1993–2000[6] (compared with only 6 in Italy and 3 in Spain).

As for the issue of the variation in size and the degree of technical change at the European level, the estimates of technical change for each class – identified on the basis of company size – are characterised by several particularly notable features.

In the first place, the values of technical change increase in accordance with increases in the size of the firm, especially in France and Germany. (Note that the impact vary across countries, although the difference in the impact is small – about 1 per cent per annum.) This implies that size is a factor explaining the impact of technical change on banks. Presumably, this result can be explained in terms of phenomena that have been extensively examined in the literature on information systems or, more precisely, the reduction in the average size of processing systems (known as IT downsizing[7]) which leads to a reduction in the production costs of a given output thanks to the lower costs of the IT (Moore's Law, originally formulated in Moore, 1965).

A comparison of the present results with those of the previous literature is possible only with reference to Altunbas *et al.* (1999, 2001). The present results confirm what was found previously, that is the scale of operations seems to be a positive factor in the achievement of better results (in terms of cost reductions) from investments in technology. In fact, all the research to date shows that levels of technical change increase in accordance with an increase in the size of firms.

Viewed in the light of the previous literature, our analysis highlights two further important considerations. In the first place, the possibility of optimising the benefits of investment in technology in association with a particular company size, although we are only arguing over a 1

Table 5.6 Size and technical change in European banks

Country	1–99,999		100,000–249,999		250,000–499,999		500,000–999,999		1,000,000–2,499,999		2,500,000–9,999,999		10,000,000+	
Number of banks (and percentage of the total number of banks)														
France	146	10.839	249	18.486	234	17.372	215	15.961	235	17.446	187	13.883	89	6.607
Germany	175	12.341	266	18.759	216	15.233	242	17.066	219	15.444	198	13.963	102	7.193
Italy	29	4.448	87	13.344	70	10.736	107	16.411	130	19.939	113	17.331	139	21.319
Spain	48	9.249	51	9.827	79	15.222	88	16.956	117	22.543	92	17.726	50	9.634
UK	51	10.669	91	19.038	51	10.669	50	10.460	63	13.180	79	16.527	101	21.130
Technical change														
France	−0.02966		−0.03235		−0.03415		−0.03683		−0.03686		−0.03744		−0.03936	
Germany	−0.01929		−0.02700		−0.02680		−0.03139		−0.03102		−0.03127		−0.03589	
Italy	−0.03415		−0.02730		−0.02988		−0.02638		−0.02697		−0.03263		−0.02881	
Spain	−0.02645		−0.02491		−0.03362		−0.02640		−0.02901		−0.02272		−0.02552	
UK	−0.03000		−0.03425		−0.03904		−0.03672		−0.03874		−0.03500		−0.03301	

The table compares the size of the banks in each European country (the banks being divided into seven classes according to size) and the corresponding estimates of technical change. The classes are identified on the basis of the value of assets (expressed in thousands of US dollars). The upper part of the table shows the number of banks that fall into each size-based class and the percentage that they constitute of the total number of banks in respect of each country. The lower part of the table shows the estimated values of technical change in respect of each size-based class. The period considered is 1993–2000.

Source: Authors own estimates.

per cent difference in the value of technical change. This means that that a specific size of banks (big for the French and German industry and small-sized for the United Kingdom) is associated with higher levels of technical change. In short, the scale of operations appears to be an important factor in the realisation of cost economies: a structural variable – size – is associated with better results in technical change.

Secondly, a significant finding lies in the fact that in two countries (France and Germany) the biggest banks (the seventh class or, in other words, those with assets greater than $10,000 million) are characterised by highest levels of technical change. Contrarily, in two other countries (Italy and the United Kingdom), the same biggest banks are characterised by levels of technical change that are inferior to those of the sixth class: although the impact of investment in technology is positive (and generates a reduction in costs), the reduction is lower than that achieved by the banks included in the sixth class (those having assets between $2500 and $9999 million). This finding may be explained in terms of the effects on investments in technology – in particular, on the human component of such investments – deriving from merger and acquisition operations that join together big banking groups in Italy and the United Kingdom.

6
Possible Explanations of the Productivity and Profitability Paradox in the European Banking Industry

6.1 Introduction

The strengthening of IT resources is associated with cost savings over the medium-to-long term (as is evident from the estimates relating to technical change) and, to a certain extent – just in respect of investments in hardware and software – over the short term as well. Nevertheless, it seems that a series of factors act as an obstacle to the transformation of technological innovation into profitability and, above all, into improvements in the various components of revenues.

The empirical results obtained up to now make it necessary to develop a series of possible explanations for why, in an industry that makes intensive use of information, there appears to be a growth in investment in technology that is not accompanied by any increase in profitability in the short term. Such an approach, which implicitly acknowledges the profitability paradox, makes it necessary to pose the following questions:

- What are the objectives associated with IT investments in banks? Careful consideration of the objectives pursued by the banks is intended to underline, on the one hand, the existence of a differentiation in the objectives attributed to technology by different banks (in general, it is possible to distinguish between the following: transactional IT, aimed at minimising costs; strategic IT, geared towards achieving competitive advantage or an increase in market share; and informational IT, intended to strengthen the information-based infrastructure necessary to manage a company)[1] and, on the other, the way in which the achievement of each of these objectives depends on the particular nature of the technological initiatives actually put in place (or, in other words, on the so-called portfolio of IT investments);

- Why – and under what circumstances – have investments in IT failed to generate an improvement in performance in banks? What factors influence the role that IT investments play in the achievement of increases in profitability? The analysis of the relationship between investments in technology and other factors relating to the firm and the institutional context is intended to identify the so-called "barriers to success" associated with investment in technology as well as evaluate their relative importance;

- In what areas of banking activity do investments in IT produce greater/lesser benefits? Here, the object is to investigate the impact of IT investments on the individual activities in the value chain of a bank, aiming in the final result to identify the factors that transform that impact on activities into variations in the bank's costs and revenues.

Interest in the benefits that can be achieved from investment in technology derives from the ever-increasing quantity of such investment as well as from the increasingly crucial role that technology itself plays in the operational activity of banks. This evolution contrasts with a number of difficulties in relation to how to evaluate and manage such investments (Willcocks and Lester, 2001). In the first place, while many organisations – for reasons of competition – cannot afford not to invest in IT, they are actually not able to justify such investment from a strictly economic point of view. Secondly, given that IT infrastructures have become an integral part of the structure and processes of organisations, it has become more and more difficult for many of the more advanced and intensive users of IT – the banks included – to separate the impact of IT from that of other assets and activities. Finally, despite the high level of investment in IT, there persists a limited understanding of the role technology plays as a fixed asset.

In short, the logic of the analysis conducted up to this point, which in an initial phase empirically identified a negative (positive) relationship between the investments in technology and the profitability (costs) of European banks, leads us in this chapter to analyse the objectives and the obstacles associated with IT initiatives so as to arrive at an identification of the factors that determine the particular direction of the relationships in question.

6.2   The objectives of investment in technology and the corresponding types of IT initiatives

So far as the first issue is concerned – that is, the objectives of investment in IT – it is evident that the increase in such investment effected by European banks in the second half of the 1990s can be linked to an extensive set of precisely targeted objectives. This is laid out clearly in the New Cronos database that gathers together the results of an analysis conducted on the matter by Eurostat (2000).[2] In particular, there emerge the following major objectives, listed in descending order of importance, as communicated by the banks that put the investments in place:

1) improvements in quality through the management of information on customers (customer information management) and the automation of distribution channels;
2) business management and the rationalisation of internal processes;
3) e-banking;
4) product innovation.

6.2.1   Improvements in quality

Table 6.1 lists the objectives perceived by the European banks as "very important" in the adoption of technology (elaborated on the basis of the data presented in the New Cronos database [Eurostat, 2000]), and conversely, Table 6.2 outlines the objectives perceived as "not important". From these tables, it is clear that a joint focus on the "customer" and "sales and commercial activities" aimed at achieving "improvements in quality" (point 1 above) has constituted the key feature in the strategic plans of European banks in the period after 1995.[3] In line with the focus on the "customer" and "sales and commercial activities", the principal objective attributed to investments in technology was "improvements in the products or the quality of services": 82 per cent of those interviewed indicated that quality was the fundamental objective. This objective assumed a particularly high degree of importance in two countries: the United Kingdom (where 96 per cent of respondents associated investments in technology with the achievement of improvements in quality) and Germany (88 per cent). By contrast, in France it was assigned less importance (only 56 per cent of respondents made the association).[4]

The focus on the customer[5] has lead to a profound change in banks at the level of strategic orientation: a passage from product-centric institutions to customer-centric organisations. Before this change banks were

Table 6.1 Objectives perceived as very important by the European banks that invest in IT

	EU		France		Germany		Italy	Spain	UK	
	No.	Ratio	No.	Ratio	No.	Ratio	No.	No.	No.	Ratio
Total no. of banks with IT investments	8462	1	772	0.0912	3680	0.4349	n.a.	n.a.	1953	0.2308
Objectives										
1. Improving product or service quality	6924	0.8182	429	0.5557	3244	0.8815	n.a.	n.a.	1871	0.9580
2. Improve production or internal business process flexibility	3881	0.4586	225	0.2915	2442	0.6636	n.a.	n.a.	453	0.2320
3. Open up new markets or increase market share	3890	0.4597	316	0.4093	1360	0.3696	n.a.	n.a.	1259	0.6446
4. Extend product and service range	3679	0.4348	426	0.5518	1834	0.4984	n.a.	n.a.	499	0.2555
5. Reduce labour cost	3451	0.4078	226	0.2927	1708	0.4641	n.a.	n.a.	1009	0.5166
6. Fulfilling regulations and standards	2007	0.2372	182	0.2358	694	0.1886	n.a.	n.a.	757	0.3876
7. Replacing products or services being phased out	1577	0.1864	159	0.2060	638	0.1734	n.a.	n.a.	256	0.1311
8. Reduce material consumption	641	0.0758	86	0.1114	357	0.0970	n.a.	n.a.	122	0.0625

The table displays the list of the objectives perceived as very important by the European banks that invest in technology. The objectives are listed in descending order of perceived importance. For each national banking industry, figures are provided both for the number of banks that held a particular objective to be very important and for the relationship (given as a ratio) between that number and the corresponding aggregate number of banks. The data provided relates to the entire EU banking industry and to the industries of three particular countries (France, Germany and the United Kingdom).
Source: Eurostat (2000).

Table 6.2 Objectives perceived as not important by the European banks investing in IT

	EU		France		Germany		Italy	Spain	UK	
	No.	Ratio	No.	Ratio	No.	Ratio	No.	No.	No.	Ratio
Total no. of banks with IT investments	8462	1	772	0.0912	3680	0.4349	n.a.	n.a.	1953	0.2308
Objectives										
1. Improving product or service quality	333	0.0394	220	0.2850	43	0.0117	n.a.	n.a.	0	0.0000
2. Extend product and service range	567	0.0670	219	0.2837	85	0.0231	n.a.	n.a.	70	0.0358
3. Open up new markets or increase market share	565	0.0668	216	0.2798	122	0.0332	n.a.	n.a.	4	0.0020
4. Improve production or internal business process flexibility	746	0.0882	266	0.3446	204	0.0554	n.a.	n.a.	67	0.0343
5. Reduce labour cost	1256	0.1484	233	0.3018	329	0.0894	n.a.	n.a.	413	0.2115
6. Fulfilling regulations and standards	1919	0.2268	364	0.4715	852	0.2315	n.a.	n.a.	97	0.0497
7. Replacing products or services being phased out	2737	0.3234	452	0.5855	959	0.2606	n.a.	n.a.	669	0.3425
8. Reduce material consumption	4382	0.5178	390	0.5052	1247	0.3389	n.a.	n.a.	1397	0.7153

The table displays the list of the objectives perceived as not important by the European banks that invest in technology. The objectives are listed in ascending order of perceived non-importance. For each national banking industry, figures are provided both for the number of banks that held a particular objective to be not important and for the relationship (given as a ratio) between that number and the corresponding aggregate number of banks. The data provided relates to the entire EU banking industry and to the industries of three particular countries (France, Germany and the United Kingdom).

Source: Eurostat (2000).

organised around product lines, with the result that information on customers did not circulate readily between the various lines. The development of a unitary and integrated perspective on the customer meant that the banks began to modify their processes and to integrate their IT systems. The integration of IT systems has led to an increase in actual investment in IT as well as a higher level of complexity in the systems themselves.

In the banking industry, the objective of achieving a focus on customers has taken the form of two initiatives: customer information management and the automation of sales. These two lines of action – which constitute the principal reasons for the realisation of IT investment in the industry – have been geared primarily towards the integration, sharing and management of information on customers, the adoption of software in support of customers and the development of analytical tools aimed at increasing cross-selling and up-selling.

The IT initiatives associated with this strategic approach, known as Customer Relationship Management (CRM [see Inset 1]), have developed at different levels. In the first place, with a view to achieving customer loyalty, increasing sales and realising cross-selling, the banks, on the one hand, have adopted tools such as databases with information on customers, software in support of customers, call management systems and analytical instruments for forecasting the behaviour of customers. On the other hand, various sales support systems such as tools used as analytical instruments for the management of sales promotion campaigns, the automation of sales and the handling of contracts have also been developed. Such initiatives have required an enormous effort to integrate systems and an equally huge investment in personal computers, servers and pre-packaged software. In addition, front-end operations have required additional functionalities enabling use of the information acquired on customers. In turn, these have obliged the banks to frequently update their servers and personal computers.

6.2.2   Business management and the rationalisation of internal business processes

The second objective of IT initiatives (point 2 above) is represented by business management and the rationalisation of internal processes: 46 per cent of respondents attributed to investment in technology the objective of "Improved production and internal business process flexibility" (Table 6.1). The importance given to this objective varies according to country: while the banking industry in the United Kingdom attributed to this objective a level of importance lower than the European average (only 23 per cent of respondents considered it very important), the German banks perceived it as more important than did the EU banks on average. From a comparative perspective, the different importance assigned to this objective – read in conjunction with what has been noted in respect of the "Improving quality" objective – suggests that there has been some variation in the nature of the strategies pursued by the banking industries in the different European countries.

Inset 1   Customer Relationship Management

"Customer Relationship Management" is a term used by the information systems industry to refer to the IT infrastructures, the procedures, the software applications and the communication channels that help a firm to manage its relations with its customers in an organised manner. For example, a firm can construct a database on its own customers so as to describe its relations with them in such a detailed manner that the management, sales staff, service providers and even the customers themselves can have direct access to the information, draw connections between customer needs and preferences and projected products and special sales offers, remind clients about service features, know what other products the client has already purchased and so on. In essence, this means that CRM makes provision for the following (www.whatis.com, mimeo):

a) helping a firm to enable its marketing division to identify and analyse its best clients, manage marketing campaigns with clear aims and objectives and specify quality criteria for sales staff;

b) assisting the organisation to improve telesales and the management of sales by exploiting to the full the information shared between the various staff members and simplifying the existing processes (for example, taking orders by way of mobile electronic instruments);

c) facilitating the formation of customised relationships with customers with a view to improving customer satisfaction and maximising profits by way of identifying the more

> profitable customers and providing them with a higher level of service;
> d) providing staff with the information necessary to know their customers, understand their needs and establish effective relations between the firm, the customers and distribution partners.

Investments in IT put in place as initiatives in business management constitute instruments for planning and control as well as for risk management. Examples of information systems aimed at business management include DSS (Decision Support Systems or, in other words, systems to support decision-making [see Inset 2]) and, so far as more recent times are concerned, EIS (Executive Information Systems, or, in other words, information systems oriented towards satisfying the needs of senior management [see Inset 3]).

Inset 2   Decision Support Systems

A Decision Support System (DSS) may be defined as a software application that makes provision for analysing the data relating to the activity of a firm and presenting it in such a way that the users can take decisions with greater ease. This type of application constitutes an "informational application" (which is to be distinguished from an "operational application", whose purpose is to collect data in the course of the normal operations of a firm), and it is generally aimed at the managers of firms or other groups of staff involved in management. The typical forms of information that a decision-making support application can collect and analyse include the following (www.whatis.com, mimeo):

a) comparative data on variations in volumes of sales;
b) data on expected revenues due to the sale of new products;
c) data on the possible implications of alternative decisions projected on the basis of past experience in a given context.

Inset 3 Executive Information Systems

An Executive Information System (EIS) is an information system based on IT infrastructures and designed to provide senior managers with access to information relating to their management activities. Generally, an EIS offers support for strategic activities like the definition of strategic policies, planning and the preparation of financial statements. The purpose of such a system is to collect, analyse and integrate internal and external data in terms of dynamic profiles of key indexes. Although different EISs vary greatly in terms of the sophistication of their particular features, their most common characteristic is to provide immediate access to a single database where it is possible to recover a vast amount of financial and operational data. In many cases, the information in question has already been available in the past, but it has not been possible to access and make use of it with great ease. The particular technical capacities of EIS include the following: drill-down analysis (i.e. the incremental examination of data taking into consideration different levels of detail), the analysis of trends (in other words, the examination of data in terms of selected intervals of time), extended graphics capabilities, the provision of data from multiple sources and the detailed analysis of information considered critical by management (www.whatis.com, mimeo).

While Management Information Systems (MIS) have been used prevalently for the filing and treatment of large quantities of information, EIS have been used to search for specific information relating to the daily status of the operational activities of organisations. In addition, as against the role of a DSS in supporting ad hoc decisions and routine analysis, the scope of an EIS is to examine and analyse the environment and any external variables so as to provide the directors of firms with an immediate evaluation of their exposure to changes.

So far as the rationalisation of internal business processes is concerned, the reasons for the adoption of IT initiatives consist in a concern to increase productivity and reduce activities characterised by low added value as well as to improve the production of documentation and the efficiency of services. The two IT initiatives aimed at rationalising business processes are Business Process Re-engineering (BPR [see Inset 4]) and, so far as more recent times are concerned, Enterprise Resource Planning (ERP [see Inset 5]).

Inset 4   Business Process Re-engineering

Business Process Re-engineering (BPR) consists in the analysis and redefinition of processes and work flows within an organisation and between different organisations (Davenport and Short, 1990). The phenomenon of BPR reached its apex at the beginning of the 1990s when Hammer (1990) advanced the idea that at times a radical reorganisation and redesign of a firm is necessary in order to reduce costs and increase the quality of services, and that it was technology that constituted the key ingredient in order for such radical change to come about (www.whatis.com, mimeo). This may find concrete expression in the fact, identified by Davenport and Short (1990), that BPR necessarily installs an integrated outlook in respect of technology and the activities of a firm, and the relations between them. IT should be seen as something more than just an automating and mechanising factor and, in particular, should be viewed as a force that in essence makes provision for redefining the modalities in which business is conducted. In this light, the activities of firms should not be viewed as a set of tasks of an individual or even functional nature, but rather, should be characterised in accordance with a process-oriented perspective. In this sense, IT and BPR are characterised by a relationship of reciprocity. The capabilities of IT should support the processes of the firm, and the processes in turn should be defined on the basis of the IT infrastructures. Davenport and Short (1990) referred to this extended and reciprocity-oriented perspective on IT and BPR as the new industrial engineering.

Note, however, that from the second half of the 1990s on, BPR basically took on the role of an instrument for effecting so-called "downsizing" (or, in other words, the reduction of personnel). The reasons for the demise of BPR, according to Hammer (1996), consisted in a lack of support on the part of management, the absence of adequate leadership and resistance to change: all this led management to abandon BPR and to adopt a new methodology known as "Enterprise Resource Planning" (ERP) (see Inset 5).

Inset 5   Enterprise Resource Planning

Enterprise Resource Planning (ERP) is a term adopted by the information systems industry to designate the broad set of activities supported by modular software applications that help a firm to manage the various phases of the production process. ERP may also include application modules for finance and for matters relating to human resources. The development of an ERP system involves a thorough analysis of the production process, a retraining of human resources and the introduction of new work procedures. Typically, an ERP system uses – or is integrated with – a relational database system such as Oracles. SAP, Peoplesoft and J.D. Edwards are producers of ERP, and are involved in the attempt to increase the penetration of ERP services in banks. Nevertheless, ERP is not yet widely used in the banking industry, although its importance continues to increase. In particular, whereas ERP systems are already used in the human resources and accounting departments of banks, strategic planning and procurement are the areas with the lowest current ERP usage (European Business School, 2004).

6.2.3   e-banking

Forty six per cent of the respondents to the questionnaire published in New Cronos survey (Eurostat, 2000) included among the very important objectives associated with the adoption of technology "Opening up new markets or increased market share" (see Table 6.1). This objective was assigned a particularly high importance by the banking industry in the United Kingdom (64 per cent of the respondents considered it very important). This strongly suggests that there is a more positive attitude towards the introduction of on-line banking in the Anglo-Saxon banks than there is on average in the banks of continental Europe.

At the end of the 1990s, the appearance of the Internet – a new channel for the provision of on-line services – led to a range of IT initiatives that varied in accordance with the nature of the different banks. First of all, the Internet made possible the emergence of a new type of bank, known as a "virtual bank" or "e-bank", which operates exclusively on-line. This new type of bank, still of relatively little importance in the European market, had to effect enormous investments in IT in order to create the infrastructures necessary to compete with the traditional banks.[6] Secondly, the traditional banks, known as "bricks and mortar" banks, invested heavily in on-line banking services in order to avoid a loss of market share in favour of the new e-banks.[7] Finally, as a parallel activity, the big traditional banking groups gave life to joint (non-independent) e-banks, set up with the intention of establishing on a separate plane activities involving an intensive use of IT.[8]

A structural analysis of the new phenomenon of the virtual bank shows that the start-up, marketing and advertising costs associated with on-line activities are particularly high and that the habits of customers are often very difficult to alter. Moreover, where the bank pursues a very competitive pricing strategy with a view to increasing market share, it may well run the risk of compromising profitability, in particular, if an increase in the margin as a result of cross-selling does not materialise. On the other hand, the virtual bank enjoys a wide range of advantages, which can be classified on the basis of their intangible character (Prometeia, 2001). Amongst the benefits of a monetary nature are the revenues deriving from the Internet banking service subscription fees, the revenues deriving from the charges applied to individual banking operations, the reduction in personnel costs and, more generally, the reduction in costs tied to the physical structure of the distribution network. Amongst the advantages of a partially monetary nature are (particularly, for the joint e-banks) the acquisition of new customers, cross-selling and an increase in the average number of operations per customer as well as, from a more general perspective, an improvement in the image of the bank and the possible elimination of constraints of a geographic nature.

In regard to the expenditure that banks expect to undertake to sustain e-banking, it is interesting to note that a large majority estimate that they will maintain expenditure at current levels and that only a small number foresee an increase in expenditure. This finding, which emerged from a study on a large sample of European banks conducted by E-Business W@tch (2003a), is presented in Table 6.3.[9] In this regard, however, it needs to be pointed out that there is a widespread perception that e-banking is not very important at present and a similarly widespread perception that it will not be particularly important in the future (Table 6.4): in the study in question 49.9 per cent of banks did not

Table 6.3 Expenditure on e-banking technology in the EU

	Increase in expenditure on e-banking	Decrease in expenditure on e-banking	Constant expenditure on e-banking
e-business expenditure – all industries			
EU7	29.7	2.2	62.5
e-banking expenditure – according to country			
France	33.2	1.8	64.7
Germany	25.9	3.1	69.9
Italy	40.2	0.0	58.0
Spain	48.1	1.1	69.9
UK	38.9	4.9	54.6
EU7	36.9	2.7	59.1
e-banking expenditure – according to size			
0–49 employees	36.2	2.9	59.7
50–249 employees	34.7	0.4	63.4
+250 employees	40.9	1.6	55.8

The table shows the percentage of banks – divided according to country and size – that forecasted increases, decreases or stability in expenditure on e-banking technology. The table includes figures for the banking industries of the five countries considered in the survey and of the EU7 in respect of the year 2002. In addition, figures are provided for expenditure on e-business in respect of all industries in the EU7.
Source: E-Business W@tch (2003a).

Table 6.4 Perception of the current importance and expectations of the future importance of e-banking in the EU

	France	Germany	Italy	Spain	UK	EU7
Current importance						
e-banking plays significant role	5.1	19.2	18.6	6.9	3.2	8.6
e-banking plays limited role	42.4	56.7	23.5	37.0	47.0	41.0
e-banking plays no role	52.4	23.1	56.1	56.1	49.8	49.9
Expectations for the future						
e-banking will play a significant or limited role	21.9	16.7	21.4	42.8	53.2	33.8
e-banking will not play a role	71.3	58.1	51.4	41.3	41.9	33.9

The table shows the perception of the current importance (significant role, limited role and no role) and the expectations of the future importance (significant or limited role, and no role) of e-banking in the five countries considered in the study as well as in the EU7 in respect of the year 2002.
Source: E-Business W@tch (2003a).

attribute to e-business an important role in their operational activity, only 8.6 per cent attributed a significant role to it and as many as 41 per cent of banks declared that e-business had a marginal role. On the basis of such data it is possible to conclude that in essence banking activity is predominantly based on traditional commercial operating activities and that the new technology has a more significant impact on the efficiency of the internal processes of banks than on their commercial activity as a whole. Such considerations also allow us to cast doubt on certain common but misleading assertions to the effect that the banks will substitute their traditional modes of operating with forms based exclusively on the Internet. This finds confirmation in Filotto (2002), where it is argued that the impact on sales and, therefore, on revenues brought about by the Internet is still extremely weak and that the financial industry has displayed a marked incapacity to transform Internet-based operational activity into profitability, even though on face value financial products seem to be particularly suitable for being sold through Internet.[10]

In regard to the e-business solutions that have been widely adopted by the European banks, the E-Business W@tch (2003a) study – as laid out in Table 6.5 – showed that CRM[11] and Application Service Providers

Table 6.5 Various e-business solutions adopted in European banks

	France	Germany	Italy	Spain	UK	EU7
1. CRM (Customer Relationship Management)	7.1	17.5	12.4	10.6	7.0	9.4
2. Plans to adopt CRM systems	3.5	5.9	5.6	11.1	1.9	3.9
3. ASP (Application Service Provider)	7.1	13.0	10.8	6.9	10.2	9.7
4. Plans to make use of an ASP	0.1	2.9	3.5	6.9	3.3	2.6
5. ERP (Enterprise Resource Planning)	4.0	6.0	11.6	11.1	1.8	5.3
6. Plans to use an ERP system	0.1	0.9	4.9	9.0	0.1	1.5
7. Knowledge Management Solution	0.4	6.9	12.5	8.0	3.6	5.1
8. Plans to use a Knowledge Management Solution	3.6	4.0	1.6	9.0	0.2	2.2
9. SCM (Supply Chain Management)	1.7	0.0	0.2	5.2	0.0	0.8
10. Plans to use an SCM system	0.1	0.0	0.0	6.3	1.7	0.9

The table shows percentage of banks that adopted the various e-business solutions in the EU7 and in the five countries considered in the study in respect of the year 2002.
Source: E-Business W@tch (2003a).

(ASP [see Inset 6]) were the most commonly used solutions, followed by ERP systems[12] and knowledge management solutions (see Inset 7). This finding, too, supports the thesis, already advanced a number of times, that banks adopt the most advanced technological solutions available and use technology so as to improve the quality of their services for their customers. In this regard, it is significant that CRM constitutes the solution that is most widely featured in the plans that the European banks have for the future.

Inset 6   Application Service Provider

An Application Service Provider (ASP) is a company that offers to individuals or firms access via Internet to applications – as well as other related services – that would otherwise have to be placed on the computers of the individuals or firms. Operators in the information systems industry expect that ASP services will become an important alternative not just for firms that have limited budgets to invest in technology but also for bigger firms disposed to make use of them as a form of outsourcing. Amongst the applications/services offered are the following:

a) remote access serving for the users of a firm;
b) a local area network to which mobile users can be connected, with a common file server;
c) access to specialised software which would be costly to install and maintain within a single firm (or on the computer of a single user).

Inset 7   Knowledge Management

Knowledge Management is a concept that refers to the gathering, organisation, sharing and analysis – both conscious and comprehensive – of knowledge by a firm on the basis of resources, documents and individual skills. At the end of the 1990s, it was thought that very few firms were really in a position to put into effect comprehensive practices of knowledge management. Advances in technology and new modalities for accessing and sharing information have modified this early situation such that today it is thought that many firms do have at their disposal some form of knowledge management. Knowledge management requires the adoption of data mining and operating methods to deliver information to users. A traditional knowledge management plan requires an examination of the goals of the firm and a detailed analysis of the tools, both traditional and technical, necessary to satisfy its needs. The object of such a close examination is to select and construct a software that fits in well with the general framework of the overall plan and that encourages the users to share information (www.whatis.com, mimeo).

With reference to the objectives pursued by European banks through the adoption of e-business solutions, we draw attention to the data in Table 6.6, which was originally presented in E-Business W@tch (2003a). In the first place, this reveals that on-line sales and on-line purchases

Table 6.6 Impact of on-line sales and on-line purchases in European banks

	France	Germany	Italy	Spain	UK	EU7
On-line sales						
Volume of sales (very positive)	0.0	13.7	30.5	27.1	0.0	10.0
Number of customers (increase)	0.0	4.9	30.5	27.3	0.7	8.6
Geographical extension of sales (very positive)	0.0	4.5	35.8	9.2	0.7	7.8
Quality of service to users (very positive)	0.0	12.9	47.9	9.9	0.7	13.1
Efficiency of internal business processes (very positive)	1.1	17.4	48.0	19.7	59.1	31.1
Costs in relation to logistics and inventories (very positive)	1.4	5.4	43.9	41.8	0.0	10.2
On-line purchases						
Costs of supplies (very positive)	0.0	8.8	16.4	18.0	18.6	12.3
Relations with suppliers (very positive)	0.0	0.0	34.9	6.3	11.0	9.2
Internal business processes (very positive)	0.0	12.3	27.1	16.6	14.9	12.2
Costs in relation to logistics and inventories (very positive)	0.0	8.1	11.4	21.6	0.2	3.1
Number of suppliers (increase)	16.7	19.5	31.6	23.9	19.3	20.2

The table shows the impact of on-line sales and purchases expressed in terms of the number of banks (given as a percentage of all banks) that reported a very positive impact. The figures relate to the five countries under investigation and the EU7 in respect of the year 2002.
Source: E-Business W@tch (2003a).

have had a very positive impact on internal business processes. This tends to confirm the idea that the adoption of new technology is primarily intended to increase the efficiency of the operational activity of banks. In the second place, the objective of realising on-line commercial operations with end-users appears to play a role as an incentive to provide higher quality services and as an instrument for reducing logistical and inventory costs (especially for Italian banks). One controversial point at the level of the different national banking systems is the importance of on-line sales in so far as they relate to volumes of sales and, consequently, the number of customers. In fact, in this regard, the impact of e-business solutions has been very positive so far as Italian and Spanish banks are concerned, but it seems that in the United Kingdom and France it has not resulted in any significant increase either in volumes or in the capacity of the bank to attract further customers. Presumably, this result is to be explained by the fact that these two banking systems, especially that of the United Kingdom, are characterised by a considerable amount of oscillation in the degree of customer loyalty.

Given that the efficiency of internal business processes is cited as the aspect of banking that more than any other extracts benefit from e-commerce, one further point of particular interest lies in the impact of on-line operational activity on the organisational structure of the bank (in this regard, see the data in Table 6.7). Overall, the greatest advantages are manifest in internal work processes, to which can be added benefits – albeit of a limited nature and, in any case, inferior to those

Table 6.7 Impact of e-banking on matters of an organisational nature

%	France	Germany	Italy	Spain	UK	EU7
Organisational structure of the bank	3.3	12.2	10.6	7.9	3.3	5.7
Internal work processes	6.7	19.1	10.5	9.0	8.4	9.3
Relations with customers	3.8	15.0	7.4	2.1	3.4	5.3
Relations with suppliers	3.4	6.0	10.0	2.1	5.0	5.5
Products/services offered	8.7	9.0	10.6	4.7	1.6	6.3

The table shows the perceived impact of e-banking on matters of an organisational nature. The figures are expressed as the percentage of banks that associate a significant impact of e-banking on several matters of an organisational nature (organisational structure, internal work process, relations with customers, relations with suppliers, range of products/services offered) in relation to the banks that reported an overall significant impact of e-banking. The values relate to the EU7 and the five countries under investigation in respect of the year 2002.
Source: E-Business W@tch (2003a).

registered in other industries of the economy – associated with other factors of an organisational nature. This latter group includes relations with customers and suppliers as well as the variety of products and services offered. Moreover, purchasing supplies on-line has a positive impact on costs and encourages suppliers to put on-line operations in place, thereby reducing what was identified previously as one of the most important barriers to on-line purchases.

6.2.4   Product innovation

With a view to satisfying the needs of customers in a comprehensive manner, European banks have progressively increased the degree of customisation in the products they offer, and have developed, as well as marketed, structured products that contain various combinations of technical features and pricing. The impact of the customisation of bank products on investment in technology is shown by an empirical finding reported in the New Cronos questionnaire (Eurostat, 2000): 43 per cent of respondents identified "Extend product or service range" as a very important objective to ascribe to investments in IT (see Table 6.1). Compared with the other European banks, the importance attributed to this factor is quite low in the Anglo-Saxon banks, where only 25 per cent of respondents identified it as very important.

The notion that IT investment is an important means through which to effect product innovation is something that brings with it a range of implications. In the first place, it implies an increase in the cost of design, maintenance and testing. Secondly, the creation of combinations of products and prices leads to an increase in the complexity of the system as well as the need for additional capabilities for processing information. Finally, the offer on the part of banks of insurance products and investment products produces a further increase in complexity. This renders necessary the adoption of more sophisticated applications that operate as instruments for forecasting trends in the financial market and for selecting the best combination of financial instruments for each customer, given the return and the level of risk exposure desired.

6.3   Barriers to success in investment in IT

After considering the principal objectives that guide banks in their realisation of investments in technology, logically, the next problem to consider takes the form of the barriers – as well as obstacles – that condition IT initiatives and, as a consequence, the impact that such initiatives have on the banks. To this end, some purpose may be served by an analysis of the causes of the high rate of failure of the major IT initiatives put in place by the European banks in the last decade. The causes of such failure – which can be characterised as barriers and obstacles – by their very nature make it possible to identify and comprehend the factors that have determined the profitability paradox established empirically in relation to European banks in Chapter 4.

6.3.1 Empirical evidence

In this section, we once again make use of the New Cronos questionnaire (Eurostat, 2000),[13] which, amongst other things, explicated the factors that have impeded technological innovation in the European banking industry. In particular, these barriers to success were specified in terms of three levels of analysis delineating what might be classified as increasingly acute forms of failure in the initiatives undertaken, namely:

a) barriers which provoke serious delays in the adoption of technology;
b) barriers which lead to the abandonment of projects;
c) barriers which prevent projects even from being started.

The first barrier takes the form of a delay in the adoption of IT, as illustrated in Table 6.8.[14] In this regard, the first thing to note is the marked differences in the levels of failure registered in the various national banking industries. In fact, the German banking industry was characterised by a high rate of instances of delay in the realisation of investments in technology in respect of the total number of initiatives (as much as 57 per cent of the total number of EU projects were delayed), the figures for France and the United Kingdom were much lower (7.6 per cent and 12 per cent, respectively). In contrast with the notable variation in the degree of failure, however, there was substantial agreement about the factors – identified above as barriers and obstacles – that determined the delays; in fact, all the European banks identified in order of importance the following two factors as the major obstacles to the success of projects: rigidities of an organisational nature and lack of qualified personnel.

The barriers to investment in technology which lead to the abandonment of projects, as specified in (b) above, are listed in Table 6.9.[15] The first thing to note is that, in keeping with what has been observed in relation to the lack of success inhering to delays in the adoption of technology, the situation in the German banking industry was far more prone to failure than that in the UK or French industries (for the three countries, the rates of failure as percentages of the total for European banks were, respectively, 58.9 per cent, 9.3 per cent and 6.8 per cent). Secondly, in regard to the relative importance of each of the barriers,

Table 6.8 Factors provoking serious delays in the realisation of IT projects in European banks

	EU		France		Germany		Italy	Spain	UK	
	No.	%	No.	%	No.	%	No.	No.	No.	%
Serious delays in investments in technology	2777	100	211	7.60	1587	57.15	n.a.	n.a.	343	12.35
				Causes						
1. Organisational rigidities	1472	53.01	64	30.33	1037	65.34	n.a.	n.a.	171	49.85
2. Lack of qualified personnel	1261	45.41	51	24.17	710	44.74	n.a.	n.a.	197	57.43
3. Problems in fulfilling regulatory requirements	490	17.64	46	21.80	323	20.35	n.a.	n.a.	35	10.20
4. Lack of information on technology	474	17.07	26	12.32	235	14.81	n.a.	n.a.	26	7.58
5. Excessive economic risk	401	14.44	50	23.70	240	15.12	n.a.	n.a.	61	17.78
6. Lack of customer responsiveness to new products	250	9.00	36	17.06	147	9.26	n.a.	n.a.	11	3.21
7. Lack of information on markets	210	7.56	33	15.64	155	9.77	n.a.	n.a.	0	0.00
8. Excessive costs of innovation	199	7.17	37	17.54	n.a.	–	n.a.	n.a.	3	0.87
9. Lack of adequate sources of financing	168	6.05	8	3.79	68	4.28	n.a.	n.a.	65	18.95

The table shows the number and the percentage of European banks with investments in technology characterised by serious delays as well as the factors identified as causes of the delays (listed in descending order of importance). Data is provided for the entire EU banking industry and for the three countries considered in the study (France, Germany and the United Kingdom) in respect of the year 2000.
Source: Eurostat (2000).

Table 6.9 Factors leading to the abandonment of IT projects by European banks

	EU		France		Germany		Italy	Spain	UK	
	No.	%	No.	%	No.	%	No.	No.	No.	%
Abandonment of investments in technology	1168	100	109	9.33	688	58.90	n.a.	n.a.	79	6.76
Causes										
1. Excessive economic risk	343	29.37	14	12.84	212	30.81	n.a.	n.a.	26	32.91
2. Organisational rigidities	332	28.42	32	29.36	243	35.32	n.a.	n.a.	4	5.06
3. Lack of customer responsiveness to new products	267	22.86	17	15.60	190	27.62	n.a.	n.a.	8	10.13
4. Lack of qualified personnel	247	21.15	15	13.76	134	19.48	n.a.	n.a.	30	37.97
5. Excessive costs of innovation	164	14.04	42	38.53	n.a.	–	n.a.	n.a.	63	79.75
6. Lack of information on markets	138	11.82	0	0.00	112	16.28	n.a.	n.a.	2	2.53
7. Lack of information on technology	124	10.62	6	5.50	67	9.74	n.a.	n.a.	30	37.97
8. Problems in fulfilling regulatory requirements	87	7.45	2	1.83	49	7.12	n.a.	n.a.	0	0.00
9. Lack of adequate sources of financing	67	5.74	15	13.76	37	5.38	n.a.	n.a.	0	0.00

The table shows the number and the percentage of European banks with investments in technology subject to abandonment as well as the factors identified as causes of the abandonment (listed in descending order of importance). Data is provided for the entire EU banking industry and for the three countries considered in the study (France, Germany and the United Kingdom) in respect of the year 2000.
Source: Eurostat (2000).

an analysis of the analogies and differences between the delays in the realisation of investments in technology, on the one hand, and the abandonment of IT projects, on the other, throws light on a range of important issues. First of all, it is interesting to note that, while for the French and the German banks the principal obstacle continued to be identified in the form of rigidities of an organisational nature, the banking industry in the United Kingdom perceived excessive economic risk as a far more unfavourable factor (in keeping with what can be seen at the level of the entire European banking system). In addition, in keeping with the tendency, as discussed in Section 6.2, to attribute priority in investment in technology to the objectives of customer satisfaction and product innovation, the lack of customer responsiveness to new products/channels assumed greater importance in relation to the abandonment of IT projects than it did in relation to delays in the realisation of projects. Finally, a marginal role continued to be attributed to the lack of adequate sources of finance (Note that in the United Kingdom, such a barrier was actually characterised as having no importance). This means that considerations of a financial nature are not to be included among the principal reasons for lack of success – be it in terms of delays or abandonment – in the realisation of investments in technology.

The barriers to investment in technology that actually prevented projects from being started, as specified in (c) above, and that, as such, constituted the most acute case of failure for the European banks are illustrated in Table 6.10.[16] First, it is apparent that the German banks, in keeping with what has been observed in respect of the previous two cases, were characterised by a particularly high rate of failure (the level of failure as a percentage of the total for European banks was 71 per cent compared with figures of 4 per cent and 9 per cent, respectively, for France and the United Kingdom). So far as the relative importance of the different barriers is concerned, the situation that emerges is practically the mirror image of what has been observed in relation to the IT projects that were abandoned: in fact, while for the Anglo-Saxon banking industry the rigidities of an organisational character again constituted the most important barrier overall, for the French and German banks it was economic risk that formed the biggest obstacle to setting in place investments in technology (in keeping with what can be observed for the European banking industry as a whole). Also, in contrast to what has emerged in relation to the other barriers to success, it appears that the lack of adequate sources of finance assumes a quite significant role in impeding technology initiatives in the initial phase.

Table 6.10 Factors preventing European banks from starting IT projects

	EU		France		Germany		Italy	Spain	UK	
	No.	%	No.	%	No.	%	No.	No.	No.	%
Non-realisation of invest-ments in technology	1484	100	60	4.04	1052	70.89	n.a.	n.a.	135	9.10
				Causes						
1. Excessive economic risk	462	31.13	17	28.33	346	32.89	n.a.	n.a.	23	17.04
2. Organisational rigidities	391	26.35	2	3.33	255	24.24	n.a.	n.a.	96	71.11
3. Problems in fulfilling regulatory requirements	387	26.08	2	3.33	351	33.37	n.a.	n.a.	2	1.48
4. Lack of qualified personnel	370	24.93	0	0.00	257	24.43	n.a.	n.a.	62	45.93
5. Lack of adequate sources of financing	311	20.96	2	3.33	271	25.76	n.a.	n.a.	16	11.85
6. Lack of customer responsiveness to new products	192	12.94	2	3.33	135	12.83	n.a.	n.a.	7	5.19
7. Lack of information on technology	185	12.47	0	0.0000	141	13.40	n.a.	n.a.	2	1.48
8. Excessive costs of innovation	107	7.21	2	0.0333	n.a.	–	n.a.	n.a.	37	27.41
9. Lack of information on markets	144	9.70	0	0.0000	105	9.98	n.a.	n.a.	0	0.00

The table shows the number and the percentage of European banks with proposed investments in technology that were not even embarked upon as well as the factors identified as causes of the non-realisation (listed in descending order of importance). Data is provided for the entire EU banking industry and for the three countries considered in the study (France, Germany and the United Kingdom) in respect of the year 2000.
Source: Eurostat (2000).

The barriers to the success of investments in IT relating to e-banking constitute a separate issue. This emerges clearly from an enquiry conducted by E-Business W@tch and is presented in Table 6.11.[17] So far as on-line sales are concerned, the two barriers that the banks in their

Table 6.11   Barriers to on-line sales and purchases in European banks

	France	Germany	Italy	Spain	UK	EU7
On-line sales						
1. The unsuitability of the products/services being sold on-line	86.6	60.4	69.5	74.6	66.9	72.7
2. The hesitation of customers to buy on-line	75.0	61.2	61.7	84.1	63.4	66.7
3. The limited revenues deriving from on-line sales	55.1	71.7	66.4	62.4	59.7	61.2
4. The excessive financial costs of technology	58.2	46.6	47.6	49.2	58.5	54.8
5. The difficulty of adapting the bank culture to e-commerce	53.9	53.8	61.5	58.1	42.2	51.3
6. The limited number of on-line customers	54.2	25.9	57.3	54.0	50.1	50.6
7. Problems involved in processing payments for on-line orders	53.0	33.8	49.9	42.3	42.8	46.1
8. Problems involved in the delivery process	33.3	18.0	49.3	32.8	21.9	30.9
On-line purchases						
1. Concerns relating to the protection of data and issues of security	77.5	41.2	66.3	82.0	71.9	69.9
2. The need for face-to-face interaction	64.6	57.0	77.8	59.7	40.1	57.3
3. The lack of on-line suppliers	55.2	38.1	69.6	65.1	46.9	53.7
4. The excessive financial costs of technology	55.3	42.8	46.6	49.2	47.1	49.3
5. Non-compatibility with suppliers' systems	30.0	24.9	35.9	27.5	30.1	30.7
6. Insignificance of the cost advantage	42.9	42.8	44.2	44.4	46.3	44.4

The table shows the barriers to on-line sales and purchases in terms of the percentage of the banks totally or partially in agreement as to their importance. The figures relate to the EU7 and the five countries considered in the study in respect of the year 2002.
Source: E-Business W@tch (2003a).

aggregate perceived to be of greater importance were identified as the unsuitability of bank products and services to be sold on-line and the hesitation of customers to make purchases on-line. It is evident that the relative importance of the two factors was the same for all the countries considered in the enquiry with the exception of Germany, where there was a more marked concern for the behaviour of customers as opposed to the suitability of the product. In regard to purchases on-line, in aggregate terms the barrier perceived to be by far the most important was that constituted by concerns in relation to the protection of data and the security of on-line transactions. Nevertheless, even in this case two exceptions are apparent: in fact, in the Italian and German banking systems, the major barrier was identified in terms of the need to maintain a personal and direct relationship with the supplier.

6.3.2   Theoretical perspectives

On the basis of the empirical evidence discussed so far in relation to the relative importance of the barriers to success encountered by European banks investing in technology, it is necessary at this point to investigate the theoretical perspectives that the literature on banking systems has developed on the subject. In particular, it seems that attention might profitably be directed to the studies on what is referred to in the Anglo-Saxon literature as "technology effectiveness". The definition of IT success has required the establishment of a well-defined measure of success, for without this many of the related studies would be merely speculative. Unfortunately, in the attempt to arrive at a measure of the success of IT, rather than light upon a single measure, one encounters – as Delone (1988) and DeLone and McLean (1992) put it – as many different measures as there are studies on the subject. The reason for the existence of such a great variety of specifications derives from the fact that information, understood as the output of an information system, can be measured at different levels. Viewed in terms of this interpretative approach, information inheres to the technical level, the semantic level and the level of effectiveness.[18] Indeed, starting out from this framework, the level relating to effectiveness has been renamed "influence" and, as a result, a further concept has been introduced: the level of the influence of information (Mason, 1978). In particular, this concept identifies "A hierarchy of events which take place at the receiving end of an information system which may be used to identify the various approaches that might be used to measure output at the influence level" (Mason, 1978, p. 227). The series of events that relates to the level of effectiveness (influence) of information includes the receipt, the evaluation and the application of the information, which, in their turn, determine a change of behaviour in the subject who receives the information and a modification in the performance of the organisation.

The concept of levels of output proposed by the theory of information makes provision for highlighting the serial nature of information itself. The information system creates information, which is communicated to the recipient, who may or may not be influenced by it. In this way, information passes through a series of phases: from production, to use and even to the influence on the user or, in other words, on the performance of the organisation. Reproducing a synthetic and incisive graphic representation proposed by DeLone and McLean (1992), Figure 6.1 illustrates the three levels of information (as in the formulation of Shannon and Weaver, 1949) together with the concept of the level of effectiveness or influence (as proposed by Mason, 1978). From this one can arrive at a specification of the categories of the success of information systems: the quality of the system, the quality of the information, the use, and the satisfaction of the user, the impact on the user and the organisational impact.

On the basis of what has been observed so far it is possible to focus attention on the level of effectiveness (or influence) that relates to the interaction of the information product with its recipients, measured by way of the specification of the following categories of IT success: the use, the satisfaction of the user, the influence on the decisions of the user (individual impact) and the effect of the information on the performance of the organisation (organisational impact).

In adopting these categories of IT success in relation to the European banking industry, the theoretical problem takes the form of an analysis, on the one hand, of the individual impact, the use of the information

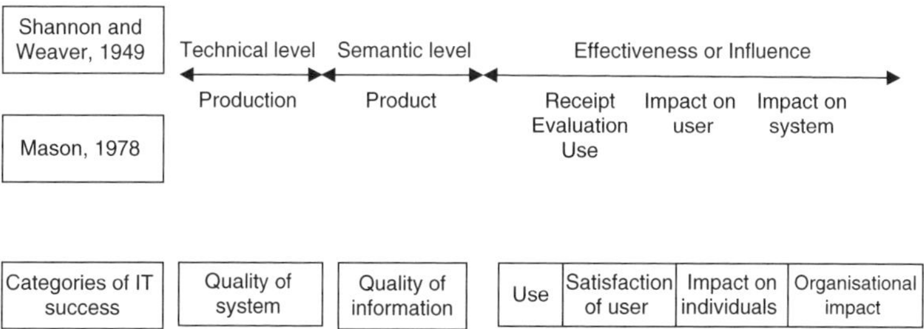

Figure 6.1   Categories of IT success

and the satisfaction of the user and, on the other, of the impact on the organisation. In fact, these two macro-categories seem to be of equal importance in determining the success of investments in technology. Their utility lies in the fact that they make provision for identifying the factors that interact with technology and which provide for an improvement in individual or organisational performance.[19]

By way of concluding on these observations on the success of IT investments, it should be noted that there is another factor that is perceived as important by European banks, namely, economic risk (in this respect, see Section 6.3.1). Although this element has not typically been taken into consideration in the literature relating to IT success, in this book we emphasise that it is clearly an important element that must be borne in mind in the context of investments in technology.

6.4 The impact of investments in IT on transactions

Having identified the objectives of IT initiatives and the barriers that stand in the way of successfully realising them, it is necessary to move on to analyse how investments in technology impact upon the operational activities – understood as the individual operations/services – of banks, so as to provide explanations of the empirical evidence regarding the previously measured technology/performance relationship. In this way, it will be possible in Section 6.5 to provide a comprehensive account of the nature of this relationship in terms of the factors which determine the impact that it has on the costs and revenues of banks.

If we consider the impact of technology on banking transactions, it is evident that in the last decades investments in technology have made it possible to increase operating cost efficiency and that, at the same time, they have influenced to an ever greater degree the evolution in the channels of distribution. Moreover, in recent years, investment in technology in banks has been progressively shifting away from the management of essential operational activities towards the improvement of internal business processes, the management of relations with customers and the quality of the products offered.

Before embarking upon an analysis of the impact of technology on the costs and revenues of banks, which will be dealt with in Section 6.5, it is necessary to indicate precisely which investments in technology impact positively on individual banking activities and which impact negatively.

6.4.1 Investments in IT which impact positively on banking activities

The following are among the investments in technology that have a positive impact on banking activities:

1) Investments aimed at reducing the unit costs of operations through the transformation of standardised activities with a high level of labour content and a low level of value added into computerised operations. Such a transformation implicitly involves an increase in productivity, in particular on the part of labour.

Among the banking activities where increases in labour productivity bring about clear benefits in terms of unit costs per operation are, in particular, those activities related to the provision of payment services (in the first place, bank cheques). The reduction in the costs of storage and labour has been rendered possible primarily by the use of imaging technology.[20] In fact, the banks used microfilm systems to store and recover bank cheques from 1928 to the mid-1990s. New imaging technology for cheques, which has replaced the previously used microfilm systems, has led to a reduction in storage and labour costs of about 40 per cent. Moreover, it has reduced the time needed to retrieve cheques by up to 70 per cent.[21] Such cost savings, moreover, could be extended if the banks put in place centralised and shared operations for storing and retrieving cheques.

2) The introduction of alternative channels of communication and delivery, which involve substantial savings in terms of costs. To be included in this category is the significant reduction in bank operating costs derived from the use of innovative technology for communication and delivery as well as of e-business channels. Considerable reductions in the unit costs of operations seem to be achievable, but the estimates offered by the relevant studies vary substantially (European Central Bank, 1999; McKinsey Global Institute, 2001; E-Business W@tch, 2002). According to the estimates provided by E-Business W@tch (2002), if the cost of an operation in a branch is one, this figure is halved by way of phone banking, it is reduced to one quarter by way of home banking and it is reduced to one sixth by way of Internet banking. According to the analysis provided by the European Central Bank (1999), if the cost of an operation performed by an employee in a branch is put at 100 units, the cost of the same operation by way of a call centre (with personnel present) varies between 40 and 70 units, the cost by way of an ATM varies between 28 and 40 units, the cost by way of

a (completely automated) call centre varies from 14 to 25 units and finally, the cost by way of Internet varies from 1 to 25 units. Referring specifically to the call centre channel in the United States banking industry, McKinsey Global Institute (2001) estimated that the banking industry has effected a substantial reduction in permanent staff by way of the use of call centres equipped with mechanisms for giving automatic responses (VRUs, Voice Response Units). In particular, in 1999, 55 per cent of the enquiries directed to bank call centres were dealt with by way of VRUs. If such technology had not been employed, McKinsey Global Institute (2001) estimated that the banks would have had to increase the number of staff in the call centres by as much as 86 per cent. This would have led to a decrease in the growth of labour productivity of about 1 per cent a year starting from the beginning of the 1990s, and it would have further accentuated the deceleration in productivity in the US banking industry in the period following 1995 (from 1.4 to 1.6 per cent). Such dramatic variations in cost structures show how the use of remote channels makes it possible to put in place aggressive pricing policies and strategic plans aimed at gaining market share by focusing attention on those customers who are prepared to switch banks on the condition that they are offered more competitive products.[22]

At this point, for reasons of methodological rigour, it is necessary to make explicit a very important qualification. The benefits – in terms of reduction in costs – associated with the use of technology are achievable only when the particular channel in question enjoys a very high level of traffic and operational activity. There is no doubt that the unit cost per operation is lower when recourse is made to remote channels as opposed to traditional operating procedures. However, the creation of virtual channels requires very high levels of investment in the initial phases. Such financial backing is provided by way of internal financial sources or by separate external sources. In these circumstances, the longer is the period of time necessary to reach the break-even point, the greater is the risk that the bank has to sustain.

6.4.2 Investments in IT which impact negatively on banking activities

In addition to the investments in IT that have a positive impact on individual banking activities, there are a number that have a negative impact:

1) A certain amount of excessive, or even unnecessary, investment in personal computers.[23] There are many reasons that induce staff to request personal computers: the management of information on customers, the support and automation of sales activity and even the need to obtain greater processing power and memory for the running of more powerful software. In actual fact, however, there is considerable evidence to suggest that the personal computers deployed in European banks have an excessive amount of processing power. It is thought that there are essentially two situations that lead to an over-investment in personal computers in the banking industry (McKinsey Global Institute, 2001).

First, conscious of the need to maintain and develop their computer resources, banks fix specific and predefined standards for the purchase of personal computers. Responsibility for determining such standards, however, is given to the skilled IT staff, who usually request personal computers that are very powerful. In this way, when the banks acquire what are established as the standard personal computers, the ordinary users end up having a lot more functional capacity than they really need. This mechanism has directly contributed to the rise in the processing capacity available to the banks, measured in terms of the stock of capital. On the other hand, this has probably contributed to reducing maintenance costs for the banks by increasing the capacity and skills of IT staff in terms of specialisation and the efficient resolution of common problems.

Secondly, it has been customary to establish only a limited number of rigorous controls in relation to the purchase of personal computers. In fact, decisions relating to purchase are typically taken at the level of the division/department, and the related costs are capitalised. This means that they are viewed as having minimal impact on the immediate revenues of the bank. In addition to this, the rapid decline in the price of personal computers has the effect in itself of making them appear relatively economical.

2) Some investments in software and hardware have not been able to generate the benefits that were expected of them in terms of profitability at least over the short term. In particular, in this category of investments in technology, it is possible to place investments that are oriented predominantly towards the realisation of improvements in the relations with customers and in quality, for example, projects like those involving CRM, the automation of sales and product innovation. The challenge that is inextricably bound up with such investments in technology presupposes the existence of a strategic and

cultural orientation on the part of the bank towards the customer, without which the initiative itself often ends in failure. Banks which do not have an approach oriented towards customers should not try to put in place such types of projects. CRM, in particular, should not be treated just as a mere sales instrument but rather as a vehicle for putting in place a competitive strategy that re-engineers the bank orienting it towards the customer (ABI, 2003; ABI and Università di Parma, 2003).

The acceptance of such a distinction between investments in technology – an orientation towards the reduction of costs or towards the maximisation of profitability – implies, above all, the assumption that the realisation of a monetary return on IT initiatives will be subject to varying time scales. In order that the related benefits be achieved, projects oriented towards revenues will require longer time lags than will projects aimed at reducing costs. In the second place, IT projects oriented towards revenues are characterised by additional implementation difficulties – in other words, the barriers to success that were identified empirically in Section 6.3, amongst which the following should be recalled:

a) lack of clarity in the focus and the objectives associated with the IT initiatives;
b) complexities and rigidities of an organisational nature and the consequent tendency to abandon IT projects, especially in the course of merger and acquisition operations;
c) costs associated with the management of unexpected complexities related to IT projects.

The first consideration derives from the fact that the majority of commercial banks have invested in IT projects oriented towards profitability – this is particularly so in respect of CRM projects – without conducting a comprehensive analysis of expected revenues and without specifying clearly what the objectives are. These omissions have resulted in a flawed process of selecting investments and, in turn, have led to an increase in the costs of realising projects – consequences which essentially account for the high rates of financial failure that up to now have been registered in relation to CRM initiatives.[24]

So far as the technical aspects of the projects are concerned, the banks have mainly concentrated their efforts on the creation of databases for collecting information, the implementation of analytical instruments for forecasting the behaviour of customers and the automation of sales and marketing functions. As of today, however, very few banks have developed the capacities and processes necessary for effectively using the existing information and tools.

The lack of clarity in the objectives of such investments in technology accounts for the failure of a large number of the projects to achieve the expected results in terms of revenues. This, in turn, accounts for the high rate of failure of CRM projects. In this regard, MetaGroup (1998)[25] estimated that CRM projects were subject to a worrying level of failure (55 to 75 per cent in the period in question),[26] even though such investments (when implemented correctly) were characterised by one of the highest levels of ROI (Return on Investment) in the entire banking context (higher even than that of projects like enterprise resource management and supply chain planning). The high failure level was basically due to the relative immaturity of the CRM applications market. Nonetheless, in a more recent study, Gartner (2002a) confirmed the original finding, even if adjusting it somewhat: in 2002, 40 per cent of firms that had already developed CRM solutions had reworked them in a substantial manner, placing emphasis on the balance between guaranteeing privacy and increasing the forms of customisation.

The second consideration derives from the fact that the commercial banks, which by their very nature are multi-channel and multi-product, face considerable organisational complexities when they realise investments in IT, especially if the investments are aimed at increasing customer loyalty and improving quality. The problems, in fact, are not merely of a technical nature but rather of an organisational nature. While different product lines may share and integrate data, they are still generally structured in an autonomous manner and with a view to pursuing their own objectives. Because of this it is difficult to develop an approach that is oriented towards the customer.

This consideration relating to complexities and rigidities of an organisational nature calls to the fore the enormous efforts of integration that are associated with the instruments for the automation of sales, IT initiatives in support of customers and sales and CRM projects.[27] The integration of new software and databases with the old systems inherited from the traditional architectures of the banks has required new interfaces and further changes in software, which, in turn, have increased the complexity of the systems in question as well as the development costs.

Moreover, the organisational complexity consequent upon the series of recent merger and acquisition operations has led to a re-evaluation, if not abandonment, of pre-existing investments in technology. Many banks involved in merger processes have been obliged to confront problems connected with decentralised systems, redundant data and non-standardised applications run on non-integrated platforms. In the context of such restraints of an organisational nature, there emerges a consideration of a financial character: on the one hand, the pre-existing but incomplete IT projects have consumed a substantial amount of IT capital but, on the other, they do not appear to offer any possibility of generating profit.

The third barrier, the high costs associated with the management of the unexpected complexities deriving from investments in technology, can be traced back essentially to the spread of product and pricing combinations as well as to multi-channel operational activity. The pursuit of these objectives – characterised by an ever-greater complexity – makes it necessary to make use of additional processing power so as to compensate for the reduction in performance. The complexity in the product/channel combinations also causes increases in the costs of maintenance and testing.[28]

3) The impossibility or, at any rate, the difficulty involved in measuring the benefits that are obtained by customers. In this context, it is necessary to consider those advantages that have already been noted as benefits for consumers of a purely soft nature and that have been identified as IT impacts (in this regard, see Section 4.3). Amongst these are increases in the quality of products and services, the greater convenience associated with non-traditional distribution channels, and the increase in the comprehensiveness and the quality of information.[29] Such IT impacts cannot be fully captured by traditional accounting methods (as has already been amply discussed). Indeed, it is from this that our interest in measuring correlation between IT investments and non-traditional measures of profitability and cost (X-efficiencies) arose.

In conclusion, the apparent predominance of the negative effects of IT investment on the operational activity of banks, as has emerged above, finds confirmation in a study by the McKinsey Global Institute (2001). In fact, in this study, which dealt with the problem of measuring the impact of IT investments on single banking activities, it emerges that, even if quality and convenience were valued at a maximum level or, in other words, even if IT impacts were included fully in the calculation, this would still not be sufficient to allow one to discount the existence of a productivity paradox in respect of the US banking industry.

This result stands as a preliminary confirmation – at the level of single banking activities – of the empirical evidence that has emerged from the present study or, in other words, of the existence of a negative relationship between investments in technology and profitability in European banks.[30] This makes it necessary to extend our enquiry into the impact of investment in technology on the components of costs and revenues.

6.5 Factors that determine the impact of investments in IT on costs and profitability of individual banking services/operations

In order to bring to a logical conclusion the analysis of the determinants of the relationships that have been identified between investment in technology, on the one hand, and costs and profits, on the other, it is necessary to analyse these features in more detail.

6.5.1 The impact on costs

Investment in technology in banks – as was discussed in Section 6.4 – has traditionally been associated with the possibility of obtaining significant reductions in the production costs of various banking services/operations. This has led analysts to forecast a reduction in total operating costs. Indeed, in this study, we have provided a clear empirical confirmation of this in relation to European banks over the medium-to-long term (see the estimates in relation to technical change provided in Chapter 5). In order to understand the objective of operational and structural factors underlying such a reduction in overall banking costs, it is interesting to examine the reasons that the banks themselves offer – these emerge in an enquiry conducted by the European Central Bank (1999) – for their expectation of reductions in the unit costs per transaction consequent upon the adoption of technology. It is necessary to appreciate at the outset that European banks expect that the adoption of technology will lead to a clear reduction in costs per operation in respect of all banking activities, in particular in respect of services relating to the retail securities business, retail (and wholesale) payment transactions and the retail deposit business. In this regard, Table 6.12 shows the European banks' medium-to-long-term expectations in relation to the production costs of individual banking services/operations: the figures shown do not represent expected reductions in costs in percentage terms but rather the intensity (from very intense to non-existent) of the expectations of cost reductions.

Table 6.12 The medium-to-long-term expectations of European banks in regard to the costs of various banking services/operations

Retail securities business	−2.79
Retail payment transactions	−2.31
Retail deposit business	−2.15
Wholesale payment transactions	−1.96
Retail lending business	−1.90
Money/asset management	−1.64
Insurance/administration of e-money	−1.62
Wholesale securities business	−1.27
Wholesale deposit business	−1.22
Wholesale lending business	−0.86
(Non-weighted) average value	−1.77

The table shows the expectations of the European banks in regard to the production costs of single banking operations/services over the medium-to-long term. The figures reported do not represent the expected reductions in cost in percentage terms but rather the intensity (from very intense to non-existent) of the expectations of cost reductions. The table also shows the (non-weighted) average value of the expectations. The figures presented in the table were obtained by means of the attribution of a positive or negative value to the expectation of a variation in costs: +, expectation of an increase in costs; and −, expectation of a reduction in costs. To each value in the range (4–0), there were attributed the following meanings: ±4 – very significant; ±3 – significant; ±2 – moderately significant; ±1 – slightly significant; 0 – neutral. The banks included in the study belonged to the following countries: Germany, Spain, France, Italy, the United Kingdom, Austria, Portugal, Finland, Sweden and Greece. *Source*: European Central Bank (1999).

By way of completing the framework of analysis of the (empirically verified) positive relationship between investments in technology and costs in European banking, we identify below various factors that determine that relationship. These include the following:

a) the lower overall cost associated with the automated – as opposed to labour-intensive – processing of banking services/operations resulting from the reduction in physical distribution networks and the consequent fall in the size of banks' labour force (European Central Bank, 1999);

b) the greater economies of scale made possible by the automated processing of transactions as opposed to the use of human labour, as well as the related savings in costs achieved by way of the centralisation of information collection and transaction processing functions (European Central Bank, 1999);

c) improvements of an organisational nature including the rationalisation of production and distribution structures and the standardisation of banking processes (European Central Bank, 1999);

d) improvements in the quality and convenience of the products/ services offered to customers (European Central Bank, 1999) including the greater ease of use and convenience of on-line distribution channels, the reduction in the time required to address customer requests, the comprehensiveness of the information provided and improvements in the use made of that information by customers and the customisation of the products offered in accordance with the particular needs of customers. In this way, in respect of Internet e-banking, the factors perceived by customers as more useful relate to the expectation of accuracy, security, velocity in the network, ease of use and involvement of the user (Liao and Cheung, 2002);

e) the offer of combinations of products, also by way of cross-selling of products provided by external suppliers (such as credit cards and insurance products), which allow the bank to benefit from economies of scope and, at the same time, to strengthen the loyalty of customers by means of an offer of products that is able to respond to their needs in a comprehensive manner (European Central Bank, 1999).

Although reductions in cost per transaction are indisputable in the medium-to-long term, there is greater doubt as to the effects on the total operating costs of banks in the short term, as is testified to by the non-uniformity of the direction of the relationship empirically verified in different countries (as explained in Section 4.6, the association between cost efficiency and IT investment is positive in France and the United Kingdom, but negative in Germany and Italy). It is apparent that the European banks are characterised by a kind of excessive optimism both in relation to the overall amount of the reduction in costs that is potentially achievable and in relation to the speed with which such cost savings may be realised. A careful, critical look at the relevant literature and actual banking practice suggests that this excessive optimism may be due to the following factors:

a) A relatively substantial volume (known as "critical mass") must be reached in order that total costs diminish in the areas of business where economies of scale are practicable (Ciocca, 2001). This consideration relates to activities where substantial initial investments (and maintenance costs) accompany low unit costs for the execution of single transactions, as, for example, in the handling of mass-scale payment services put in place through networks of computers. In this case, the estimate of the cost per operation does not include the fixed costs, and by default it is close to the average service cost. When the fixed costs tied to investments in IT are taken into consideration, the unit cost per operation depends very much on the number of clients. This accounts for the emphasis that the administrators and directors of virtual banks put on the magnitude of "the number of accounts managed", even at the cost of countenancing conditions that are not remunerative (Resti, 2001).

In regard to the achievement of a critical mass in relation to investments in technology, it is interesting to note that there is very little awareness of the overall size of the IT capital accumulated in previous years. Moreover, this is accompanied by a marked concentration of attention on the part of bank directors in the direction of the annual investments in technology (Keen, 1991; Willcocks, 1994). These errors in the evaluation of the dimensions of such investments lead to an inadequate management of the technology present in the bank (as well as a management that fails to fully exploit the potential available), a lack of attention to the evaluation and control of investments in IT and a very limited effort to identify how to make use of the existing IT in accordance with its full potential;

b) The full pursuit of cost savings may require the elimination of existing duplications, including, most importantly, redundant capabilities and obsolete functions. Such purely organisational exercises, which come to the fore particularly as a consequence of merger and acquisition operations, often require rather long-time lags to be brought to a conclusion;

c) Quite long-time lags have to be conceded to customers in order that they might modify their own behaviour in relation to everyday banking habits and, thereby, make greater use of the new distribution channels. This situation obliges banks to maintain some duplication in their distribution capacities for the various segments of their customers (European Central Bank, 1999). As Resti (2001) effectively pointed out, no financial group, even in the case that the decision was made to develop on-line banks through independent subsidiary banks, has taken into consideration the idea of dismantling in the short term its network of branches. Rather, their strategy has been to induce customers to shift towards automated channels that are typically repetitive and of low value added. It was thought that, once such a transfer had been effected, it would be possible to re-absorb excessive production capacity (dedicating it to commercial activity or simply dismantling it), thereby reducing the costs of branches. In many cases, however, the transactions conducted through the

Internet have not substituted those conducted in branches but rather have simply constituted additional work flows;[31]

d) The apparent strengthening of the quality, professionalism and skills of bank staff leads to increases in salaries[32] and greater opportunities for staff development and training (European Central Bank, 1999). There takes place a shift from activity of a strictly administrative nature towards the use of more highly qualified human resources capable of using more complex information systems in all the areas of activity in the bank. A further, related phenomenon that the banks have to confront takes the form of an increase in salaries, resulting from the need to avoid the so-called "brain drain" in favour of competitors. This involves an increase in the cost of existing personnel, even though the total cost of labour may fall as a result of a decrease in the number of employees.

e) Banks are often obliged to invest in the most recent versions of hardware and software, which in the initial phase of market introduction are generally offered at relatively high prices, or/and may have to contribute to the development costs of new software so as to be able to compete effectively in the IT-related areas.

f) The substantial costs that are tied to the marketing and affirmation of the trademark in the case of newly formed virtual banks (Resti, 2001). A single indicator can demonstrate these costs: expenditure in customer acquisition. As emerges in a study by Morgan Stanley DeanWitter (2000), the case of the big European virtual banks, whose success has been substantially based on very aggressive marketing and pricing policies, shows that expenditure in promotion (including bank accounts remunerated at a loss) primarily eats up net profits.

In demonstration of the empirical results presented previously, it appears that the banks may undergo a reduction in total costs prevalently in the medium-to-long term. So far as the short term is concerned, however, no such clear tendency is apparent. In fact, it seems that the main effect of investments in technology on banking costs can be identified in a reduction of the (variable) costs associated with the execution of payment services as well as with all the standardised mass operations. Associated with all this, however, is an increase in the fixed costs for maintaining relations with customers and the IT-based services themselves.

6.5.2 The impact on profitability

Having examined the factors that determine the impact of investments in technology on the costs of European banks, it is now necessary to investigate how investments in technology impact upon the generation of new revenue and, thus, upon profitability of individual banking activities/operations.

As emerges in the above-mentioned study in the European Central Bank (1999), many European banks expect that the major influence of IT investments in the medium-to-long term will be on the revenue rather than the cost side (Table 6.13). In keeping with the intuition that the effects of investment in IT are more marked in respect of retail sales than wholesale sales, the forecasts of increased profitability were generally believed to be higher for retail than for wholesale activity. Moreover, in line with what has already been observed for costs, the biggest increases in profitability were expected in respect of retail payment transactions, the retail securities business and the retail lending business. It seems reasonable to argue, then, that in respect of such areas of activity the expectations of increases in profitability were induced primarily by expectations of reductions in costs rather than increases in revenues. By contrast, the expectations relating to the retail deposit business were for a reduction in profitability, because it can be assumed that the customers

Table 6.13 The medium-to-long-term expectations of European banks in regard to the profitability of various banking services/operations

Retail payment transactions	+2.58
Retail securities business	+2.02
Retail lending business	+1.67
Wholesale payment transactions	+1.57
Money/asset management	+1.50
Off-balance sheet business	+1.08
Wholesale securities business	+1.05
Retail deposit business	+0.95
Wholesale deposit business	+0.65
Wholesale lending business	+0.63
(Non-weighted) average value	+2.06

The table shows the expectations of the European banks with regard to the profitability of single banking operations/services over the medium-to-long term. The figures reported do not represent the expected increases in profit in percentage terms but rather the intensity (from very intense to non-existent) of the expectations of increases in profit. The table also shows the (non-weighted) average value of the expectations. The figures presented in the table were obtained by means of the attribution of a positive or negative value to the expectation of a variation in profit: +, expectation of an increase in profit; −, expectation of a reduction in profit. To each value in the range (4–0), there were attributed the following meanings: ±4 – very significant; ±3 – significant; ±2 – moderately significant; ±1 – slightly significant; 0 – neutral. The banks included in the study belonged to the following countries: Germany, Spain, France, Italy, the United Kingdom, Austria, Portugal, Finland, Sweden and Greece. *Source*: European Central Bank (1999).

will have a greater opportunity to access alternative forms of deposits capable of offering higher returns. In regard to the optimistic expectations of increases in the profitability of European banks, it is necessary to make some qualifications. In particular, compared with the smaller banks, the larger banks tend to assume positions that are more cautious or even neutral. Possible explanations of these cautions are that larger banks are proportionately bigger spenders on IT, and also tend to be the market leaders.

Calling to mind the empirical evidence of a negative relationship over the short term between investment in technology and profitability performance measures expressed in terms of profitability and profit efficiency – something that makes it difficult to share the above-mentioned optimistic expectations in regard to the impact over the long term – logically, it becomes necessary to investigate the factors that might explain the negative direction of this relationship. In particular, from an operational and structural point of view the following factors appear to be the most important:

a) the increase in the degree of competition, which has characterised the European banking industry in the last decade, has induced the banks to think that the adoption of new technology is an essential requirement in order to maintain customers over the long term. If it were not so (i.e. if investments in technology were not put in place or were realised later than they were by other banks), it is assumed that the market position of the bank – both in the present and especially in the future – would be put in danger.

b) Although there is still no evidence of there having been any substantial diminution in the degree of loyalty shown by customers (recall the evidence provided at endnote 22: the average EU consumers have maintained their current account with the same bank for around 10 years), and although in respect of lending transactions about one-third of the market share of banks is due historically to established relationships with customers (Kim *et al.*, 2003), there are ever more frequent signals to the effect that the customers of banks are beginning to show a greater degree of mobility in their search for better offers on the market. For example, it is enough to think of the shift of a hypothetical potential client towards institutions that offer the possibility of adhering to mutual funds or other alternative forms of investment. In addition, in view of recent experience in the American and European financial systems, one might also reflect on how the level of competition between banks and non-banking financial institutions has considerably increased (Allen and Santomero, 2001), and how there is an expectation that over time there will be a further erosion of the lines of demarcation between financial and non-financial institutions;

c) The possibility of making use of remote channels (especially, e-banking) could erode the established competitive advantages of the banks that are linked to the existence of a physical network of branches. In fact, this characteristic has traditionally represented an extremely important barrier to entry – one which has had a range of important ramifications both in terms of the entry costs necessary to establish a distribution network and in terms of the pursuit of merger and acquisition policies that have made it possible to avoid the establishment of such a network. The emergence of multi-channel policies and the consequent spread of operational activity through remote channels would reduce the importance of the physical network of branches as a point of contact with customers and would thereby increase the opportunity to gain access to the industry (Padoa-Schioppa, 1999; Solans, 2002);

d) The increased competition could generate pressure to change the present policy of cross-subsidisation. This would result in a lower differentiation in price between the remote channels and the traditional channels (with the exception in some countries of Internet banking).[33] The trend should be towards pricing on the basis of costs and, at the same time, towards a diminution in the level of cross-subsidisation. If the new entrants in the form of e-banks were to gain significant market shares, the fact that they do not have to sustain costs connected to the physical network of branches leads one to suppose that the traditional banks would be obliged to apply differentiated prices so as to maintain their competitiveness.

e) High start-up costs mean that technology leaders – essentially identifiable as the category that is defined in institutional terms as e-banks – do not necessarily constitute the most profitable institutions (at least in the short term). One reason is due to the decision to amortise the implementation costs of the new IT infrastructure, applying only a low initial price or even no fees at all with a view to increasing the level of acceptance (as opposed to applying a high price to a small number of customers). Consequently, the specialised banks that offer their products and services only or prevalently through remote channels are not profitable in the initial years of activity on account of the high start-up costs and as a consequence of the impossibility of adopting policies of cross-subsidisation.

7
Conclusion

7.1 A framework for the investigation of the relationship between IT investments and bank performance

An enquiry into the relationship between IT investments and performance in respect of European banking is an exercise of particular interest because the banking industry is typically considered to involve an intensive use of technology. It is widely accepted that technological developments have had a major impact on re-shaping banks' front- and back-office operations and the relevant data bears this out clearly. In the first place, the banks represent the industry in the European economy that has the highest share of overall investment in IT. Moreover, this feature is characterised by a trend that is decidedly upward, and it seems that this will continue for a considerable time to come. Although various European countries are characterised by different levels of investment, the overall amount of investment in IT in the European banking industry doubled over the period between 1995 and 2005.

Nevertheless, there still remains some doubt as to whether the massive spending on IT by banks has positively influenced performance or productivity in the sector. In fact, there is some evidence that the so-called productivity paradox still exists in US banking – where IT appears to have had a negative impact on bank productivity. This evidence, however, contrasts with the demise of the productivity paradox for other industries in the US economy and, in particular, for those characterised by an intensive use of IT.

The existence of scarce empirical evidence on IT spending in banking and the surprising persistence of the productivity paradox in US banking provides the major motivation for this study which has attempted to shed some light on whether significant IT spending really boosts

European bank performance. At this end, we investigated the relationship between IT investments and performance in five European countries (France, Germany, Italy, Spain and the United Kingdom) during the 1990s. In particular, we have sought to provide answers to the following questions: How much does a given IT investment impact on accounting profitability in the short-to-medium time period? How much does it impact on costs and profit operating efficiency over the same period? And finally, how does it impact on costs over a longer time frame?

This book makes several contributions to the investigation of whether significant IT spending really boosts bank performance. First, it extends the scope of the established literature by examining at a cross-country level the experience of EU banking industries and IT investment during the 1990s to see if such spending has had an influence on performance. Although investment in IT is an important issue for banks throughout the world, as far as we are aware, up to now, there has not been any attempt to empirically examine the contribution it has made to profit performance and productivity in the European banking industry.

Furthermore, a second contribution relates to the fact that in the past an emphasis on the theory of production led to the use of quantitative models of a deterministic nature that centred on a relationship between the inputs of the production process (including technology) and the outputs of that process. The abandonment of such an approach has been rendered necessary by the scale and the variety of the phenomena in terms of how technology impacts on banks (e.g. via its influence on the quality of products and services, the multiplicity of delivery channels, customisation and the rationalisation of organisational processes). In this context, the conceptual space offered within the theory of strategic competition appears the most appropriate means by which to capture the qualitative component of the phenomenon and, thereby, evaluate the performance of IT investments in banking. In other words, we seek to investigate whether IT investments improve business performance (and not simply productivity, as traditionally investigated) and impact positively on organisational capabilities resulting in improved competitive advantage.

In addition, this study investigates the influence of IT spending on bank competitive advantage by considering various business performance measures other than financial ratios, which are the measures traditionally used in the established literature. In particular, we analyse the performance of banks using both traditional financial profitability measures (such as ROE and ROA) and a more advanced global measure of operational productivity – the so called X-efficiency (both cost and alternative profit efficiency) to investigate the influence of IT investments on EU bank performance. In fact, X-efficiencies make it possible to capture delays, errors and uncertainties in the decision-making process or, in other words, to measure the capacity of management to control costs (cost X-efficiencies) or to maximise profits (profit X-efficiencies). We argue that those are, in fact, better measures of the impact of IT (or improvements/deterioration in organisational capacities) as they take into account the quality and variety of the products and services offered, the speed and flexibility of delivery, the simplification of administrative processes, the productivity of labour and operational productivity in general. Thus, X-efficiencies are capable of capturing the degree to which technology impacts on operational productivity. As far as we are aware, these have never before been used for the measurement of the impact of IT investments.

Finally, in contrast with the previous approaches to measuring the influence of IT investments, in this book investments in technology have not been treated as a monolithic entity but rather have been broken down into various distinct components: hardware, software and IT services. In this way, it has been possible to take into account how the various components of overall investment in IT contribute in different ways to the creation of value in banks. Considering the investment figures for the various categories in the period 1995–2005, it has been noted that the average level of IT investment by European banks (expressed as a percentage of total investment in IT) stood at 24.60 per cent for hardware, 16.75 per cent for software and 58.65 per cent for IT services. The trend in this period clearly reveals an increase in the resources dedicated to IT services and a reduction in investment in hardware. The figure for software, on the other hand, was stable. The United Kingdom was the banking system with the highest proportion of resources destined to the acquisition of IT services (i.e. in respect of total investment in IT). Germany, on the other hand, has traditionally invested less in IT services and more in hardware.

7.2 The short-to-medium-term impact of investments in IT on bank performance

This study has provided a range of significant empirical results. As far as profit X-efficiencies are concerned, it is clear first of all that the evidence clearly confirm the existence of the profitability paradox: the impact of investments in IT was negative in respect of operational efficiency in terms of profit; profit X-efficiencies did not improve when investment in IT increased. Moreover, results confirm the finding of a negative relationship between IT investment and profit efficiency over time when we take into account assimilation, learning and adjustment factors. Finally, there is no causality bias: the Granger causality Wald test suggests the existence of unidirectional causality (i.e. increased IT investments cause a decline in profit efficiency, but increased profit efficiency does not cause a decrease in IT investments).

The previous findings emphasise that banks are not able to increase their revenues (by applying a price premium) despite the (presumed) greater quality of outputs produced (achieved thanks to an increase in investment in technology) for a given mix of inputs. In fact, the introduction of IT into European banking in the latter part of the 1990s does not seem to have been geared towards improving short-term profitability but rather towards meeting a broad range of other needs. In particular, it seems legitimate to characterise the banks as engaged in a strategic alignment of their information systems in response to competitive pressures and in accordance with a policy of maintaining customers and making them more loyal by way of improvements in the quality and the variety of the services offered. Moreover, it may well be that initiatives of this kind offer economic benefits that are indirect and that emerge over time. It becomes important not only to rationalise production by lowering unit costs but also to produce products and services when, how and where the market requires. In this way, there is a shift from the use of technology in keeping with a paradigm involving the rationalisation of productive processes to the use of technology in accordance with a paradigm privileging operational adequacy and the market. Thus, banks do not invest in technology so as to be able to apply a premium price. On the contrary, it seems that generally technology represents a strategic necessity as opposed to a variable capable of generating a competitive advantage over the short term. The adoption by the banks of information systems that are more and more expensive seems to be a structural component of the form of competition that exists in the industry. In short, these investments in technology seem increasingly to assume the form of attributes that are essential in order to enter the industry. If one adopts this assumption, it follows that the banks should seek to reduce the costs involved in the customisation of the technology, accepting that certain systems may function as standards for the industry and that these may be developed in conjunction with competing banks and shared with them. However, it is clear that, in the absence of a guiding body that operates in an impartial manner and at the national level, it will be very difficult to overcome the obstacles that stand in the way of developing joint IT projects and not least the obstacle represented by the supposed strategic importance that is traditionally attributed to technology as a factor in competitiveness.

From the perspective of the traditional accounting measures of profitability (ROE and ROA), the relationship between investment in IT and performance is not so clear and unambiguous, as suggested in previous studies. It is not possible to identify a unidirectional relationship – whether positive or negative – between technology spending and (contemporaneous and/or lagged) accounting profitability.

As far as the explanatory power of the models estimated is concerned, it is interesting to note the high value of the statistical parameter R^2 relating to profit efficiency. This indicates that variation in IT spending explains a large portion of the banks' variation in profit efficiency. Also, the explanatory power of our models that link IT spending to profit efficiency appears to be larger than compared to when traditional profitability measures are used. This suggests that investments in IT are not reflected in traditional accounting measures of profitability (ROE and ROA) to the same extent as far estimates of profit efficiency. From this point of view, too, then, the choice to use profit X-efficiencies as a measure of performance is appropriate: the empirical test bears out the arguments in relation to the superiority of this measure – in terms of its capacity to capture IT impacts – compared with traditional accounting measures.

In contrast to the situation relating to profitability, the IT performance paradox has not been confirmed with the same degree of clarity in relation to costs. In the short term, the impact of investments in IT on cost efficiency was not uniform and homogenous in respect of all the banking systems analysed. In the medium-to-long term, on the other hand, it is evident that there was a marked tendency for investments in IT to reduce costs.

In fact, the relationship between IT investment and short-to-medium-term cost efficiency was positive only in France and the United Kingdom (in relation to which it thus renders invalid the paradox). By contrast, in Germany and Italy it was negative. It is quite possible that improvements in efficiency as a result of cumulative investment in IT require an accumulation of competencies and extended periods of learning and adaptation as well as the realisation of a critical mass in the investments themselves. All of which, presumably, did not come about to the same extent in the various European banking systems.

7.3 The positive impact of technical change

Regarding the estimate of the reduction in total long-term costs attributable to technical change, we quantified the shifts in the efficient frontier attributable to technical change as measured by a time trend variable. However, this technique, which had traditionally been proposed for measuring the effects of IT on cost efficiency, needs to be used with caution because the time variable captures not only the effects of technological progress but also the effects produced by other factors such as environmental changes. It is apparent that overall technical change had a positive impact in the various European banking systems, facilitating a reduction in real production costs of about 3.1 per cent per annum. The United Kingdom and France are the two systems that experienced the biggest reductions – in the order of 3.5 per cent per year.

The impact of technical change on the systematic reduction of costs in European banks increased over time – from –2.5 per cent in 1993 to –3.9 per cent in 2000. Comparatively speaking, it was again the United Kingdom that benefited to the greatest extent from the effects of technical change. In fact, not only did technological change impact positively on the cost structure of British banks in a more marked manner than took place in other European countries but also this trend strengthened over the period 1993–2000. In contrast, the Spanish banking industry constantly experienced smaller cost improvements resulting from technical change compared to the European average.

The relationship between levels of technical change and the size of firms shows that cost reductions increased in tandem with bank size. We might well assume that this finding can be attributed to the phenomenon of IT downsizing (or, in other words, to the reduction in the average size of the processing systems which facilitate a reduction in the production costs of a given output), and this, in turn, possibly be traced back to the continual downward trend in the costs of IT processing power, known as Moore's Law.

Secondly, a very significant finding lies in the fact that in two countries (France and Germany) the biggest banks (the seventh class or, in other words, those with assets greater than $10,000 million) are characterised by highest levels of technical change. Contrarily, in two other countries (Italy and the United Kingdom), the same biggest banks are characterised by levels of technical change that are inferior to those of the sixth class: although the impact of investment in technology is positive (and generates a reduction in costs), the reduction is lower than that achieved by the banks included in the sixth class (those having assets between $2500 million and $9999 million). This finding may be explained in terms of the effects on investments in technology – in particular, on the human component of such investments – deriving from merger and acquisition operations that join together big banking groups in Italy and the United Kingdom.

7.4 The heterogeneous performance of hardware, software and IT services

The distinction between the various components of investment in technology (hardware, software and IT services) makes it possible to elaborate the previous findings. This is essential in order to explain how strategic choices relating to technology spending impact upon performance, and, in this way, useful information can be provided to managers responsible for IT investments. On the one hand, IT services provided by external suppliers impact positively on the profit efficiency of banks (and also on traditional accounting profitability). On the other hand, the acquisition of hardware and software has a negative influence on the profitability of banks.

A number of interesting considerations have emerged with respect to our study of the profitability paradox in the European banking industry. It appears that the paradox relates not to all the components of investment in technology but only to some. This seems to suggest that the opportunities associated with the purchase of hardware and software can be fully exploited when they take place in conjunction with the purchase of IT services from external providers. If one accepts the hypothesis that the potential of hardware and software investments can be exploited fully in conjunction with IT services, then the implication for information system managers is that an increase in the expenditure on IT services will lead to an increase in profitability and productivity. It goes without saying that such a finding should lead to an increase in the amount of resources allocated to IT services (as a percentage of the total amount of investment in technology), as has happened, for that matter, in recent years in the banking industries of all European countries and, in particular, in that of the United Kingdom. In this regard, however, it is necessary to note various qualifications. In the first place, there are certain technical relations between IT services and hardware and software components (some of which derive from the very nature of the components themselves and some of which are imposed by the suppliers) that basically oblige the banks to make certain decisions in relation to the composition of their IT portfolio. One obvious example is the relationship between systems of CRM (in their hardware and software components) and implementation services and operational services available through outsourcing. Another significant practice to take account of in this regard is that of bundling. Widely practised in the information systems industry, this consists in selling several IT products and services at a single price. In this way, the bank is constrained to purchase a range of IT products and services which is wider than what it needs. This places the bank in the position of being able to benefit from the so-called option value of the investment, in other words, the possibility of using certain IT components at a point subsequent to the initial acquisition without having to undergo any additional cost.

***

In conclusion, the strengthening of IT resources in banks is associated with cost savings over the long term. On the other hand, it seems that in the short-to-medium-term investment in technology has the potential to impact more positively on costs than on revenues. Thus, there are good reasons for believing that the principal effect of investment in technology takes the form of a reduction in the variable costs relating to mass standardised operations. This, however, is accompanied by an increase in the fixed costs relating to the promotion of client loyalty and the improvement in the quality of the products offered, factors, moreover, which are not easily transformed into profitability increases over the short term. Presumably, a number of factors are involved in impeding the transformation of technological innovations into profitability: scale issues, the habits of customers, the maintenance costs of various bank structures dedicated to particular client segments and costs associated with bank staff training and so on. Paradoxically, then, IT investment does not lead to improvements in profitability over the short-to-medium term in European banking but hopefully it should in the longer term.

Notes

1 Introduction: Banks and investment in IT

1. Note that in what follows we refer without distinction to "technology" and "information technology", not neglecting, however, to take full account of the fact that "information technology" represents a subset of the more extensive category of "technology", from which it inherits (and with which it shares) the properties we discuss below.
2. For example, as pointed out in Orlikowski (1992, p. 399), Perrow (1967) viewed organisations as environments in which the processes of production take place and, thus, defined as the "technology of organisations" the activities and very processes of transformation. Thompson (1967) characterised technology in terms of interdependencies between activities.
3. Note that for Orlikowski (1992), on the other hand, the scope of technology encompassed only the material artefacts: in the author's words, hardware and software.
4. This view is typical of early work in the field. The relevant literature is vast (as is extensively laid out by Markus and Robey, 1988): among others, see Perrow (1967) and Foster and Flynn (1984). An interesting confutation of the deterministic relationship between technology and organisation (as well as work) can be found in Butera (1990).
5. This view is put forward in a series of more recent studies, as pointed out in Orlikowski (1992): among others, see Bijker *et al.* (1987) and Hirschheim *et al.* (1987).
6. Without wishing to enter into a detailed analysis of the position advanced by Orlikowski (1992) – given that it falls outside the scope of this book – it might be noted, nonetheless, that the author considered both views to be incomplete and, as a consequence, proposed a reconceptualisation of technology, known as the structurational model of technology. Drawing on some of the fundamental principles of sociological theory (Giddens, 1984) or, more precisely, structuration theory, her reformulation makes provision for taking both views into consideration.
7. For example, while, on the one hand, it is easy to understand how users can make use of calculators to perform arithmetic calculations, obtaining more or less predictable and uniform results, on the other, different users will tend to 'interpret' and use in a personalised manner more sophisticated technology such as spreadsheets and Web pages. If users are in a position to be able to interpret technology freely (it is enough to think of the creation of an archive of clients by means of a spreadsheet), the results that emerge will be to a considerable extent unpredictable and inconsistent.
8. According to an hypothesis recently put forward in De Marco *et al.* (2003), it appears that the degree of interpretative flexibility in relation to technology – and, therefore, the difficulty of foreseeing its effects – is gradually increasing with the passing of time.

9. The literature in this regard is extensive and it unfolds in terms of the particular definition of technology that is adopted. Nonetheless, it is worth noting the following: from the objectivistic point of view, the concept of interdependence between separate organisational units (Thompson, 1967); from the phenomenological perspective, the concept of ambiguity (Gallino, 1983) or equivocation (Weick, 1990).

10. The theme of the ubiquity of technology has emerged in the international literature on information systems only in recent years (Lyytinen and Yoo, 2002), but its enormous importance and its extensive implications have been keenly felt for a long time.

11. The concept of the intensity of use of information was introduced by Porter and Millar (1985). The authors characterised the various degrees of intensity, making use of a matrix, in which the vertical axis represents the activities of the value chain in a given industry, while the horizontal axis represents the products of the industry. The scale for each axis is fixed on the basis of distinct values: the physical component, on the one hand, and, on the other, the information-processing component. So far as the activities of the value chain are concerned, an elevated information-processing component takes the form of the existence of a large number of clients, a wide range of products and services and a high level of informational interdependence between products and related processes. The informational component of the products, on the other hand, defined in a very general way, involves everything that the buyer has to know in order to be able to take possession of the product and to use it to obtain the desired result. In other words, the product includes information about its features and about how it should be used and supported. The authors concluded that the banking industry is located in the quadrant of the matrix where the information-processing component – as opposed to the physical component – assumes a dominant position in respect of both the dimensions (the products and the activities of the value chain).

12. It is known that the production and distribution processes of a great number of banking products (and services) are based on the use of technology. In addition, it should be recognised that the structure of the information system in a bank significantly conditions the types of products/services offered (as well as their features), the degree of customisation possible and the speed with which the banks can respond to competitive opportunities (or threats).

13. Note that this implication regarding the strategic use of technology in the banking industry has been fully allowed for by the central European monetary authority (European Central Bank, 1999). It has been acknowledged that the strategic use of technology has modified the competitive nature of the industry in accordance with the three modalities referred to. As well as being an extremely important component in the cost structure of banks, technology exerts a strong influence on strategies of differentiation and on the possibility of bringing into existence new forms of production and distribution. On the one hand, in fact, the adoption of automated procedures to substitute labour-intensive work methods based on paper documents has led to a reduction in the costs associated with the management (collection, storage, processing and transmission) of information. On the other, the development of remote delivery channels has resulted in a differentiation

in distribution policies (multi-channel delivery) or, rather, a change in the modalities by way of which bank customers access the products and services offered.

14. This position is advanced not only in the academic literature on the subject but also by the central European monetary authority (European Central Bank, 1999), as has been observed in the previous note.

15. There is a vast body of literature on this subject. Nonetheless, it is worth noting the following: ABI and Università di Parma (2003), Dedrick *et al.* (2002), Willcocks (1992), Hochstrasser and Griffiths (1991), Vowler (1990) and Kearney (1990). The research group co-ordinated by Munari observed that 41.4 per cent of the Italian banks that were active in the field of CRM (Customer Relationship Management. See Inset 1 in Chapter 6) declared that they had not managed to estimate the extent of the economic commitment they had made in the past or would have to make in the future and that 8.5 per cent did not provide an answer to the question posed (ABI, Università di Parma, 2003). Hochstrasser and Griffiths (1991) estimated that as much as 84 per cent of their sample did not use rigorous methods to evaluate the benefits of IT. Vowler (1990) indicated that 66 per cent of the organisations in the sample were characterised by limits in the way that they evaluated the benefits that IT brought to their activity.

16. The only exception is a recent empirical work – relating, moreover, just to the Italian banking industry – contained in "Temi di discussione della Banca d'Italia" (Casolaro and Gobbi, 2004).

17. We have chosen for the study a period of time analogous to that adopted in the recent research conducted in the field (for a review of works relating to the US economy, see, among others, Dedrick *et al.*, 2003; for a study on the Italian banking system, see Casolaro and Gobbi, 2004).

18. For reasons of methodological rigour, it should be noted that our interest in this book is not limited just to the empirical examination of the above-mentioned relationship, but extends to the development of a methodology capable of isolating the effect of IT investments on the performance of banks.

19. Note that the terms X-efficiencies and X-inefficiencies express the same concept and, in particular, that the value of X-inefficiencies represents one minus the percentage estimate of the X-efficiencies.

20. Among others, see Shin (2001), Tam (1998), Rai *et al.* (1997), Hitt and Brynjolfsson (1996), Barua *et al.* (1995), Ahituv and Giladi (1993), Dos Santos *et al.* (1993), Markus and Soh (1993), Weill (1992), Alpar and Kim (1990a,b) and Strassmann (1985, 1990).

21. In particular, see Williams and Gardener (2003), Berger and De Young (1997), Altunbas *et al.* (1999), Wagenvoort and Scure (1999), McKillop *et al.* (1996), Berger and Humphrey (1991), Humphrey (1993), Bauer *et al.* (1993) and Hunter and Timme (1991).

22. This concept was introduced into the literature on information systems by Sambamurthy and Zmud (1994). See Section 4.4.

23. As will be made clear in what follows, on the one hand, X-efficiencies make it possible to estimate a measure of productivity that takes account of the various inputs and outputs that form part of the production process and, on the other, they provide results that are more objective and all-inclusive (Berger and Humphrey, 1997; Thanassoulis *et al.*, 1996).

2   New strategic and structural tendencies in the European banking industry and investment in IT

1. The biggest operations in the relevant countries, listed in terms of the total value of the deal, were in descending order:

   - The merger of DG Bank and GZ Bank (Germany, 6.2 billion Euro).
   - The merger of Banca Intesa and Banca Commerciale Italiana (Italy, 3.6 billion Euro).
   - The creation of Eulia, the third biggest banking group in France, following upon an agreement between Caisse d'Epargne (CNCE) and Caisse des Dépots et Consignations (CDC) (France, 3.5 billion Euro).

2. The Cruickshank Report – a study sponsored by the Treasury Ministry in the United Kingdom – concluded that in 2000, problems relating to bank competitiveness had impacted negatively on the market in respect of money transfer services and retail services (HM Treasury, 2000). Similarly, the Dutch government body for the analysis of political economy pointed out that segments of the operational activity of the banking industry were characterised by rigid forms of oligopoly and that the competitiveness of the institutions tends to be limited (Canoy *et al.*, 2001).

3. This is especially so for those customers who value the qualities of spatial, temporal and procedural liberty that characterise the alternative distribution channels, in particular remote channels. The emergence of this preference is to be accounted for partly in terms of changes in income levels and the availability of time and partly in terms of the increasingly widespread use of personal computers and acceptance of the Internet on the part of bank clients belonging to younger generations.

4. By contrast, in Germany the number of branches has been falling considerably as a consequence of endeavours to reduce costs. In Spain, on the other hand, different trends are apparent in the various segments of the banking industry: while commercial banks have reduced the number of branches, savings banks have increased theirs (European Central Bank, 2002b).

5. Indeed, because of the difficulties that pure Internet banks are experiencing, some of them – by way of bringing their business to completion – are actually trying to set up a network of branches (European Central Bank, 2002b).

6. Such constraints involve an evaluation of the requirements of the market on the part of external authorities and a kind of centrally controlled strategic planning that artificially distorts the competitive forces operating in the industry.

7. In a multi-channel strategy, the three remote channels are more or less complementary, in that the bank offers its own customers the possibility of purchasing banking products and services by way of using various channels in accordance with the type of service/product offered, the time and place it is acquired/used and the cost attaching to it.

8. In reference to the Spanish banking industry over the period 1992–2000, it has been estimated that the combined passage from the use of physical networks of branches to the use of ATMs and from the use of paper-based payment instruments to the use of electronic ones allowed savings on unit operating costs of 45 per cent (on average). For the Spanish banking industry

as a whole this translated into cost savings in the order of 6 billion Euro (Carbo Valverde *et al.*, 2003).

9. As far as we are aware, there are no more recent estimates available on the spread of phone banking services at the European level.
10. On-line PC banking consists in enabling customers to perform banking transactions by way of using a personal computer (furnished with a modem) and making use of software provided by the bank. Internet banking, on the other hand, involves the use of Internet as an instrument through which customers can directly manage their own banking transactions. The software employed in the Internet banking channel is not memorised on the personal computer of the user (as in the case of on-line PC banking) but on the server of the bank.
11. It should be recognised that the definition given by E-Business W@tch (2003a) of on-line sales and on-line procurements needs to be specified – and this is by no means a simple exercise – in respect of the banking industry. In fact, the report, which was produced in relation to a range of industries, defines on-line sales as "the percentage of total sales that was effected through Internet or through other on-line distribution channels". On-line procurements, on the other hand, are represented in terms of "the percentage of banks that purchase goods and services on-line". In an effort to propose an adequate definition in respect of the banking industry, on-line sales are assumed to cover all the activities that are typically associated with e-banking or, more precisely, the direct sale of products or the offer of customer assistance services through the Internet channel or other on-line distribution channels. In particular, this definition includes standardised products and services such as savings accounts, on-line trading and payment services (in particular, bank transfers). On-line procurements, on the other hand, refer to any direct purchase by the bank that takes place on-line. This includes, among other things, the real-time connections with external providers by using Internet and Extranet (i.e. the transferring of data to archives managed by external providers). This enables banks to consistently reduce (up to 90 per cent) the costs associated to communication systems (telephone, fax, etc.) and to improve the workflow.
12. Similarly, in the United States there has been a switch from paper payments (checks and cash) to electronic payments (credit and debit cards) as argued by Berger (2003). In particular, between 1995 and 2000, in the United States the number of checks fell by an annual rate of 3.0 per cent, whereas the estimated credit card payments grew by an average annual rate of 7.3 per cent and debit card payments by an annual growth rate of 35.6 percent (Gerdens and Walton, 2002).
13. Humphrey *et al.* (2006) document that banking operating costs are US$32 billion lower in 1999 due to the shift to electronic payments (electronic giro and card transactions) from paper based payments (check and paper giro) and the expanded use of ATMs which permitted banks to conserve on building new branches. The estimated US$32 billions in cost saving is equal to 0.38 percent of the 1999 GDP of the 12 EU nations in their sample. As a result banks may have experienced a 7.8 per cent reduction in an indicator of their real average total (operating plus interest) cost.

14. The magnetic card has an adhesive magnetic band inserted onto its reverse side. The magnetic band contains information to identify the card and the user. Passing the card under a reader provides for the codification of that information.
15. The "chip and PIN" cards, known as "smart cards", incorporate a chip and a PIN (Personal Identification Number) for the confirmation of the identity of the holder. The system provides for the card to be inserted in a terminal and for the client to simply type in the PIN in the appropriate apparatus. There is no need to effect a signature: this reduces the responsibility of the staff involved in the transaction and increases the speed with which it is processed. A substantial reduction in the amount of fraud is expected to take place following upon the introduction of the "chip and PIN" cards. Europe leads the world in the introduction the "chip and PIN" technology, which has been based both for credit cards and for debit cards on the EMV standard (Europay/Mastercard/Visa).
16. It is worth pointing out, nonetheless, that at the level of the individual European country the same technology is generally used for credit and debit cards as well as for the systems dealing with information relating to transactions effected by way of credit and debit cards.
17. The term "e-money" refers to the use of electronic cards within the context of the Internet banking channel. Usually, a distinction is made between "e-money based on electronic cards" and "network e-money". E-money based on electronic cards represents value stored in credit or debit cards that makes provision for consumers to effect transactions that are generally of a limited amount. By contrast, network e-money refers to transactions conducted through networks, in particular the Internet (European Central Bank, 1999).
18. Policy debate among the principal operators in the industry is co-ordinated by Eurosystem, an organ of European origin that sees its statutory role as that of promoting harmony in the operational features of payment systems. Thus, the Eurosystem fulfils a fundamental role in the pursuit of efficiency and security in the use of e-money (European Central Bank, 2002a).
19. Credit card companies (Visa, Mastercard and others) have recently introduced "contactless cards" for purchases under $25 (The Economist, 2006). In less than 2 seconds, with a tap or a wave, these cards wirelessly beam data to a receiving device on the retailer's counter. Customers appreciate the reduction in queues enabled by the use of these cards, whereas retailers like the lower risk of theft associated to the fewer notes and coins to be banked each day.

3   Evaluating the performance of investments in IT: Reflections on the productivity and profitability paradox

1. It is worth noting, as evidenced in De Marco (1993), that in this same period the issue of the performance valuation of technology – in particular, the hardware component – attracted very little attention even in the classic texts on information systems that were calling for a justification of the use of very powerful hardware for the running of highly inefficient software (Lucas, 1985).

2. See the survey in Loveman (1994), where an outline is offered on numerous studies that provide empirical evidence in relation to the putatively negligible (or non-existent) benefits derived from investment in technology.

3. Gross marginal output is the additional output produced by the last Euro invested. This should be distinguished from average output, which is to be understood as the average for all the Euro invested.

4. Note that the net marginal productivity of technology should be zero, once all the related costs have been deducted.

5. In the original article Moore (1965) pointed out that the price of electronic data-processing technology decreases by about a half every 2 or 3 years. Since then, this relationship has been named Moore's Law – after the author himself, John Moore, who first documented the trend in relation to the microprocessors used in computers. Further studies are on information systems reiterates the same prediction in respect of the future trend in the cost of hardware (among other studies, see Gordon, 1987). In fact, over the last 35 years the cost (adjusted for quality) of computer hardware has decreased more than 6000 times compared with the price of equipment produced by industries other than the computer industry.

6. This follows directly from Porter (1980). In a competitive market without restrictions on entry, firms are not able to generate abnormal profits in the medium term, because the availability itself of such anomalous profits induces other firms to enter the market, provoking as a consequence a fall in prices. Although there may well exist the possibility of realising an unusually high profit in the short term, the overall profit in the long term will only be sufficient to cover the cost of capital and to compensate the providers of all the inputs used in the production process (including, for example, the providers of managerial expertise).

7. A barrier to entry can be defined broadly as any circumstance that permits firms to realise abnormal profits, like patents, economies of scale, expenditure in research and development, product differentiation or favoured access to limited resources (Bain, 1956).

8. Amongst the other works originally proposed, see Baily and Chakrabarti (1988) and Osterman (1986).

9. For studies on the relationship between productivity and technology in the services sector, see Cron and Sobol (1983), Strassmann (1990), Harris and Katz (1989), Brynjolfsson and Hitt (1993) and Noyelle (1990).

10. The author was well aware, given conventional hypotheses on rates of productivity, that very substantial variations in the amount of capital are necessary in order for there to be any significant impact on total production.

11. In relation to this, Alpar and Kim (1990a,b) argue that under the accounting ratio approach there is no basis to assume that the results of one year could be generalised for a longer time period. Instead, especially in the case of large and strategic IT investments, one would expect that benefits of IT investments accrue over a longer time period.

12. Brynjolfsson, 1993, p. 67.

13. It would appear that even in terms of an optimal model of investment strategy, short-term marginal costs may be higher than short-term marginal benefits as a consequence of the effect – among others – of the phenomenon known as "learning by doing".

14. By measurement on a short-term basis we mean that the benefits of IT investment are measured in the same period in which the investment itself takes
place.
15. Note that in another study Brynjolfsson *et al.* (1994) stated – on the basis of
an empirically grounded econometric model – that time lags of at least 2–3
years are necessary in order for technology to impact on organisations in a
significant way.
16. In the author's words: "IT rearranges the shares of the pie without making it
any bigger" (Brynjolfsson, 1993, p. 75). This line of argument is supported by
the following possible explanations of the effects of redistribution associated
with IT investments. First of all, information, more than other goods, is liable
to the dissipation of returns, or, in other words, the gains of one firm take
place at the expense of other firms rather than through the creation of new
wealth. Knowledge in advance about demand, supply or other circumstances
that impact upon asset pricing can be very profitable at the level of individual
firms, without, however, contributing to increasing total output. Secondly, IT
can be used to a disproportionate extent for marketing and market research –
both activities that may generate extremely positive results for the individual
firm but which do not contribute to total output.
17. From this point of view it is highly likely that investments in technology
are best seen as a public good whose benefits are enjoyed by the whole
community.
18. The book value of technology is given by the cumulated value of the assets
constituting the technology as expressed in the balance sheet and by the
cost of the technology as expressed in the income statement.
19. By way of example, a productivity index expressed in terms of revenues in
respect of the total number of employees does not take into consideration
other inputs in the production process. Another productivity index, like total
revenues on total costs, is not capable of distinguishing between the impacts
on productivity of various inputs and outputs.
20. The estimate of this type of inefficiency is essentially based on the measure of
the distance between the position of each firm and the efficient production
frontier (among others, see Beccalli, 2001, 2004).
21. In recent research (Berger *et al.*, 1993; Bauer *et al.*, 1993) it has been estimated
that X-inefficiencies may be equivalent in value to as much as four times
that of inefficiencies of scale and scope. In particular, the overview shows
that, when parametric techniques are used, X-inefficiencies account for 20
per cent of costs. When non-parametric approaches are adopted, the figures
vary from between 10 and 50 per cent (or more).
22. With the exception of the banks, as will be detailed in Section 3.6.
23. Note that performance is defined as the growth in the productivity of labour,
expressed as the average annual percentage variation in value added in relation to each full-time employee (Council of Economic Advisors, 2001).

4 The evaluation of the performance of IT investments: An empirical analysis of the European banking industry

1. See Section 3.6, where this is discussed extensively.

2. There is also the further problem of actually identifying the particular variables that represent the various activities involved in the production process in banking. This is a difficulty that is no less present in the studies dealing with the banking industry in the United States.
3. The methodology and main results of this chapter are taken from Beccalli (2007).
4. See the discussion in Section 3.4.3.
5. We are well aware, as pointed out clearly by Brynjolfsson (1993), that it may take a number of years for the benefits deriving from some forms of IT investment to assume significant dimensions in financial terms. Our reference to the theory of strategic competition, however, requires that we consider the short-term effects, as is demonstrated by the studies relating to the US economy over recent years (among others, see Hitt and Brynjolfsson, 1996; Rai *et al.*, 1997).
6. In the model proposed by Soh and Markus (1995), relating to the ways that technology creates value, IT impacts essentially constitute the third phase of a three-stage process through which investments in technology are transformed into positive payoffs for the company (note that IT conversion and appropriate use constitute the first two stages, as is specified in Note 7). In our view, the acceptance of such a phase necessarily implies the use of a measure of performance for the firm as a whole.
7. In terms of what was discussed in Note 6 in reference to the model proposed by Soh and Markus (1995) in relation to the ways that technology creates value, IT conversion and appropriate use constitute, respectively, the first and the second stages of the model.
8. ROA is algebraically correlated to Economic Value Added (EVA), a concept that has been attracting increasing interest on the part of the managerial community (as is evident from Tully, 1993; Fiordelisi and Molyneux, 2006a,b).
9. In fact, as has already been explained in Section 3.4.3, in the macroeconomic literature the term X-inefficiencies is deliberately generic, because it is simpler to define X-inefficiencies in terms of what they are *not* (distance, error, delay, disturbance, etc.) than it is to identify them positively (cf., for example, Resti, 1997a,b).
10. In this regard, Tirole (1988) points out a range of factors resulting in the large gap between a situation involving perfect rationality and reality. In large-scale organisation (such as financial institutions tend to be), the causes of the gap involve the following: (1) delays and errors in communication constraining the regular flow of information from the higher echelons to the lower; (2) the inertia of actors in their reactions to external changes, taking the form of delays in the adoption of new technology or in the innovation processes; (3) a falloff in the commitment to objectives passing from the upper echelons to the lower as a result of problems in the principal-agent problem (Jensen and Meckling, 1976); (4) increases in execution times and deterioration in the quality of the information transmitted (in proportion to the increase in the distance between actors responsible for making decisions and those who execute the decisions); and (5) forms of rationality that are different from that aiming at the maximisation of profit and that correspond,

instead, to the strategic behaviours of the various actors operating within the organisation (once again, as a consequence of the principal-agent problem).

11. In fact, in his original contribution to the debate, Leibenstein (1966) noted that the actors of organisations generally do not work as efficiently (or as much) as they could. Reciprocal adjustments to interpretative processes on the part of different actors – which inhere to the organisational structure as a whole and to mechanisms of integration – determine a situation of equilibrium for the firm.

12. In the evolution of Leibenstein's (1980) theorisation, the situation of equilibrium of a firm "may arise for reasons outside the knowledge or the capability of managers attempting to do the management. It may arise for reasons entirely outside the firm, or for reason having to do with choices made by employees who are not themselves managers." For an organisational re-interpretation of the economic theorisation proposed by Leibenstein, refer to Ciborra (1990).

13. The two overall classes of measurement approaches are:

    A) Parametric approaches, including (1) the Stochastic Frontier Approach (SFA), also known as the Econometric Frontier Approach; (2) the Distribution Free Approach (DFA); and (3) the Thick Frontier Approach (TFA);
    B) Non-parametric approaches, including (1) Data Development Analysis (DEA); and (2) Free Disposal Hull (FDH).

    Following Berger and Mester (1997), we have preferred to choose a parametric approach – as opposed to a non-parametric approach – because it is particularly effective in representing the concepts of cost and profit efficiency. Non-parametric methods do not generally take account of prices. Thus, on the one hand, they take account only of technical efficiency (ignoring allocative efficiency) and, on the other, do not make it possible to compare banks that are inclined to specialise in different inputs and outputs (given that the comparison of different inputs and outputs requires recourse to relative prices).

    See Berger and Mester (1997) and Beccalli (2001) for an overview of the main methods that characterise parametric and non-parametric approaches.

14. Again, there is no agreement in the literature as to what is the best technique to use, but this method has been the most frequently used in the empirical studies on banks (cf. Berger and Humphrey, 1997).

15. Note, however, that in the literature various hypotheses have been formulated and employed in relation to this assumption (for greater detail, see Coelli *et al.*, 1998).

16. The econometric software package used in this study was FRONTIER Version 4.1 (Coelli, 1992, 1996).

17. In particular, v_i is assumed to be distributed as two-sided normal with zero mean and variance σ^2, while u_i is assumed to be distributed as a truncated normal.

18. The 1992 Battese and Coelli model, as illustrated in Coelli (1996), makes use of the parameterisation of Battese and Corra (1977), where σ_v^2 and σ_u^2 are replaced by $\sigma^2 = \sigma_v^2 + \sigma_u^2$ and $\gamma = \frac{\sigma_u^2}{\sigma_v^2 + \sigma_u^2}$. The parameter γ, lying between

0 and 1, can be searched to provide a good starting value for the iterative maximisation process used (Coelli, 1996). See Resti (1997a) for an illustration of the benefits associated with this model.

19. The utility of the concept of alternative profit efficiency is evident in the following cases (Berger and Mester, 1997): (1) a highly differentiated and not easily measurable quality of financial services; (2) outputs that are not completely variable or, in other words, banks that are not capable of producing a full range of output scales and mixes; (3) non-perfect competition in the market of the outputs: banks having a certain power to fix production prices; and (4) output prices that are not measured accurately.

20. The main functional forms proposed in the literature are the following: the Cobb-Douglas, the Constant Elasticity of Substitution, the Transcendental Logarithmic (known as translog) and the Fourier flexible. For the relevant literature, see Berger and Mester, 1997.

21. Cf., for example, Gallant, 1981, 1982; McAllister and McManus, 1993; Mitchell and Onvural, 1996; Berger and DeYoung, 1997; Berger *et al.*, 1997; Berger and Humphrey, 1997; Berger and Mester, 1997; Berger and Mester, 1999; Altunbas *et al.*, 2000; Berger and Mester, 2001.

22. Note that an estimate has also been made of the sensibility to the form of the distribution, by way of including the third-order trigonometric term.

23. Likewise, Mitchell and Onvural (1996) did not impose restrictions on the trigonometric coefficients of the input prices for reasons connected with the complexity of the calculation. Support for such an approach also comes from Gallant (1982), whose results show that the exclusion of these restrictions should not prevent a cost function estimated by way of a Fourier flexible from correctly approximating the true cost function of a bank.

24. In keeping with the hypothesis advanced in Note 23, the variable relating to financial capital (E) is not included in the Fourier terms. Nonetheless, in this analysis, in order to test the robustness of the model, we have included the adjusted values of the natural logarithm of the output variables ($\ln Q_i$) and of the natural logarithm of the financial capital coefficient ($\ln E$) in keeping with what was proposed in Altunbas *et al.* (2001). The two models provide consistent empirical results.

25. In regard to the different positions taken in the debate dealing with the specification of the productive process in banks, see the more recent literature in general (Cossutta *et al.*, 1988; Molyneux *et al.*, 1996; Goddard *et al.*, 2001).

26. One of the main difficulties in the application of the model relates to the impossibility of attributing null values to the outputs of the function. The existence of null values corresponding to some of the activities exercised, however, is an important element of differentiation between banks. We have sought to resolve this problem by substituting the null values with a small positive value (equal to 1).

27. For a more extensive discussion, see Section 4.4.2.4.

28. For an overview of the studies in question, cf. Berger and Humphrey (1997), where an analysis is presented of the frequency of distribution in respect of 131 average values of efficiency relating to the banks of 14 non-US countries.

29. One of the first studies to examine the banking industries of a range of countries from a comparative perspective – though just with reference to the Scandinavian countries and using a parametric approach – is to be attributed

to Berg *et al.* (1993). The literature dealing with single countries – characterised by the use of non-parametric approaches – is vast. In this regard, see Pastor *et al.* (1997) (for Spain) and Drake and Howcroft (1994) (for the United Kingdom).

Even though Resti (1997b) points out that parametric and non-parametric approaches provide similar estimates of efficiency, only a few studies use a stochastic cost frontier for comparisons between the different European banking industries: Dietsch and Weill (1998) and Altunbas *et al.* (2001). Thus, as well as providing a test of the profitability paradox on the basis of this index of operating productivity, our study fills a gap in the literature on productivity as a whole. In the treatment of the existing literature, the reference to Altunbas *et al.* (2001), then, is inevitable, in that it constitutes the most recent study in the field.

30. Note that the empirical analysis of the relationship between IT investments and performance is then restricted to the period 1995–2000, for consistency with previous studies on the US banking industry.

31. The methodology followed by IDC makes it possible to produce estimates of a supply-side nature or, in other words, on the basis of information relating to the turnover of the vendors of IT products (classified in terms of hardware, software and IT services) in respect of each country at an international level. Subsequently, these estimates are broken down in terms of the various industries of the economy on the basis of information of a statistical nature (the contribution of each industry to gross national product or the number of employees in the industry) or of investigations conducted within IDC (dealing with issues such as, for example, the priority given to the acquisition of IT by the various industries).

    Note that the methodology that CIPA, the Information Services and Data Elaboration Unit of the Bank of Italy, uses to measure the costs of and investment in IT differs from that of IDC. In fact, each year CIPA conducts a "Survey of the state of automation in the credit system" (Rilevazione dello stato dell'automazione del sistema creditizio) on a sample of Italian banks adhering to the Convention. In particular, data is collected in relation to "costs" and "investments" attaching to the EDP (Electronic Data Processing) department. These are divided into the following categories: hardware, software acquired externally, the cost of permanent EDP staff belonging to the EDP department, the cost of permanent EDP staff external to the EDP department, the cost of training EDP staff, the cost of services performed by third parties and miscellaneous costs.

32. It follows from this that the accounting distinction between expenditure and investment is not relevant in this context. Thus, we refer to "investment in IT" and "IT expenditure" without distinction, keeping in mind, though, that from an accounting point of view the two categories are clearly separate.

33. One measure of investment in technology that is commonly used (cf. Hitt and Brynjolfsson, 1996) is made up of just two components. The first of these is computer capital or, in other words, the value of the central processors and personal computers owned by a firm. The second is the work force dedicated to IS (Information Systems) or, more precisely, the portion of total labour

costs accounted for in the IS budget. This results in the following:

$$\text{IT Capital} = \text{Computer capital} + (3 \times \text{IS Labour}) \qquad (4.17)$$

where the factor of 3 represents the usability period of the good created by IS Labour.

34. The following are some examples of information access tools: spread sheets, Executive Information Systems (EIS) and statistics. Programmer development tools include database engines and AMD (Analysis, Modelling and Design).

35. Examples of consulting services tied to IT include the evaluation IS organisation of the help desk of an organisation as well as the examination of the technology that is best able to help a firm to deal with the processing of its orders. IT consulting can also relate to specific IT products: advice on how to incorporate a new software product into an existing operating system or the evaluation of the performance of a network and the fine-tuning of the equipment for accessing it.

36. Examples of these implementation services include the creation of the prototype of a new system before starting the installation and the configuration of the features of a new software package.

37. For example, the installation of a single PC is to be considered as a standalone installation service. On the other hand, a system integration project involving the construction of a new data-processing centre requires a series of implementation activities such as the preparation of the site, the installation of new equipment and software applications, the development of new interface drivers, the testing of the system, the documentation of the final configuration and the management of the entire project.

38. The activities specifically included in the category of operating services are the following: help desk management, outsourcing, asset management services, systems management, network management, software update management, information systems outsourcing, processing services, backup, archiving and business recovery services.

39. Staff development and training services can be provided by way of an instructor in a class or through indirect methods (such as Internet, satellite-based communication or use of educational software). The content of the initiatives may relate to specific technologies or to the ways in which to make better use of IT.

40. Many of the activities included in this category are considered as "traditional services", because the suppliers of the IT products have traditionally had to supply a certain level of assistance to their customers in critical and problematic situations. The use of packaged software has added a new meaning to this category of services.

41. Note that an interesting development in this same direction is represented by the breakdown of the macro-categories of IT investment (hardware, software and IT services) themselves into their own components with a view to measuring their relation to performance in an even more precise manner. In this case, the interest lies in an examination of the so-called "portfolio of IT investments" (McFarlan, 1981). This intuition was originally proposed by Weill (1992), where investments in IT are classified in terms of three categories on the basis of the objectives of management: "Transitional IT",

aimed at minimising costs, "Strategic IT", geared towards the achievement of competitive advantage and an increase in market share, and "Informational IT", aimed at providing the informational infrastructure necessary to manage a firm and realise management objectives different to the two previously mentioned ones. Amongst the other analytical studies on this subject, it is worth mentioning the following: Gurbaxani *et al.* (1998), where a subdivision of the hardware category is proposed, Lucas (1993) and Strassmann (1990).

42. Total costs include personnel expenses, operating costs, total administrative costs and interest expenses. Operating costs include total operating (non interest) expenses and total administrative costs. Although the ratio of IT to operating costs has not been used in previous IT studies, we believe this ratio may be informative, and we calculated it.

43. Note that a similar estimate is proposed by CIPA (2002) in its "Survey of the state of automation in the credit system" (Rilevazione dello stato dell'automazione del sistema creditizio), where for the Italian banks the percentage of expenditure in technology on operating costs is estimated at 9% (Ciocca, 2001; Casolaro and Gobbi, 2004).

44. An even more marked situation is apparent in the case of the US banks, where IT investments represent 15% of general operating costs (Hitt *et al.*, 1999).

45. Note that the coefficient of the linear regression between profit efficiency and investment in IT (as the independent variable) is always negative, though not significant.

46. This follows from what Butera (1990) argued in relation to the affirmation of the model of an "economy of flexibility": management, formerly based on production, is centred more and more on the market and, as such, it is compelled to accept the variability of demand and the consequent product variety that this brings about.

47. CRIF is an international group specialising in the design, development and management of information solutions, decision-making models, outsourcing, software and consulting services in support of banks and financial firms operating in retail credit markets. Founded in Bologna in 1988 and today present in a large number of European countries as well as in the United States, Gruppo CRIF numbers over 440 adherents (banking and financial institutions). Each day 85% of bank branches in Italy make on-line contact with CRIF. EURISC – the CRIF credit information system – manages over 51 million credit standings, monitors much of the Italian retail credit market and maintains contact with the credit referencing of the major European countries (creating the network Key Factor).

    CDB Software INC., founded in Texas in 1985, is an international group that provides solutions in the emerging market of database systems management. The solutions in question make it possible to completely automate the DB2 environment (the IBM database platform) with a view to increasing its ease of use and cost efficacy (the reduction of CPU and processing times and the automation of routine functions).

48. On the basis of the theory of strategic competition (which is the perspective that from a theoretical point of view justifies the methodology adopted here), the lack of a relationship between investment in IT and accounting

measures of profitability is consistent with – and confirms – what has been sustained by way of the extension of the theory on competitive advantage to investment in technology or, more particularly, that the impact of technology on barriers to entry is unambiguous. As already argued in Section 3.2.1, the only situation in which technology (or any other input) makes it possible to achieve abnormal profit is where there exist barriers to entry into the industry. In particular, the theory of strategic competition does not enable us to predict in a clear manner the impact of technology on the barriers to entry in a given industry and, therefore, is not capable of identifying a mono-directional relationship – positive or negative – between technology and accounting profitability. Thus, our analysis confirms the hypothesis that technology is not correlated with abnormal profits.

49. It should be noted that this result leads us to hypothesise a case of inadequate accounting definition which, however, strictly speaking, cannot be inferred from the proposed interpretative model.

50. In particular, regarding ROE in respect of the IT ratio to total costs, the banking industry in the United Kingdom was characterised by values that, in respect of those pertaining to the other national industries, were lower to the following degrees: Germany, -14.80%; France, -13.70%; Italy, -13.30%; and Spain, -7.04%. So far as cost efficiency is concerned, given the coefficient for the United Kingdom as a benchmark, the highest values for the other European banking industries were as follows: Italy, $+22.7\%$; Germany, $+18.4\%$; Spain, $+10.4\%$; and France, $+6.91\%$.

51. It is interesting to note that the value of R^2 in the model that employs ROA as the dependent variable and the absolute values of the three IT components actually rises up to 80 per cent.

52. Note, moreover, that in respect of the entire sample on an aggregate basis, the sign of the correlation between ROA and the IT ratios is negative and statistically significant, while the sign of the correlation between ROE and IT investment is positive and statistically significant.

5 Technical change in the European banking industry: methodological problems and empirical results

1. For an overview of the principal technological applications – understood as milestones of technical change – that have been developed since the 1950s, see the survey by De Marco *et al.* (2003).

2. Even though the variable T may seem of little importance in the measurement of technical change, this methodology is the only one employed in the banking literature to quantify the phenomenon in question. It is for this reason that we are interested in developing an alternative methodology – as outlined in the previous chapter – that, on the one hand, integrates the models used in the literature on information systems and, on the other, gears those models in accordance with the specific characteristics of banks so as to isolate the effects of investments in IT on performance.

3. The Thick Frontier Approach (TFA) assumes that deviations from predicted performance values – within the highest and lowest performance quartiles of firms in a size class – represent random error, while deviations in predicted

performance between the highest and the lowest quartiles constitute inefficiencies (Berger and Humphrey, 1991, 1992; Berger, 1993; Bauer and Hancock,
1993).

4. Note, however, that in the measurement of technical change we do not adjust
   for quality.
5. In the study by Altunbas *et al.* (1999) the sample relates to the period 1989–
   1996.
6. For reasons of methodological rigour, it should be noted that this figure seems
   to be coloured by the presence in London of various international banks.
7. As Due (1992, p. 65) puts it: "Downsizing, in the IS world, is usually the
   movement of applications and data from mainframes to minicomputer or
   microcomputer hardware."

6 Possible explanations of the productivity and profitability paradox in the European banking industry

1. Note that this categorisation corresponds to what Weill (1992) proposed.
2. As far as we know, this database constitutes the only source of data at the
   European level on issues relating to technology. We thank the London School
   of Economics and Political Science for making it available for consultation.
3. Note that this study on the objectives associated with investment in IT
   deals with the same period as that taken into consideration in the empirical
   research on the evaluation of technology reported in the previous chapters.
4. Unfortunately, data on Italy and Spain is not available – the banking industries of these two countries not being included in the data set provided by
   Eurostat (2000).
5. In the first place, it is necessary to consider the nature of the reasons that
   underlie such a strategic orientation. As pointed out clearly in a study by
   Gartner (2001), firms that have reached the objective of securing customer
   loyalty are in a position to achieve a higher level of profit – up to 60 per cent –
   than their competitors and can even surpass the forecasts of financial analysts
   by as much as two times. This strongly suggests that, generally speaking,
   the achievement of customer loyalty is a highly desirable objective. By the
   same token, a subsequent study by Gartner (2002b) revealed that only 46
   per cent of customers declared that they were satisfied with the services they
   received, even though 70 per cent of the relevant firms believed that they
   had a customer service centre that was well organised and able to provide
   good service to customers. In the face of such data, it would appear that
   in regard to the realisation of the strategic objective of achieving customer
   loyalty there is a marked discrepancy between the perceptions of the firms
   providing services and the customers themselves.
6. Similarly in the United States, as of March 2002, there were 20 Internet-only
   banks and thrifts and approximately a dozen other such institutions have
   failed, been acquired or voluntarily liquidated (Berger, 2003).
7. In regard to the "bricks and mortar" banks which implement Internet
   banking, it is necessary to recognise two distinct situations: internal development and complete outsourcing (Prometeia, 2001). "In the first case investment costs take the form of costs relating to the evaluation and choice of the

suppliers of hardware and software, the costs of the purchase of such items, the costs of the internal development of the software and the costs of the installation, testing, customisation and checking of the system. Investment in Internet banking involves a further series of costs of an organisational nature such as those relating to the possible employment of new staff or the redeployment of existing staff or, indeed, to an overall reduction of staff in general. Finally, not to be forgotten are the costs relating to the redesign of the organisational structure (sales network) and, in consequence of this, those further costs relating to marketing and consultation with customers.

In the second case (outsourcing), it is necessary to consider the costs relating to the choice of supplier, the costs of the technology itself and the costs relating to the contract. The costs of an organisational nature are similar to those of the first case.

So far as management costs are concerned, it is again necessary to distinguish between the two cases. In regard to internal management, the major costs relate to the following: the Internet connection, the external communications infrastructure, the information security certification, the updating of the Website, the customer help desk, the employment of IT staff and the maintenance of the systems. In the case of outsourcing, the management costs consist in the following: fees paid to service providers, the costs involved in the information security certification and the costs relating to the staff of branches charged with providing assistance to customers" (Prometeia, 2001, p. 85).
   8. It is interesting to note that in the United States, a few large banks set up Internet units, and then integrated them into the main bank after poor performance (Berger, 2003).
   9. It should also be noted that this study dealt with e-business initiatives in 15 different industries in Europe and that the forecasts for future expenditure in relation to e-banking were amongst the highest that were identified.
  10. As Filotto effectively put it in E-Business W@tch (2003b, p. 4): "At the very beginning it looked like the bank's Promised Land: the burden of costly and often inefficient branches was gone or at least could be progressively eased. The Internet could combine richness of content, full availability of service, low cost services, new products, new profitable customers and markets. Yes, of course, some [huge] investments had to be made but nobody expected a free lunch. What is left now? The trading on-line frenzy of the second half of the nineties is gone and with it the only real source of revenues for all the e-finance activities. So, not only was there no free lunch in the beginning, but it looks like banks have invited everybody out for dinner. One striking point arising from the E-Business W@tch statistics: the financial industry has an overall digitalisation and e-Business intensity that compares with and often outperforms that of many other industries; but then, when it comes down to the real thing, to selling on line, well, things turn gloomy. The impact on sales and thus on revenues of the internet is still extremely weak and the financial industry is underperforming despite its products being apparently the best of breed in Internet terms: everything is information based, perfectly digitalisable, and there are no logistics problems (the nightmare of all e-merchants)." For a comprehensive analysis, see Filotto (2002).

11. See Inset 1.
12. See Inset 5.
13. It should be noted that the Eurostat (2000) analysis did not specify what instances of failure took place or the relative magnitude of them. As such, its value is limited to that of a qualitative survey, albeit one conducted in an accurate and reliable manner.
14. It is worth listing (in descending order of importance) all the barriers to success that manifested themselves in terms of delays in the realisation of initiatives, as reported by the European banks: (1) Organisational rigidities (53 per cent); (2) Lack of qualified personnel (45 per cent); (3) Problems relating to the fulfillment of regulatory and legislative requirements (18 per cent); (4) Lack of information on the technology itself (17 per cent); (5) Excessive economic risk (14 per cent); (6) Lack of customer responsiveness to new products/channels (9 per cent); (7) Lack of information on the markets to which the products and services are destined (8 per cent); (8) The excessive costs of innovation (7 per cent); and (9) Lack of adequate sources of financing (6 per cent).
15. In regard to barriers that lead to failure in the form of the abandonment of investments in technology, in aggregate terms the European banks identified in descending order of importance the following factors: (1) Excessive economic risk (29 per cent); (2) Rigidities of an organisational nature (28 per cent); (3) Lack of customer responsiveness to new products/channels (23 per cent); (4) Lack of qualified personnel (21 per cent); (5) The excessive costs of innovation (14 per cent); (6) Lack of information on the markets to which the products and services are destined (12 per cent); (7) Lack of information on the technology itself (11 per cent); (8) Problems relating to the fulfillment of regulatory and legislative requirements (7 per cent); and (9) Lack of adequate sources of financing (6 per cent).
16. The barriers that led to a lack of success in the form of a failure to realise investments in technology were identified by the European banks in aggregate as follows (the factors being listed in descending order of importance): (1) Excessive economic risk (31 per cent); (2) Rigidities of an organisational nature (26 per cent); (3) Problems relating to the fulfillment of regulatory and legislative requirements (26 per cent); (4) Lack of qualified personnel (25 per cent); (5) Lack of adequate sources of financing (21 per cent); (6) Lack of customer responsiveness to new products/channels (13 per cent); (7) Lack of information on the technology itself (12 per cent); (8) Excessive costs of innovation (7 per cent); and (9) Lack of information on the markets to which the products and services are destined (10 per cent).
17. The barriers leading to the lack of success of on-line sales were identified by the aggregate of European banks as the following (in descending order of importance): (1) The unsuitability of the products/services being sold on-line (72.7 per cent); (2) The hesitation of customers to buy on-line (66.7 per cent); (3) The limited revenues deriving from on-line sales (61.2 per cent); (4) The excessive financial costs of technology (54.8 per cent); (5) The difficulty of adapting the culture of the bank to e-commerce (51.3 per cent); (6) The limited number of on-line customers (50.6 per cent); (7) Problems involved in processing payments for on-line orders (46.1 per cent); and (8) Problems involved in the delivery process (30.9 per cent). As far as on-line

purchases are concerned, the barriers to success were as follows: (1) Concerns relating to the protection of data and issues of security (69.9 per cent); (2) The need for face-to-face interaction (57.3 per cent); (3) The lack of on-line suppliers (53.7 per cent); (4) The excessive financial costs of technology (49.3 per cent); (5) Non-compatibility with suppliers' systems (30.7 per cent); and (6) Insignificance of the cost advantage (44.4 per cent).

18. Shannon and Weaver (1949) defined the technical level in terms of the accuracy and efficiency of the system that produces information, the semantic level in terms of the success of the information in transferring an intentional meaning and the level of effectiveness in terms of the effect of the information on the recipient.

19. For an overview of the models that investigate the technology–performance relationship, it is worth mentioning the following studies: Ciborra and Pugliese (1996) and, with a particular focus on IT success, Heine *et al.* (2003), Raymond (1985, 1990), Ein-Dor *et al.* (1984), Ein-Dor and Segev (1978), Robey and Zeller (1978) and Tait and Vessey (1988).

20. Note, however, that in regard to the proof of deposits, imaging technology has been employed with very little success.

21. Autor *et al.* (2000) examined the effects of the use of imaging technology in the processing of bank cheques in 20 principal banks in the United States. They maintained that computers effectively substitute human labour in the case of standardised tasks and work of a low skill level but that they require the presence of a workforce that is skilled in the use of IT. Moreover, the authors emphasised the interdependencies between technological and organisational changes.

22. In this regard it is interesting, however, to refer to a recent enquiry of the European Commission about customer mobility in the retail banking market (European Commission, 2006). This analysis of customer mobility relies on data on the current account market and looks at the mobility of consumers and SMEs. Two indicators are used: a measure of mobility named "churn" (share of customers who change bank in a given year) and a measure called "longevity" (average length of existing banking relationships). As shown in the table below (in which we just reported the evidence for the countries under investigation in our study), the average churn is equal to

Customer mobility in EU banks

	Churn (%)		Longevity (years)	
	Consumers	SMEs	Consumers	SMEs
France	6.84	12.26	11.06	8.39
Germany	8.46	15.15	11.55	9.85
Italy	7.68	11.23	9.39	8.23
Spain	12.12	10.34	6.91	6.02
UK	5.07	12.72	10.66	7.66
EU15	7.55	12.21	10.40	8.56

Source: European Commission (2006, pp. 102, 104).

7.55 per cent for EU consumers and 12.21 per cent for EU SMEs in 2005. The UK banking industry is among the countries with the lowest churn for consumers (5.07 per cent) and the highest one for SMEs (13.72 per cent). As regard to longevity, the average EU consumers have maintained their current account with the same bank for around 10 years and the average EU SME for around 8 years.

23. According to the US Bureau of Economic Analysis (BEA), for each staff member in the years 1995 to 1999 commercial banks spent on average $5253 (the equivalent of 2 new personal computers per person), compared to an average expenditure on the part of firms in the private sector in the United States of $440 per staff member over the same time period. In real terms (or, in other words, taking account of the quality of the IT equipment), investment in personal computers in US commercial banks grew more than threefold in the course of the years taken into consideration (McKinsey, 2001).

24. This interpretation is confirmed in the 1998 MetaGroup Report (www.metagroup.com, mimeo), which put forward seven factors – or, in other words, barriers to success – that have to be anticipated in order to reduce the risks associated with the realisation of CRM projects. The first two factors listed are as follows (for the other factors, see Notes 27 and 28):

   1. Lack of executive sponsorship. The executive bodies of the bank are rarely involved in mandates of CRM, basically because the business performance metrics associated with CRM projects are not subject to reporting or quantification in the balance sheets of banks. In fact, CRM projects are normally led by functional heads (e.g., the director of sales or marketing). The consequence of this case of organisational rigidity is an incapacity to obtain the result desired through the adoption of CRM, namely, an approach involving a strategic orientation towards the customer.

   2. Lack of cultural preparation. Investment in CRM technology requires that the bank have a strategic and cultural orientation towards the customer, without which the initiative itself ends in failure. This approach involves, for example, the need not just to provide call centres that are well organised and equipped with adequate technology but also to staff them with competent and well-paid employees and not, as often occurs, with low-paid employees with limited skills, who, in reality, end up producing a damaging effect on customer satisfaction and loyalty. In fact, "customer care" does not take the form of a company capability guided by technology. Thus, as already argued, organisations that are not characterised by an all-encompassing customer-oriented approach should not endeavour to put in place CRM projects.

25. www.metagroup.com, mimeo.

26. It is important to underline that this failure rate related specifically to the automation of sales and not to general CRM projects.

27. Again, according to the 1998 MetaGroup Report, other barriers to the success of CRM projects can be accounted for in terms of the following:

   1. The design of applications like "inside out". A large number of CRM applications are designed to model the business processes of a particular function (e.g., the automation of sales). This methodology is characterised

by two important limitations: (a) the inclusion in the application of business processes that are potentially inappropriate or inefficient; and (b) a single external functional perspective in relation to the interaction between the customer and the bank. Instead, in reality, project managers are expected to adopt a components-based approach to the design of applications which models the interactions with the customer in terms of the perspective of the customer himself/herself with a view to putting in place a more flexible application architecture.

  2. Myopic vision of extensibility. In addition to the front office (inside sales, telemarketing, customer services) and the mobile office (sales and services in the field), CRM projects also relate to the extended office (self-service on the part of the customer). Although this application extension brings tangible benefits (reduction in the workload and in the cost of labour), it also involves numerous consequences of an organisational nature such as the collaboration between staff and customers and Web support for transactions (www.metagroup.com, mimeo).

28. Again according to the 1998 MetaGroup Report, other barriers to the success of CRM projects relate to the following:

  1. Over-automation. Many CRM application packages have been designed in such a way as to generate an over-automation of business functions. This becomes particularly problematic in relation to sales activity (given that sales processes benefit from a minimal level of automation) and call centres (where the level of staff turnover is high and where, on account of the reduced expenditure on personnel, there are considerable problems involved in ensuring that staff are sufficiently well qualified).

  2. Limited support in terms of synchronisation with portable telephones. For sales and service applications, mobile synchronisation constitutes a critical requirement for the entire CRM architecture. The majority of CRM projects, in fact, make use of a first generation system for mobile synchronisation. In this situation, it becomes necessary to distribute electronic software, to modify the design of databases, to make use of publish and subscribe service, and to set in place a team for dealing with security and authorisations (www.metagroup.com, mimeo).

29. The offer of on-line payment services by the banks (e.g, on-line bank transfer operations) may be considered more simple and convenient for customers than the mailing of a bank cheque in paper form. Similarly, customers who have access to information via on-line banking or phone banking enjoy the benefits of ease of access and a more extended period of time in which to use the service.

30. See the detailed analysis offered in Section 4.6.

31. Common operations include checking bank accounts, requesting quotes for complex products and effecting bank transfers that are of small amounts and exempt from fees.

32. Note that the cost of labour for European banks increased as a result of adjustments consequent upon the introduction of the single European currency and the need to resolve problems connected with the Year 2000 problem.

33. In fact, there have already been some cases in which the use of remote channels has been accompanied by prices that were greater than those applied to the traditional channels. This means that European banks do not appear to make widespread use of pricing policies aimed at promoting the choice of remote channels. In fact, many retail banking transactions are offered without applying a fee, because they are implicitly paid for by no or little interest paid on current accounts and by interest margins on other businesses (European Central Bank, 1999).

References

ABI (2003), *Il Customer Relationship Management nelle banche italiane*, Bancaria Editrice, Roma.

ABI, Università di Parma (2003), "Il CRM nelle banche italiane", *MK*, 1, pp. 2–13.

Aigner, D.J., Lovell, C.A.K. and Schmidt, P. (1977), "Formulation and Estimation of Stochastic Frontier production Function Models", in *Journal of Econometrics*, 6, pp. 21–37.

Ahituv, N., Giladi, R. (1993), "Business Success and Information Technology. Are They Really Related?", *Proceedings of the 7th Annual Conference of Management IS*, Tel Aviv University, Israel.

Allen, F., Gale, D. (1994), *Financial Innovation and Risk Sharing*, MIT Press, Cambridge, MA.

Allen, F., Santomero, A.M. (2001), "What do Financial Intermediaries Do?", in *Journal of Banking and Finance*, 25, pp. 271–294.

Alpar, P., Kim, M. (1990a), "A Comparison of Approaches to the Measurement of IT Value", *Proceedings of the Twenty-Second Hawaii International Conference on System Science*, Honolulu, Hi, Vol. 4, pp. 112–119.

Alpar, P., Kim, M. (1990b), "A Microeconomic Approach to the Measurement of Information Technology Value", *Journal of Management Information Systems*, Fall, 7(2), pp. 55–69.

Altunbas, Y., Goddard, J. and Molyneux, P. (1999), "Technical Change in Banking", *Economics Letters*, 64, pp. 215–221.

Altunbas, Y., Goddard, J. and Molyneux, P. (2001), "Efficiency in European banking", *European Economic Review*, 45, pp. 1931–1955.

Altunbas, Y., Liu, M.H., Molyneux, P. and Seth, R. (2000), "Efficiency and Risk in Japanese Banking", *Journal of Banking and Finance*, 24, pp. 1605–1628.

Altunbas, Y., Evans, L., Molyneux, P. (2001), "Bank Ownership and Efficiency", *Journal of Money, Credit, and Banking*, 33(4), pp. 926–954.

Andersen, A. (1993), *European Banking and Capital Markets – A Strategic Forecast*, Economist Intelligence Unit, London.

Autor, D.H., Levy, F. and Murnane, R.J. (2000), *Upstairs, Downstairs: Computer-Skill Complementarity and Computer-Labour Substitution on Two Floors of a Large Bank*, NBER Working Paper, n. 7890.

Baily, M.N., Chakrabarti, A. (1988), *Innovation and the Productivity Crisis*, Brookings Institutions, Washington DC.

Baily, M.N., Lawrence, R.Z. (2001), "Do we Have a New E-Economy?", *American Economic Review*, 91(2), pp. 308–312.

Bain, J. (1956), *Barriers to New Competition*, Harvard University Press, Cambridge, MA.

Baltagi, B.H., Griffin, J.M. (1988), "A General Index of Technical Change", *Journal of Political Economy*, 96, pp. 20–41.

Bank for International Settlements (1999), "The Monetary and Regulatory Implications of Changes in the Banking Industry", *Bis Conference Papers*, Vol. 7, March, Basle.

Bankscope (several years), *World Banking Information Source, Database*, Bureau van Djik, Electronic Publishing, London.

Barua, A., Kriebel, C. and Muk Hopadhyay, T. (1995), "Information Technology and Business Value: An Analytic and Empirical Investigation", *Information Systems Research*, 6(1), pp. 3–23.

Battese, G.E. and Coelli, T.J. (1992), "Frontier Production Functions, Technical Efficiency and Panel Data: With Application to Paddy Farmers in India", *Journal of Productivity Analysis*, 3, pp. 153–169.

Battese, G.E. and Corra, G.S. (1977), 'Estimation of a Production Frontier Model: With Application to the Pastoral Zone of Eastern Australia', *Australian Journal of Agricultural Economics*, 21, pp. 169–179.

Bauer, P.W., Hancock., D. (1993), "The Efficiency of the Federal Reserve in Providing Check Processing Services", *Journal of Banking and Finance*, 17, pp. 287–311.

Bauer, P.W., Berger, A.N. and Humphrey, D.B. (1993), "Efficiency and Productivity Growth in US Banking", in Fried, H.O., Lovell, C.A.K. and Schmidt, S.S. (eds), *The Measurement of Productive Efficiency: Techniques and Application*, Oxford University Press, Oxford.

Beccalli, E. (2001), "L'industria europea delle imprese di investimento", *Quaderni del Dipartimento di Scienze dell'Economia e della Gestione Aziendale*, ISU Università Cattolica del Sacro Cuore, Milano.

Beccalli, E. (2004), "Cross-Country Comparisons of Efficiency Evidence from the UK and Italian Investment Firms", *Journal of Banking and Finance*, 28, pp. 1363–1383.

Beccalli, E. (2007), "Does IT Investment Improve Bank Performance? Evidence from Europe", *Journal of Banking and Finance*, doi: 10.1016/j.bankfin.2006.10.022.

Beccalli, E., Casu, B. and Girardone, C. (2006), "Efficiency and Stock Performance in European Banking", *Journal of Business Finance & Accounting*, 33(1 & 2), 218–235.

Berg, S.A., Forsund, F.R., Hjalmarsson, L. and Suominen, M. (1993), "Banking Efficiency in the Nordic Countries", *Journal of Banking and Finance*, 17, pp. 371–388.

Bergendahl, G. (1995), "Dea and Benchmarks for Nordic Banks", Working Papers, Gothenburg University, Gothenburg.

Berger, A.N. (1993), "Distribution-Free Estimates of Efficiency in the US Banking, Industry and Tests of the Standard Distributional Assumptions", *Journal of Productivity Analysis*, 4, pp. 261–292.

Berger, A.N. (2003), "The Economic Effects of Technological Progress: Evidence from the Banking Industry", *Journal of Money, Credit, and Banking*, 35(2), pp. 141–176.

Berger, AN., DeYoung, R. (1997), "Problem Loans and Cost Efficiency in Commercial Banks", *Journal of Banking and Finance*, 21, pp. 849–870.

Berger, AN., DeYoung, R. (2002), "Technological Progress and the Geographic Expansion of the Banking Industry", Working Paper Federal Reserve Bank of Chicago, n. 7.

Berger, A.N., Humphrey, D.B. (1991), "The Dominance of Inefficiencies Over Scale and Product Mix Economies in Banking", *Journal of Monetary Economics*, 28, pp. 117–148.

Berger, A.N., Humphrey, D.B. (1992), "Measurement and Efficiency Issues in Commercial Banking", in GRILICHES, Z. (ed.), *Measurement Issues in the Service Sectors*, Chicago National Bureau of Economic Research, University of Chicago Press, Chicago.

Berger, A.N., Humphrey, D.B. (1997), "Efficiency of Financial Institutions International Survey and Directions for Future Research", *European Journal of Operational Research*, 98, pp. 175–212.

Berger, A.N., Humphrey, D.B. and Pulley, L.B. (1996), "Do Consumers Pay for One-Stop Banking? Evidence from an Alternative Revenue Function", *Journal of Banking and Finance*, n. 20, pp. 1601–1621.

Berger, A.N., Hunter, W.C. and Timme, S.G. (1993), "The Efficiency of Financial Institutions. A Review and Preview of Research Past, Present and Future", *Journal of Banking and Finance*, 17, pp. 221–249.

Berger, A.N., Leusner, J.H. and Mingo, J.J. (1997), "The Efficiency of Bank Branches", *Journal of Monetary Economics*, 40, pp. 141–162.

Berger, A.N., Mester, L.J. (1997), "Inside the Black Box what Explains Differences in the Efficiency of Financial Institutions?", in *Journal of Banking and Finance*, n. 21, pp. 895–947.

Berger, A.N., Mester, L.J. (1999), "What Explains the Dramatic Changes in Cost and Profit Performance of the USs Banking Industry", Working Paper Federal Reserve Bank of Philadelphia, n. 1, February, Philadelphia.

Berger, A.N., Mester, L.J. (2001), "Explaining the Dramatic Changes in Performance of US Banks Technological Change, Deregulation, and Dynamic Changes in Competition", Working Paper Federal Reserve Bank of Philadelphia, n. 6, April, Philadelphia.

Berndt, E.R. (1991), *The Practice of Econometrics Classic and Contemporary*, Addison-Wesley, Reading, MA.

Bijker, W.E., Hughes, T.P. and Pinch, T. (eds) (1987), *The Social Construction of Technological Systems*, Cambridge, MIT Press, MA.

Bresnahan, T.F. (1986), "Measuring the Spillovers from Technical Advance Mainframe Computers in Financial Services", *American Economic Review*, 76, pp. 742–755.

Bresnahan, T.F. (1999), "Computerization and Wage Dispersion: An Analytical Reinterpretation", *Journal Royal Economic Society*, 109 (456), pp. F390–F415.

Brynjolfsson, E. (1993), "The Productivity Paradox of Information Technology", *Communications of the ACM*, 35(12), pp. 66–77.

Brynjolfsson, E. (1996), "The Contribution of Information Technology to Consumer Welfare", *Information Systems Research*, 7(3), pp. 281–300.

Brynjolfsson, E., Hitt, L.M. (1993), "Is Information Systems Spending Productive? New Evidence and New Results", *International Conference on Information Systems*, Orlando, Fl.

Brynjolfsson, E., Hitt, L.M. (1994), "Computers and Economic Growth Firm-Level Evidence", MIT Sloan School of Management Working Paper, n. 3714, August, Cambridge, MA.

Brynjolfsson, E., Hitt, L.M. (1995), "Information Technology as a Factor of Production: The Role of Differences among Firms", *Economics of Innovation and New Technology*, 3(4), pp. 183–200.

228 *References*

Brynjolfsson, E., Hitt, L.M. (1996), "Paradox Lost? Firm-Level Evidence on the Returns to Information Systems Spending", *Management Science*, 42, pp. 541–558.

Brynjolfsson, E., Hitt, L.M. (1998), "Beyond the Productivity Paradox. Computers are the Catalyst for Bigger Changes", *Communications of the ACM*, 41(8), pp. 49–55, 230.

Brynjolfsson, E., Hitt, L.M. (2000), "Beyond Computation: Information Technology, Organization Transformation and Business Performance", *Journal of Economic Perspectives*, 14(4), pp. 23–48.

Brynjolfsson, E., Malone, E., Gurbaxani, V. and Kambil, A. (1994), "Does Information Technology Lead to Smaller Firms?", *Management Science*, 40(12), pp. 1628–1644.

Bukh, P.N.D., Berg, S.A. and Forsund, F.R. (1995), "Banking Efficiency in the Nordic Countries: A Four-Country Malmquist Index Analysis", Working Paper, University of Aarhus, Denmark.

Butera, F. (1990), "Nuove tecnologie ed economia della flessibilità", in de Michelis, G. and Viviani, D. (eds), *La gestione strategica della tecnologia, Quaderni di Formazione Pirelli*, 69, pp. 11–28.

Canoy, M., Van Dijk, M., Lemmen, J., de Mooij, R. and Weigand, J. (2001), "Competition and Stability in Banking", *CPB Netherlands Bureau for Economic Policy Analysis*, SDU Publisher, The Hague.

Carbo Valverde, S., Humphrey, D.B. and Lopez Del Paso, R. (2003), "Effects of ATMs and Electronic Payments on Banking Costs: The Spanish Case", *Fundaciion de las Cajas de Ahorros Confederadas, Documentos de Trabajo*, n. 177, Spain.

Carr, N.G. (2003), "IT Doesn't Matter" *Harvard Business Review*, n. 81, pp. 41–50.

Casolaro, L., Gobbi, G. (2004), "Information Technology and Productivity Changes in the Italian Banking Industry", *Temi di discussione, Banca d'Italia*, n. 489, Roma.

Cecchini, P. (1988), *The European Challenge in 1992 the Benefits of a Single Market*, Wilwood House, Aldershot.

Child, J., Loveridge, R. (1990), *Information Technology in European Services Towards a Microelectronic Future*, Basil Blackwell, Oxford.

Ciborra, C. (1990), "X-Efficiency, Transaction Costs, and Organizational Change", in Weiermair, K., Perlman, M. (eds), *Studies in Economic Rationality. X-Efficiency Examined and Extolled.* Essays Written in the Tradition of and to Honor Harvey Leibenstein, The University of Michigan Press, Ann Arbor, pp. 205–222.

Ciborra, C. (ed.) (2000), *From Control to Drift: The Dynamics of Global Information Infrastructures*, Oxford University Press, Oxford.

Ciborra, C., Pugliese, S. (1996), "La tecnologia", in Costa, G., Nacamulli, R.C.D. (eds), *Manuale di organizzazione aziendale*, Utet, Torino.

Ciocca, P. (2001), *Tecnologia, produttività, redditività delle banche italiane, alla vigilia dell'euro, Atti Assemblea Annuale, Convenzione Bancaria per i Problemi dell'Automazione (CIPA)*, Roma.

Clemons, E.K. (1991), "Evaluation of Strategic Investments in Information Technology", *Communications of the ACM*, 34(1), pp. 22–36.

Coelli, T.J. (1992), "A Computer Program for Frontier Production Function Estimation Frontier, Version 2.0", *Economics Letters*, 39, pp. 29–32.

Coelli, T.J. (1996), "A Guide to Frontier Version 4.1: A Computer Program for Stochastic Frontier Production and Cost Function Estimation", *Working Paper, Centre for Efficiency and Productivity Analysis*, n. 7, University of New England, Armidale.

Coelli, T.J., Prasada Rao, D.S. and Battese, G. (1998), *An Introduction to Efficiency and Productivity Analysis*, Kluwer Academic Publishers, Norwell.

Convenzione Interbancaria Per I Problemi Dell'automazione, CIPA (2002), *Rilevazione dello stato dell'automazione del sistema creditizio*, 1995–2001, Roma.

Cossutta, D., di Battista, M.L., Giannini, C. and Urga, G. (1988), "Processo produttivo e struttura dei costi nell'industria bancaria italiana", in Cesarini, F., Grillo, M., Monti, M., Onado, M. (eds), *Banca e mercato*, Il Mulino, Bologna.

Council of Economic Advisors (2001), "The Annual Report of the Council of Economic Advisors", *The Economics of the President*, US Government Printing Office, Washington, DC.

Cron, W.L., Sobol, M.G. (1983), "The Relationship Between Computerization and Performance: A Strategy for Maximizing the Economic Benefits of Computerization", *Information and Management*, 6, pp. 171–181.

Davenport, T.H., Short, J.E. (1990), "The New Industrial Engineering Information Technology and Business Process Redesign", *Sloan Management Review*, pp. 11–27.

De Bandt, O., Davis, E.P. (2000), "Competition, Contestability and Market Structure in European Banking Sectors on the Eve of Emu", *Journal of Banking and Finance*, 24(6), pp. 1045–1066.

De Marco, M. (1993), "Performance Valuation and Capacity Planning dello sportello bancario: origini, motivazioni e tecniche", in Arduini, A. (ed.), *Investimenti in Information Technology nel settore bancario*, Franco Angeli, Milano.

De Marco, M., Sorrentino, M. and Virili, F. (2003), *Organizzazioni e cambiamento tecnologico. Spunti di riflessione*, Libreria Universitaria Cuesp, Milano.

Dedrick, J., Gurbaxani, V. and Kraemer, K.L. (2002), "Information Technology and Economic Performance: Firm and Country Evidence", *Working Paper August 2002*, Center for Research on Information Technology and Organizations, University of California, Irvine.

Dedrick, J., Gurbaxani, V. and Kraemer, K.L. (2003), "Information Technology and Economic Performance: Firm and Country Evidence", *ACM Computing Surveys*, 35(1), pp. 1–28.

Delone, W.H. (1988), "Determinants of Success for Computer Usage in Small Business", *MIS Quarterly*, 12(1), pp. 51–61.

Delone, W.H., Mclean, E.R. (1992), "Information Systems Success: The Quest for the Dependent Variable", *Information Systems Research*, 3(1), pp. 60–95.

Denison, E.F. (1989), *Estimates of Productivity Change by Industry: An Evaluation and an Alternative*, The Brookings Institution, Washington, DC.

Dewan, S., Kraemer, K.L. (1998), "International Dimensions of the Productivity Paradox", *Communications of the ACM*, 41(8), pp. 56–62.

Dewan, S., Min, C. (1997), "The Substitution of Information Technology for Other Factors of Production: A Firm Level Analysis", *Management Science*, 43(12), pp. 1660–1675.

DeYoung, R. (1998), "Management Quality and X-inefficiency in National Banks", *Journal of Financial Services Research*, 13(1), pp. 5–22.

Dietsch, M., Weill, L. (1998), *Banking Efficiency and European Integration Productivity, Cost and Profit Approaches*, Paper presented at the Suerf Conference "The Euro: Challenge and Opportunity for Financial Markets", Frankfurt.

Dos Santos, B.L., Peffers, K.G. and Mauer, D.C. (1993), "The Impact of Information Technology Investments Announcements on the Market Value of the Firm", *Information Systems Research*, 4(1), pp. 1–23.

Drake, L., Howcroft, B. (1994), "Relative Efficiency in the Branch Network of the UK Bank: An Empirical Study", *Omega*, 22(1), pp. 83–96.

Due, R.T. (1992), "The Dangers of Downsizing", *Information Systems Management*, 9(3), pp. 65–67.

Earl, M.J. (1989), *Management Strategies for Information Technology*, Prentice Hall, Hemel Hemstead, UK.

E-Business W@tch (European e-Business Market Watch) (2002), ICT & e-Business in the Financial Sector, European Commission, Enterprise Directorate General, e-Business, ICT Industries and Services, Bonn/Brussels.

E-Business W@tch (2003a), ICT & e-Business in the Financial Sector, European Commission, Enterprise Directorate General, e-Business, ICT Industries and Services, Bonn/Brussels.

E-Business W@tch (2003b), "ICT & e-Business in the Financial Sector", *Newsletter*, n. 4, European Commission, Enterprise Directorate General, e-Business, ICT Industries and Services, Bonn/Brussels.

Ein-dor, P., Segev, E. (1978), "Organizational Context and the Success of Management Information Systems", *Management Science*, 24(10), pp. 1067–1077.

Ein-dor, P., Segev, E., Blumenthal, D. and Millet, I. (1984), "Perceived Importance, Investment and Success of Mis, or the Mis zoo", *Systems, Objectives, Solutions*, 4, pp. 61–67.

European Business School (2004), *ERP in Banking 2005 – An Empirical Survey*. Based on research conducted from March to September 2004, Oestrich-Winkel, Germany.

European Central Bank (1999), *The Effects of Technology on the EU Banking System*, European Central Bank, Frankfurt.

European Central Bank (2001), *Blue Book. Payment and Securities Settlement Systems in the European Union*, European Central Bank, Frankfurt.

European Central Bank (2002a), *E-Payments in Europe – The Eurosystem's Perspective*, European Central Bank, Frankfurt.

European Central Bank (2002b), *Structural Analysis of the EU Banking Sector. Year 2001*, European Central Bank, Frankfurt.

European Central Bank (2003a), *Structural Analysis of the EU Banking Sector. Year 2002*, European Central Bank, Frankfurt.

European Central Bank (2003b), *Blue Book. Payment and Securities Settlement Systems in the European Union*. Addendum Incorporating 2001 Figures, European Central Bank, Frankfurt.

European Commission (1997), "Credit Institutions and Banking", *The Single Market Review*, Vol. 3, Kogan Page, London.

European Commission (2006), "Interim Report II: Current Accounts and Related Services", *Sector Inquiry under Article 17 Regulation 1/2003 on Retail Banking*, Brussels.

European Information Technology Observatory, EITO (1996–2002), *European Information Technology Observatory*, Fourth Edition, 1996–2002, Frankfurt.

Eurostat (2000), "Survey on Innovation in EU enterprises", *New Cronos Database, Statistical of the European Communities*, Economic and Social Data Services (ESDS) On Line, Brussels.

Farrell, M.J. (1957), "The Measurement of Productive Efficiency", *Journal of Royal Statistical Society*, 120(A), pp. 253–281.

Fetcher, F., Pestieau, P. (1993), "Efficiency and Competition in OECD Financial Services", in Fried, H.O., Lovell, C.A.K., Schmidt, S.S. (eds), *The Measurement of Productive Efficiency: Techniques and Applications*, Oxford University Press, Oxford.

Filotto, U. (ed.) (2002), *La "nuova" web bank. Cultura, organizzazione e tecnologia dopo la crisi di Internet*, Bancaria Editrice, Roma.

Financial Analysis Made Easy, FAME (several years), *UK and Irish Company Information in an Instant, Database, Bureau van Djik*, Electronic Publishing, London.

Financial Insights – IDC (2006), *Investments in Hardware, Packaged Software and IT Services in Western Countries (1995–2005)*, Milano.

Fiordelisi, F., Molyneux, P. (2006a), *Shareholder Value in Banking, Studies in Banking and Finance Institutions series*, Palgrave Macmillan, UK.

Fiordelisi, F., Molyneux, P. (2006b), "Do Cost And Profit Efficiency Drive Shareholder Value? Evidence From European Banking", *Paper presented at the Financial Management Association Conference*, Stockholm.

Fitzgerald, G. (1993), "Evaluating Information Systems Projects: A Multidimensional Approach" Arduini, A. (ed.), *Investimenti in Information Technology nel settore bancario*, Franco Angeli, Milano.

Foster, L.W., Flynn, D.M. (1984), "Management Information Technology: Its Effects on Organizational Form and Function", *MIS Quarterly*, 8, pp. 229–235.

Fox, R. (eds) (1998), *Technological Change: methods and themes in the history of technology*, 919980 Harwood Academic, Amsterdam.

Franke, R.H. (1987), "Technological Revolution and Productivity Decline: Computer Introduction in the Financial Industry", *Technological Forecasting Soc. Change*, 31(2), pp. 143–154.

Fusconi, A. (1983), "Lo sviluppo dei sistemi organizzativi nelle aziende di credito", in AA.VV., *Strategia e organizzazione nelle aziende di credito*, ASSBB, Giuffrè, Milano.

Fusconi, A. (1985), "Caratteristiche strutturali dell'attività creditizia ed organizzazione aziendale: vincoli per una strategia", in Fusconi, A. (ed.), *Organizzazione ed efficienza nelle imprese di credito*, Franco Angeli, Milano.

Fusconi, A. (1996), "L'incidenza del fattore tecnologico nella funzione di produzione della banca", in Fusconi, A., Loddo, S.A., Rosignoli, B. (eds), *Banca e Intermediazione, Monduzzi Editore*, Bologna.

Gallant, A.R (1981), "On the Bias in Flexible Functional Forms and Essentially Unbiased Form: The Fourier Flexible Form", *Journal of Econometrics*, 15, pp. 211–245.

Gallant, A.R (1982), "Unbiased Determination of Production Technologies", *Journal of Econometrics*, 20, pp. 285–324.

Gallino, L. (1983), *Informatica e qualità del lavoro*, Einaudi, Torino.

Gartner (2001), *If They're So Satisfied, Why Are They Leaving?*, Mimeo.

Gartner (2002a), *What's Happening to CRM in 2002?*, Mimeo.

Gartner (2002b), *CRM in 2002: Redesign from the Customer Perspective*, Mimeo.

Gerdens, G.R., Walton II, J.K. (2002), "The Use of Checks and Other Retail Noncash Payments in the United States", *Federal Reserve Bulletin*, August, pp. 360–374.

Giddens, A. (1984), *The Constitution of Society*, University of California Press, Berkeley.

Goddard, J.A., Molyneux, P. and Wilson, O.S. (2001), *European Banking: Efficiency, Technology and Growth*, John Wiley & Sons, Chichester.

Granger, C.W.J., Newbold, P. (1986), *Forecasting Economic Time Series*, Academic Press Inc., California.

Gordon, R.J. (1987), "The Postwar Evolution of Computer Prices", *National Bureau of Econometric Research*, Working Paper n. 2227, Cambridge, MA.

Gordon, R.J. (2000), "Does the 'New Economy' Measure Up to the Great Inventions of the Past?", *Journal of Economic Perspectives*, 14(4), pp. 49–76.

Gurbaxani, V., Melville, N. and Kraemer, K. (1998), "Disaggregating the Return on Investment to IT Capital", *Proceedings of the International Conference on Information Systems*, Helsinki, Finland.

Hammer, M. (1990), "Reengineering Work Don't Automate, Obliterate", *Harvard Business Review*, 68, pp. 104–112.

Hammer, M. (1996), *Beyond Reengineering: How the Process-Centered Organization is Changing Our Work and Our Lives*, HarperBusiness Press, New York.

Harris, S., Katz, E. (1989), "Predicting Organizational Performance Using Information Technology Managerial Control Ratios", *Proceedings of the Twenty-Second Hawaii International Conference on System Science*, Honolulu, Hi.

Heine, M.L., Grover, V. and Malhotra, M.K. (2003), "The Relationship between Technology and Performance: A Meta-Analysis of Technology Models", *Omega International Journal of Management Science*, 31, pp. 189–204.

Hirschheim, R., Klein, H. and Newman, M. (1987), "A Social Action Perspective of Information Systems Development", *Proceedings of the Eight International Conference on Information Systems*, Pittsburg, PA.

Hitt, L.M., Brynjolfsson, E. (1996), "Productivity, Business Profitability, and Consumer Surplus: Three Different Measures of Information Technology Value", *MIS Quarterly*, 20(2), pp. 121–142.

Hitt, L.M., Frei, F.X. and Harker, P.T. (1999), "How Financial Firms Decide on Technology", in Litan, R.E., Santomero, A.M. (eds), *Brookings – Wharton Papers on Financial Services*, Brookings Institution Press, Washington, DC.

HM Treasury (2000), *Review of Banking services in the UK ("Cruickshank Report")*, London.

Hochstrasser, B., Griffiths, C. (1991), *Controlling Information Technology Investments: Strategy and Management*, Chapman and Hall, London.

Hughes, J.P., Mester, L.J. (1993), "A Quality and Risk-Adjusted Cost Function for Banks: Evidence on the 'Too-Big-To-Fail' Doctrine", *Journal of Productivity Analysis*, 4, pp. 293–315.

Humphrey, D.B. (1993), "Cost and Technical Change: Effects from Bank Deregulation", *Journal of Productivity Analysis*, 4, pp. 9–34.

Humphrey, D.B., Kim, M. and Vale, B. (2001), "Realizing the Gains from Electronic Payments: Costs, Pricing, and Payment Choice", *Journal of Money, Credit, and Banking*, 33(2), pp. 216–234.

Humphrey, D.B., Willesson, M., Bergendahl, G. and Lindblom, T. (2006), "Benefits from a Changing Payment Technology in European Banking", *Journal of Banking and Finance*, 30, pp. 1631–1652.

Hunter, W.C., Timme. S.G. (1991), "Technological Change in Large US Commercial Banks", *Journal of Business*, 64, pp. 339–362.

International Data Corporation, IDC (2000), *White Paper*, Internet Banking, Milano.

Inzerillo, U., Morelli, P. and Pittaluga, G.B. (2000), "Deregulation and Changes in European Banking Industries", in Galli, G., Pelkmans, J. (eds), *Regulatory Reform and Competitiveness in Europe*, Vol. 2, Edward Elgar, Cheltenham, UK.

Jagtiani, J., Khanthavit, A. (1996), "Scale and Scope Economies at Large Banks, Including Off Balance Sheet Products and Regulatory Effects", *Journal of Banking and Finance*, 20, pp. 1271–1287.

Jensen, M.C., Meckling, W.H. (1976), "Theory of the Firm Managerial Behaviour, Agency Costs and Ownership Structure", *Journal of Financial Economics*, 3, pp. 305–360.

Jorgenson, D.W. (1986), "Econometric Methods for Modelling Producer Behaviour", in Griliches, Z., Intriligator, M.D. (eds), *Handbook of Econometrics*, Vol. 3, North-Holland, Amsterdam.

Jorgenson, D.W., Stiroh, K.J. (2000), "Raising the Speed Limit US Economic Growth in the Information Age", *Brookings Paper on Economic Activity*, 1(1), pp. 125–211.

Jurison, J. (1996), "Towards more Effective Management of Information Technology Benefits", *Journal of Strategic Information Systems*, 5(2), pp. 263–274.

Kearney, A.T. (1990), *Breaking the Barriers: IT Effectiveness in Great Britain and Ireland*, A.T. Kearney/Cima, London.

Keen, P. (1991), *Shaping the Future Business Design Through Information Technology*, Harvard Business Press, Boston.

Kim, M., Kliger, D. and Vale, B. (2003), "Estimating Switching Costs the Case of Banking", *Journal of Financial Intermediation*, 12, pp. 25–56.

Kraemer, K., Dedrick, J. (2001a), "Information Technology and Productivity: Results and Policy Implications of Cross-Country Studies", in Pohjola, M. (ed.), "Information Technology, Productivity and Economic Growth", *Implications for Economic Development*, Oxford University Press, Oxford.

Kraemer, K., Dedrick, J. (2001b), *The Productivity Paradox: Is it Resolved? Is There a New One? What Does It All Mean for Managers?*, Center for Research on Information Technology and Organizations, Working Paper February 2001,University of California, Irvine.

Landauer, T.K. (1995), *The Trouble with Computers*, The MIT Press, Cambridge, MA.

Lang, G., Welzel, P. (1996), "Efficiency and Technical Progress in Banking: Empirical Results for a Panel of German Banks", *Journal of Banking and Finance*, 20, pp. 1003–1023.

Leibenstein, H. (1966), "Allocative Efficiency vs. 'X-efficiency' ", *American Economic Review*, 56, pp. 392–415.

Leibenstein, H. (1980), *Inflation, Income Distribution and X-efficiencies Theory*, Croon Helm, London.

Liao, Z., Cheung, M.T. (2002), "Internet-Based e-Banking and Consumer Attitudes: An Empirical Study", *Information and Management*, 39, pp. 283–295.

Lichtenberg, F.R. (1995), "The Output Contribution of Computer Equipment and Personal. A Firm-Level Analysis", *Economics of Innovation and New Technology*, 3, pp. 201–217.

Loveman, G.W. (1994), "An Assessment of the Productivity Impact on Information Technologies", in Allen, T.J, Scott-Morton, M.S. (eds), *Information Technology and the Corporation of the 1990s: Research Studies*, MIT Press, Cambridge, MA, pp. 84–110.

Lucas, H.C. (1985), *The Analysis, Design and Implementation of Information Systems*, McGraw-Hill Book Company, New York.

Lucas, H.C. (1993), "The Business Value of Information Technology: A Historical Perspective and Thoughts for Future Research", in Banker, R., Kauffman, R. and Mahmood, M.A. (eds), *Strategic Information Technology management*, Idea Publishing, Harrisburg, PA, pp. 102–123.

Lyytinen, K., Yoo, K. (2002), "Issues and Challenges in Ubiquiyous Computing", *Communication of the ACM*, 45, pp. 62–65.

Malone, T. (1997), "Is Empowerment Just a Fad?", *Sloan Management Review*, 38(2), pp. 23–35.

Markus, M.L., Robey, D. (1988), "Information Technology and Organizational Change: Causal Structure in Theory and Research", *Management Science*, 34(5), pp. 583–598.

Markus, L., Soh, C. (1993), "Banking on Information Technology: Converting IT Spending into Firm Performance", in Banker, R., Kaufmann, R., Mahmood, M. (eds), *Strategic Information Technology Management: Perspectives on Organizational Growth and Competitive Advantage*, Idea Group Publishing, Harrisburg, PA, p. 240.

Mason, R.O. (1978), "Measuring Information Output: A Communication System Approach", *Information & Management*, 1(5), pp. 219–234.

Maudos, J., Pastor, J.M. and Quesada, J. (1996), "Technical Progress in Spanish Banking 1985–1994", in Revell, J. (ed.), *The Recent Evolution of Financial Systems*, McMillan Press, UK, pp. 214–245.

McAllister, P., McManus, D. (1993), "Resolving the Scale Efficiency Puzzle in Banking", *Journal of Banking and Finance*, 17, pp. 389–405.

McFarlan, F.W. (1981), "Portfolio Approach to Information Systems", *Harvard Business Review*, 59(5), pp. 142–150.

McKillop, D.G., Glass, C.J. and Morikawa, Y. (1996), "The Composite Cost Function and Efficiency in Giant Japanese Banks", *Journal of Banking and Finance*, 20, pp. 1651–1671.

McKinsey Global Institute (2001), *U.S. Productivity Growth 1995–2000: Understanding the Contribution of Information Technology Relative to Other Factors*, McKinsey Global Institute, Washington, DC.

Meeusen, W., Van Den Broeck, J. (1977), "Efficiency Estimation from Cobb-Douglas Production Functions with Composed Errors", *International Economic Review*, 18(2), pp. 435–444.

Menon, N.M. (2000), *The Impact of Information Technology: Evidence from the Healthcare Industry*, Garland Publishing, New York.

Mester, L.J. (1996), "A Study of Bank Efficiency Taking into Account Risk-Preference", *Journal of Banking and Finance*, 20, pp. 1025–1045.

Mester, L.J. (1997), "Measuring Efficiency at US Banks: Accounting for Heterogeneity is Important", *European Journal of Operational Research*, 98, pp. 230–243.

Mitchell, K., Onvural, N.M. (1996), "Economies of Scale and Scope at Large Commercial Banks: Evidence from the Fourier Flexible Functional Form", *Journal of Money, Credit and Banking*, 28, 178–199.

Molyneux, P., Altunbas, Y. and Gardener, E. (1996), *Efficiency in European Banking*, John Wiley & Sons, Chichester.

Moore, G.E. (1965), "Cramming More Components into Integrated Circuits", *Electronics*, 38, April 19.

Morgan Stanley Deanwitter (2000), "On Line Only Banking is a Dead End", *The Internet and Financial Services*, FIG.com, New York, London.

Nelson, R.A. (1984), "Regulation, Capital Vintage, and Technical Change in the Electric Utility Industry", *Review of Economics and Statistics*, 66, pp. 59–69.

Nobes, C.W., Parker, R.H. (1988), *Comparative International Accounting*, St Martin's Press, London.

Noyelle, T. (ed.) (1990), *Skills, Wages and Productivity in the Service Sector*, Western Press, Boulder, Colorado.

Olson, R.E., Schmidt, P. and Waldman, D.M. (1980), "A Monte Carlo Study of Estimators of Stochastic Frontier Production Functions", *Journal of Econometrics*, 13, pp. 67–82.

Orlikowski, W.J. (1992), "The Duality of Technology: Rethinking the Concept of Technology in Organizations", *Organization Science*, 3(3), pp. 398–427.

Osservatorio Phone Banking (2003), *Rapporto 1, November,Università Cattolica del Sacro Cuore*, Milano.

Osservatorio Phone Banking (2004a), *Rapporto 2, May, Università Cattolica del Sacro Cuore*, Milano.

Osservatorio Phone Banking (2004b), *Rapporto 3, December, Università Cattolica del Sacro Cuore*, Milano.

Osterman, P. (1986), "The Impact of Computers on the Employment of Clerks and Managers", *Industrial and Labour Relations Review*, 39, pp. 175–186.

Padoa-Schioppa, T. (1999), "Licensing Banks: Still Necessary?", Lecture by Executive Board of the European Central Bank, Washington, DC, 24 September.

Parsons, D.J., Gottlieb, C.C. and Denny, M. (1993), "Productivity and Computers in Canadian Banking", *Journal of Productivity Analysis*, 4, pp. 95–114.

Pastor, J.M., Pérez, F. and Quesada, J. (1997), "Efficiency Analysis in Banking Firms: An International Comparison", *European Journal of Operational Research*, 98, pp. 395–407.

Perrow, C. (1967), "A Framework for the Comparative Analysis of Organizations", *American Sociological Review*, 32, pp. 194–208.

Porter, M.E. (1980), *Competitive Strategy*, Free Press, New York.

Porter, M.E., Millar, V.E. (1985), "How Information Gives You Competitive Advantages", *Harvard Business Review*, July–August, pp. 149–160.

Prasad, B., Harker, P.T. (1997), "Examining the Contribution of Information Technology Toward Productivity and Profitability in US Retail Banking", *Wharton Working Paper Series on Financial Services*, n. 97–09, The Wharton School, University of Pennsylvania, Philadelphia.

Prometeia (2001), *Analisi dei bilanci bancari. Dicembre 2001*, Prometeia, Bologna.

Rai, A., Patnayakuni, R. and Patnayakuni, N. (1997), "Technology Investment and Business Performance", *Communications of the ACM*, 40(7), pp. 89–97.

Raymond, L. (1985), "Organizational Characteristics and MIS Success in the Context of Small Business", *MIS Quarterly*, 9(1), pp. 37–52.

Raymond, L. (1990), "Organizational Context and Information Systems Success: A Contingency Approach", *Journal of Management Information Systems*, 6(4), pp. 5–20.

Resti, A. (1997a), *Linear Programming and Econometric Methods for Bank Efficiency Evaluation: An Empirical Comparison Based on a Panel of Italian Banks*, Research Papers in Banking and Finance, Ief, University of Wales, Bangor.

Resti, A. (1997b), "Evaluating the Cost-Efficiency of the Italian Banking System: What Can Be Learned from the Joint Application of Parametric and Non-Parametric Techniques", *Journal of Banking and Finance*, 21, pp. 221–250.

Resti, A. (2001), "La banca virtuale: Quale modello di business dopo delusioni e bugie?", in Resti, A. (ed.), *Banca virtuale e multicanale. Strategie, best practices, errori da evitare*, Edibank, Milano, pp. 31–72.

Roach, S.S. (1986), *Macrorealities of the Information Economy*, National Academy of Sciences, New York.

Roach, S.S. (1989), "America's White-Collar Productivity Dilemma", *Manufacturing Engineering*, August, n. 104.

Roach, S.S. (1991), "Services under Siege – The Restructuring Imperative", *Harvard Business Review*, September–October, pp. 82–92.

Robey, D., Zeller, R.L. (1978), "Factors Affecting the Success and Failure of an Information System for Product Quality", *Interfaces*, 8(2), pp. 70–75.

Ruthenberg, D., Elias, R. (1996), "Cost Economies and Interest Rate Margins in a Unified European Banking Market", in *Journal of Economics and Business*, 48, pp. 231–249.

Sambamurthy, V., Zmud, R.W. (1994), *IT Management Competency Assessment: A Tool for Creating Business Value Through IT*, Working Paper, Financial Executive Research Foundation, Morristown, New Jersey.

Schmalensee, R. (1976), "Another Look at Social Valuation of Input Price Changes", *American Economic Review*, 66(1), pp. 239–243.

Sealey, C., Lindley, J.T. (1977), "Inputs, Outputs and a Theory of Production and Cost at Depositary Financial Institutions", *Journal of Finance*, 32, pp. 1251–1266.

Shannon, C.E., Weaver, W. (1949), *The Mathematical Theory of Communication*, University of Illinois Press, Urbana, IL.

Shapiro, C., Varian, H.R. (1999), *Information Rules: A Strategic Guide to Network Economy*, Harvard Business School Press, Boston, MA.

Shin, N. (2001), "The Impact of Information Technology on Financial Performance: The Importance of Strategic Choice", *European Journal of Information Systems*, 10, pp. 227–236.

Sigala, M. (2003), "The Information & Communication Technologies Productivity Impact on the UK Hotel Sector", *International Journal of Operations and Production Management*, 23(10), pp. 1224–1245.

Soh, C., Markus, L. (1995), "How IT Creates Business Value: A Process Theory Synthesis", *Proceedings of the International Conference on Information Systems*, Amsterdam, The Netherlands.

Solans, E.D. (2002), *The New Challenges for the European Banking System*, Speech at the seminar Ambrosetti and Getronics, Vienna, April 12.

Solow, R. (1987), "We'd Better Watch Out", *New York Times Book Review*, July 12.

Stiroh, K.J. (1988), "Management Productivity as an IT Measure", in Berger, P., Kobielus, J.G. and Sutherland, D. (eds), *Measuring Business Value Information Technology*, ICIT Press, Washington, DC.

Stiroh, K.J. (1990), *The Business Value of Computers*, Information Economics Press, New Canaan, CT.

Stiroh, K.J. (2001a), "What Drives Productivity Growth?", *Economic Policy Review*, 7(1), pp. 37–59.

Stiroh, K.J. (2001b), *Information Technology and the US Productivity Revival: What Do the Industry Data Say?*, Federal Reserve Bank of New York, New York, January 24.

Strassmann, P.A. (1985), *Information Payoff, The Transformation of Work in the Electronic Age*, The Free Press, New York.

Tait, P., Vessey, I. (1988), "The Effect of User Involvement on System Success: A Contingency Approach", *MIS Quarterly*, 12(1), pp. 91–109.

Tam, K.Y. (1998), "The Impact of Information Technology Investments on Firm Performance and Evaluation: Evidence from Newly Industrialised Economies", *Information Systems Research*, 9, pp. 85–98.

Thanassoulis, E., Boussofiane, A. and Dyson, R.G. (1996), "A Comparison of Data Envelopment Analysis and Ratio Analysis as Tools for Performance Assessment", *Omega International Journal of Management Science*, 24(3), pp. 229–244.

The Economist (2006), "Panhandlers Beware; Payments", US Edition, November 18.

Thompson, J.D. (1967), *Organizations in Action*, McGraw-Hill, New York.

Tirole, J. (1988), *The Theory of Industrial Organization*, MIT Press, Cambridge, MA.

Trice, A.W., Treacy, M.E. (1986), "Utilization as a Dependent Variable in MIS Research", in Maggi, L., Zmud, R. and Wetherbe, J. (eds), *Proceedings of the International Conference on Information Systems*, San Diego.

Triplett, J.E., Bosworth, B.P. (2003), "Productivity Measurement Issues in Services Industries: 'Baumol's Disease' has been cured", *Frbny Economic Policy Review*, September, pp. 23–33, New York.

Tufano, P. (2002), "Financial Innovation", in Constantinides, G., Harris, M. and Stulz, R. (eds), *Handbook of the Economics and Finance*, Elsevier, North Holland.

Tully, S. (1993), "The Real Key to Creating Wealth", *Fortune*, September 20, pp. 30–50.

Varian, H.R., Farrell, J. and Shapiro, C. (2004), *The Economics of Information Technology*, The Raffaele Mattioli Lecture Series, Cambridge University Press, Cambridge, MA.

Vowler, J. (1990), "The Theory and the Reality", *Computer Weekly*, November 15.

Wagenvoort, R., Schure, P. (1999), "Who Are Europe's Efficient Bankers?", *EIB Cahiers Papers*, 4(1), pp. 105–126.

Weick, K.E. (1990), "Technology as Equivoque: Sensemaking in New Technologies", in Goodman, P.S., Sproull, L.S. (eds), *Technology and Organisation*, Jossey-Bass, San Francisco.

Weill, P. (1992), "The Relationship Between Investments in Information Technology and Firm Performance: A Study on the Valve Manufacturing Sector", *Information Systems Research*, 3(4).

White, W.R. (1998), *The Coming Transformation of Continental European banking?*, BIS Working Papers, n. 54, Bank for International Settlements, Monetary and Economic Department, Basle.

Willcocks, L.P., Lester, S. (2001), "Information Technology and Organizational Performance", in Galliers, R.D., Leidner, D.E. and Baker, B.S.H. (eds), *Strategic Information Management: Challenges and Strategies in Managing Information Systems*, Butterworth-Heinemann, Oxford.

Willcocks, L.P. (1992), "Evaluating Information Technology Investments: Research Findings and Reappraisal", *Journal of Information Systems*, 2(4), pp. 243–268.

Willcocks, L.P. (ed.) (1994), *Information Management Evaluation of Information Systems Investments*, Chapman and Hall, London.

Willcocks, L., Graeser, V. and Lester, S. (1998), "Cybernomics and IT Productivity: Not Business as Usual?", *European Management Journal*, 16(3), pp. 272–283.

Williams, J., Gardener, E.P.M. (2003), "A Note on Technical Change in Banking: The Case of European Savings Banks", *Applied Economics*, 35, pp. 705–719.

Author Index

Subject Index